PUBLISHING

Library of Congress Control Number: 2004104416

Developed and produced
by Miles Kelly Publishing

Publishing Director	Anne Marshall
Senior Editor	Jenni Rainford
Assistant Editor	Teri Mort
Designers	John Christopher, Jo Brewer
Picture Research	Liberty Newton
Copy Editor	Rosalind Beckman
Sub Editor	Jim Murphy
Text	Clive Carpenter, Windsor Chorlton, Peter Eldin, John Farndon, Geoff Tibballs
Indexer	Lynda Watson
Production Manager	Estela Boulton
Jacket Design	Dick Skelt for Out of House
Color Separation	DPI Colour Digital Ltd, Essex, U.K.

ISBN 1-893951-73-1

1 3 5 7 9 10 8 6 4 2

Printed in China

CONTENTS

Ripley's

BELIEVE IT OR NOT

In December 1918, while working as a sports columnist for the *New York Globe*, Robert Ripley created his first collection of odd facts and feats. The cartoons, based on unusual athletic achievements, were submitted under the heading "Champs and Chumps," but his editor wanted a title that would describe the incredible nature of the content, so after much deliberation it was changed to "Believe It or Not!" The cartoon was an instant success and the phrase "believe it or not" soon entered everyday speech.

Robert Ripley's first "Believe It or Not!" cartoon, published in 1918.

Ripley's passion was travel and by 1940 he had visited no fewer than 201 countries. Wherever he went, he searched out the bizarre for inclusion in his syndicated newspaper cartoons, which had blossomed to reach worldwide distribution, being translated into 17 different languages and boasting a readership of 80 million people. During one trip he crossed two continents and covered over 24,000 mi (39,000 km) from New York to Cairo and back to satisfy his appetite for the weird.

One of Robert Ripley's journeys included 15,000 mi (24,000 km) by air, 8,000 mi (13,000 km) by ship, and over 1,000 mi (1,600 km) by camel, horse, and donkey!

"At Chicago, one hundred people fainted every day and we had to have six beds. Here we have only three beds and hardly anyone has fainted"

Robert Ripley comparing his 1940 New York City Odditorium to his original 1933 Chicago Odditorium

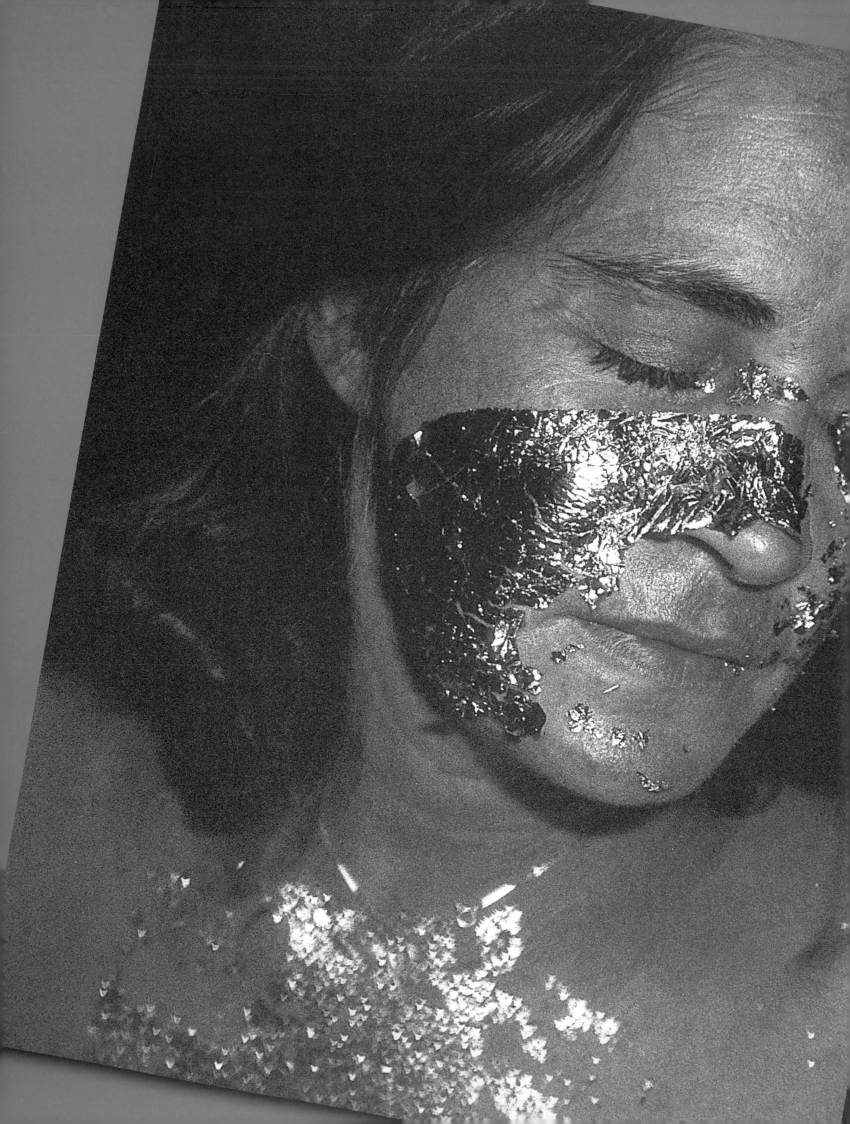

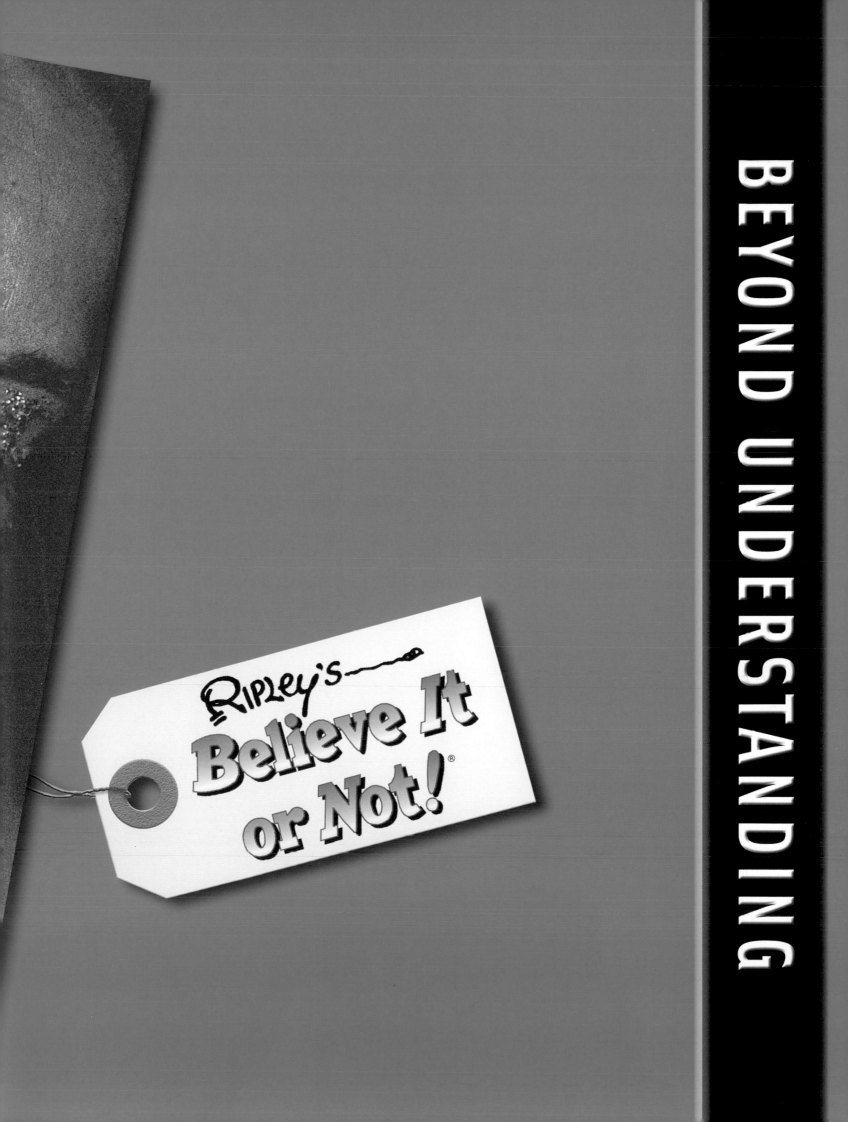

Earth's Nightlight

If humans had been around in the very earliest years of the Earth's life, nights would have been very dark for them indeed—because there was no moonlight at all.

In fact, there was no Moon. Amazingly, the Moon did not form at the same time as the Earth, but some time after. Scientists think the Moon formed when another small planet cannoned into the newborn Earth— with an impact so tremendous it melted almost instantly. Just like a stone hurled into a pond, the impact flung splashes of melted planet back out into space. As the splashes cooled down, they clumped together to form the Moon.

If you wanted to see all of Australia, Europe, and America in less than a half day, you could try sitting on the Moon. The Moon barely moves, but the Earth spins round beneath it at over 24,860 mph (40,000 km/h)!

MOON MATTERS

• With gravity just a sixth of the Earth's, the average person on the Moon could jump 13 ft (4 m) straight up—like jumping on top of a double-decker bus!

• The Sun shines for up to 360 hours on the Moon's sunny side and temperatures can reach up to 260°F (127°C)

• The Moon looks the same size as the Sun but at a staggering 870,000 mi (1.4 million km) across, the Sun is 400 times bigger than the Moon, which is just 2,175 mi (3,500 km) across. Yet at a distance of 93 million mi (150 million km) from us, the Sun is 400 times farther away than the Moon, which is just 240,000 mi (384,000 km) away

The footprints left behind on the Moon by Apollo astronauts, Neil Armstrong and Edwin "Buzz" Aldrin, more than 30 years ago are still there—just as perfect as if they were made yesterday, because there is no wind or rain to ever wipe them away. In fact, they will probably last forever.

HIGH AND DRY

The Moon is covered in scores of seas, known as maria (the latin for sea)—yet there is not a drop of water in any of them, nor has there ever been. They just looked like seas to early astronomers on Earth. The first manned mission to the Moon landed in the bone-dry Sea of Tranquillity.

Hollow Claim In 1976, two Russian scientists claimed that the Moon is not a natural satellite of Earth but a "hollowed-out planetoid fashioned by a highly advanced, technologically sophisticated civilization into an artificial 'inside out' world which was steered into orbit around the Earth aeons ago."

> **"More than 450 astronauts have traveled into space"**

First Moon Landing? According to Chinese historical tradition, a man and a woman landed on the Moon over 4,000 years ago. The engineer Hou-Yih and his wife, Chang Ngo, flew to the Moon on a celestial bird. Their descriptions of the conditions on the Moon were incredibly accurate. Was their journey the result of an over-active imagination or did they really go there using technology that was later lost to mankind?

Far Sighted View A voyage to the moon by ship was described in a work of fiction by Lucian of Samasota, Syria, in the 2nd century AD.

Moon in the Window A piece of Moon rock is enshrined in the stained glass window of Washington Cathedral.

Aztec Astronomy A calendar wheel used by the ancient Aztecs of Mexico traced the intricate orbits of the Earth and Moon and accurately forecasted eclipses.

Good Vibes After the crew of *Apollo 12* landed on the Moon, in 1969, the lunar surface continued to vibrate for almost an hour.

Long Shot When man landed on the Moon, David Trelfall won £10,000 ($18,000). In 1964, he placed a bet, on odds of 1,000 to 1, that a man would set foot on the Moon before January 1, 1971.

Since the world's first artificial satellite, the Russian Sputnik 1, was launched into space in 1957, there have been over 4,000 successful launches of spacecraft—manned missions of exploration, robot probes to distant planets, orbiting space laboratories, and satellites.

Firepower

Every second, the Sun gives out enough energy to supply all the United States' energy needs for 50 million years! To produce this, it burns up an incredible 4 million tons of its mass. However, it will take about 5 billion years to burn it all up, so we needn't worry about it running out. The weight of the Sun is 332,946 times that of the Earth and it burns up some 33 billion million tons of hydrogen in a year.

The Sun burns so brilliantly that it lights the Earth with daylight, even though it is over 93 million mi (150 million km) away. In fact, every square inch of the Sun's surface—no bigger than a postage stamp—burns with the brightness of over 1.5 million candles!

Hard Nosed The Danish astronomer Tycho Brahe had an artificial nose of solid metal. His real nose was cut off in a duel in 1566, when he was 20.

Rounded View The first person to suggest that the Earth was not flat, but actually spherical, was the Greek philosopher Philolaus of Tarentum in 450 BC.

Near Miss Our world was almost destroyed by an asteroid in 1976. The asteroid in orbit around the Sun was only 750,000 mi (1.2 million km) away, which, in space terms, is too close for comfort!

BLIND SPOTS

The first observation of sunspots had to be kept secret! They were observed by a Jesuit, Father Scheiner, in 1650 but it would have been blasphemous to acknowledge the fact because the Sun was regarded as the purest symbol of celestial incorruptibility.

Great Balls of Fire Balls of fire have been witnessed through the ages. Scientists call them "ball lightning" but no one knows what they are or how they are produced. Some cause damage but most do not and they appear to be able to pass through solid objects without harming them.

Implosion When the gravity of a star becomes too great, it collapses in upon itself. Sometimes this imploding increases until absolutely nothing can escape its force. When it reaches this stage it is known as a "black hole."

Starlets Not all stars shine. Nor are they all gigantic. In fact, there are stars out in space that are completely dark and smaller than the Moon. They can be just 17–23 mi (27–37 km) across, no bigger than a large city, and are called neutron stars because they are made almost entirely from subatomic particles called neutrons.

Light Speed It takes 4 minutes for the light of the Sun to reach Earth.

Serious Size The star Sirius is about 25 times brighter than our Sun.

Universal Age The Universe is between 12 and 15 billion years old.

Massive Crater The largest known meteorite crater, the Chixulub crater in Mexico, is 112 mi (180 km) across!

The Barringer crater in Arizona was caused by a meteorite that hit Earth 25,000 to 40,000 years ago! It is 2,625 ft (800 m) across and 656 ft (200 m) deep.

Comets streaking across the heavens were once thought to be warnings from the gods of war, plague, famine, or death—and when any occurred in a comet year (the year a comet appears), it was thought to be proof positive—even though worse things often happened in non-comet years!

Long Wait The Delavan comet returns to our Solar System every 24 million years!

Space Diet If you really want to lose weight, you could move to the planet Pluto. This is because Pluto is small and its gravity weak, so you would weigh just two-thirds of what you do on Earth. However, if you went to Jupiter, you would weigh 23 times as much!

Pocket Stars At just 10 mi (16 km) across—no bigger than a small town—the smallest stars of all are strange or quark stars, discovered in 2002, and made entirely from quarks, the tiniest subatomic particles of all.

Pioneer Guppies South American guppies were the first fish in space.

Quicktime If you're in a hurry to reach school leaving age (or collect your pension), you could try moving to Mercury. This is because Mercury is so near the Sun, so its years last less than three Earth months. So if you're 12 on Earth now, you'd be nearly 50 years old on Mercury!

Earliest Atoms Atoms were first described by the Greek intellectual, Democritus of Addesa, over 2,000 years ago

Closing the Circle

Around 250 BC the Greek philosopher Eratosthenes of Cyrene worked out the circumference of the Earth from shadows! He observed that shadows cast by the Sun at two places 500 mi (800 km) apart differed by seven degrees. From this he calculated that if Earth was a sphere and the seven degree difference equalled 500 mi (800 km) then its circumference was about 25,000 mi (40,230 km) and its diameter about 8,000 mi (12,875 km). He was incredibly close, for we now know that the circumference is 24,902.4 mi (40,075 km) and the average diameter (because the Earth is not an exact sphere) is 7,917.78 mi (12,740 km).

Super Dense Neutron stars are so compressed that they squeeze a tenth of the matter that made up the original giant star (before it imploded) into a ball 1.5 billion times smaller.

Cubic Weight Neutron stars are so dense that a fragment the size of a sugar cube would weigh as much as all the people on Earth put together.

Tight Ball At just 20 mi (32 km) across, the average neutron star packs one tenth of the amount of matter as the Sun into only a billionth of the space.

Whirling Stars Spinning at more than 1,000 times a second, some neutron stars rotate ten times faster than a compact disc.

Sunny Days Our Solar System is about 4.6 billion years old.

Two amazed, and rather scared Russian farm workers, Anna Takhtarova and her granddaughter Rita, were the first people to meet Yuri Gagarin when he landed on Earth in his landing apparatus (shown here) after the world's first ever manned space flight in April 1961.

MOONLIGHT MAGIC BY COLUMBUS

The discovery of America might not have been announced had it not been for an eclipse of the Moon. Knowing that an eclipse was due, Columbus announced to hostile natives in Jamaica that he would make the Moon "lose her light." When it happened as predicted, the natives caused no more trouble and Columbus eventually sailed back to Europe to announce his discoveries.

Pulling Power Neutron stars called magnetars may be a million times smaller than the Earth, but they have a thousand trillion times the magnetic power!

Heavenly Beat Like the flashing lights on police cars, pulsars are neutron stars that send out signals in regular pulses because they rotate at high speed.

Spaceman's Breakfast Before he entered the *Vostok 1* spacecraft on April 12, 1961, Yuri Gagarin had chopped meat, blackberry jam, and coffee for breakfast.

Happy Birthday *Apollo* 9 astronauts sang "Happy Birthday to You," in space for the first on March 8, 1969.

Space Hop America's first manned space venture lasted only 15 minutes, 22 seconds. The 302-mi (483-km) sub-orbital flight was made in the Mercury spacecraft, *Freedom 7*, by astronaut Alan B. Shepherd on May 5, 1961.

Weightless Tummy The medical kits that were issued to America's *Skylab* crew included pills intended to control travel sickness.

Greetings on High "Capriadno was vidit" were the first words spoken by an American to a Russian the first time they met in space in 1975. They mean "How nice to see you again" and were spoken by the American General Tom Stafford to Russian Colonel Alexei Leonov when an *Apollo* spaceship docked with a *Soyuz* spaceship.

A former tire factory worker was the first woman in space— Valentina Tereshkova. In the late 1950s Tereshkova took up parachuting and in 1960 was selected for space training, becoming the first woman in space just two years later.

Flashy Rings

Made entirely of light gases such as hydrogen and helium, the planet Saturn is so light it would actually float—if you could find a swimming pool big enough! Saturn is 1,000 times as big as the Earth but less than 100 times as heavy. Saturn is the farthest planet from the Earth that we can sometimes see with the naked eye. Although the other planets can be seen from Earth they do not emit any light. The light that enables us to see them is reflected sunlight. The amount of sunlight decreases as it travels through the Solar System so the planets beyond Saturn are so faint they are not visible to the naked eye.

It has been suggested that the pygmies of the Ituri Forest in Central Africa called Saturn "the star of the nine moons"—before scientists even knew about Saturn's moons!

Encounters of the Alien Kind!

A short drive in New Hampshire in 1961 took seven hours out of two people's lives!

Betty and Barney Hill were confused about why it had taken them so long to reach their destination. However, it wasn't until two years later when they sought the advice of psychiatrist Dr. Benjamin Simon to deal with their reoccuring and strangely similar nightmares, that they were hypnotized to get to the root of their night-time stirrings. While hypnotized, they both told how they had been pulled from their car by strange beings and subjected to intense medical examination. Betty, in her hypnotic state, also told how the origin of the aliens was the zeta reticuli, which is a star system in space. It was not actually officially discovered until 1969!

Betty and Barney Hill were the first people to speak out in public about their apparent alien encounter, and since then, many other "abductees" have stepped forward to speak of their similar experiences.

Flying Pancakes Joe Simonton said he met aliens in 1961 and they gave him several salt-free pancakes. Joe was thereafter nicknamed "Pancake Joe."

Fellow Traveler George Adamski, a hotdog seller at the Mount Palomar Observatory near San Diego, California, claimed that he made many contacts with beings from other worlds and even flew with them throughout the Solar System. His first contact was apparently near Desert Center, Arizona, on November 20, 1952.

Dead Language The Martian written language was first copied down by Catherine Muller of Geneva, Switzerland, who insisted she learned it from a departed associate during a seance.

This strange creature was discovered in northern Israel in 1998. At 4–5 in (10–12 cm), it has what appear to be arms, legs, fingers, and a head. Many believe that this strange creature was an alien.

REAL SAUCERS JUST WON'T FLY

Just before 1960, the Canadian government financed a program to build an advanced flying saucer. This jet-power disc would fly incredibly fast—1,500 mph (2,414 km/h)—and take off and land vertically. However, the project became so expensive that it was sold to the U.S.A. for further development. Unfortunately, the craft proved unstable at speeds above 30 mph (48 km/h), and could not rise higher than 4 ft (1 m) without tipping dangerously.

Group Sighting More than 50 people confirmed the sighting of an object that flew around Trindade Island in the South Atlantic on January 16, 1958. The crew of the Brazilian Hydrographic and Navigation Service vessel, the *Alminante Saldanha*, and a team of divers on board claimed to have seen the object.

True Believers A poll revealed that 92 percent of Americans believe that aliens are living among us.

Official Stamp Equatorial Guinea was the first country to depict flying saucers on its stamps.

Hot Craft Carl Farlow was driving a truck between Avon and Sopley, in Britain, on November 6, 1967 when the vehicle's lights went out. An oval object floated across the road then flew away and disappeared. Police later discovered that it had burned the ground, melting the tarmac™.

Letter from Mars The letter B on the side of a Martian rock was clearly seen when a Viking space probe transmitted pictures of the surface of Mars to Earth in 1976. The Pasadena Space Center was inundated with telephone calls about this apparent evidence of life on the red planet.

UFO Triggered Crash American pilot Captain Thomas Mantell chased an unidentified flying object at Godman Air Force Base, Kentucky, on January 7, 1948. During the chase Mantell's plane exploded and the wreckage was found 90 mi (145 km) away. The official explanation was that the pilot had been chasing the planet Venus, but it was later shown that Venus was not visible at that time.

The Mystery of Roswell?

In July 1947, a mysterious object crashed in a remote part of New Mexico. A local rancher from the town of Roswell reported to the sheriff that he might have recovered the remains of a flying saucer. The sheriff promptly reported this to the nearby military airbase, which sent out a team to examine the wreckage. The world was soon astonished by an official report telling of the recovery of the remains of a "flying disc." By the next day, the military were officially denying everything and claimed that it was just the remains of a weather balloon. The actual remains were of shiny metallic plastic material, but they seem to have disappeared since. From then on, argument has raged about the significance of the incident.

This is alledgedly the remains of the "flying disc" that landed in Roswell in July 1947. However, many believe it to be material from a weather balloon.

Paul Villa is a true believer in the existence of alien life. He has spent years photographing what he claims to be UFOs. He sends his photographs to important heads of state, as well as distributing copies to the public. He is determined to one day capture an image of a UFO that he believes will prove, beyond doubt, that UFOs and, consequently, aliens, exist! Meanwhile, people inevitably believe that his photographs are fakes, including this one taken in Albuquerque, New Mexico.

Nazi Secret Weapon In 1959, reports leaked out that the Nazi regime had created several mysterious flying discs, which were said to have phenomenal performance, though no evidence of their existence was ever found. They were said to have been designed by several scientists: Schreiver, Miethe, Bellonzo, and Habermohl, although none of these individuals was ever traced after the war. One such flying disc certainly existed. It was designed by German farmer, Arthur Sack, and tested by Luftwaffe pilots in 1944. Unfortunately, it was very reluctant to leave the ground and the project was abandoned!

Saucer Eyes While flying over the Cascade Mountains in Washington state on June 24, 1947, pilot Kenneth Arnold saw several shining lights that looked like bat-winged craft. He described them as moving "like a saucer would if you skipped it across the water." That observation coined the term "flying saucer."

Wheel of Light Men on a British steamer sailing through the Persian Gulf in 1906 witnessed an enormous wheel of light revolving under the water. Beams from the wheel, which was bigger than the steamer, passed through the vessel but did not harm it or the crew in any way!

New World? Explorer Christopher Columbus saw a UFO the night before his discovery of the New World.

" UFO left grid pattern of dots on chest of American man "

Stephen Michalak claimed to have approached a landed UFO at Falcon Lake, Manitoba, in 1967. As he got closer, he was apparently burned, leaving a grid pattern of dots on his chest.

This photograph purports to show an alien that was recovered from a UFO that crashed in 1950 near New Mexico. The "alien" was apparently sent to Germany for examination, but it is believed to be a hoax.

WHAT'S GOING ON IN AREA 51?

Each working day, at least 500 people are flown in to work at a mysterious base in Nevada, which officially does not exist. This place, called Area 51, is part of the Groom Lake airbase, where the U2 spy plane was first tested in conditions of great secrecy, and where new stealth aircraft are rumored to be tested. Very heavy security keeps curious people away but there are rumors that several alien spacecraft are kept at Area 51 for test purposes, so their workings can be understood and applied to new projects. There have even been reports that a dead alien has been dissected, studied, and contained at this secret base.

Lights Out A red flying object disabled the lights, radio, and engine of a car driven by a schoolteacher in Cochcrane, Wisconsin, on April 3, 1968.

Waving Aliens There were numerous witnesses to the appearance of a strange flying vessel over an Anglican mission in Papua New Guinea in June 1959. Father Gill, the mission staff, and all the congregation saw a circular vessel with rails, "like the bridge of a boat." The crew of four were leaning over the rails and when the people on the ground waved to them, they waved back!

Vanishing Author After a meeting with an alien in February 1954, Cedric Allingham disappeared! The meeting took place near Lossiemouth, Scotland, and Allingham then wrote a book about the event but was then never heard of again!

Light Bells Canadian Second World War soldier Lance Corporal Carson Yorke saw a ball of light floating in the air near Antwerp, Belgium. It was joined by four other glowing balls, but to this day no one knows what they were.

- *UFOs were apparently sighted in 1989, flying above Russia.*

Playful Ghosts Go Bump in the Night

There have been many reports of poltergeist activity in countries around the world, terrifying families with their antics.

In 1973, in an ordinary suburban house in Enfield, North London, England, psychic investigators looked into a case of poltergeists (a German word meaning "noisy ghost") who were harassing Peggy Harper, a divorced woman living with her four children. Her children's beds jumped up and down and objects flew about mysteriously. The police were called in, and one police officer reported seeing a chair float into the air. Next, the children floated into the air, too. The poltergeist activity ended suddenly in 1979, at about the same time that one of the girls entered puberty.

This upended furniture in the Webster's living room was apparently the work of a poltergeist. The haunting of this cottage in Chester, England, began in late 1984 and continued for a couple of years. The residents of the cottage tracked the "poltergeist" back to a man named Tomas Harden, who lived in a cottage that was on the same plot of land in the 16th century. The couple had been renovating their property and believe that this disturbed the poltergeist.

In 1985, Ken Webster had a computer in his home, rare for the time, and would often find messages written on the screen from Tomas Harden. The messages were always in an old style of English and would have to be translated to make sense. Not content with writing messages on the computer screen, Harden would often write them on the floor of the cottage as well. Between 1984 and 1987, the Websters received around 300 messages from their poltergeist!

The Magic Word The word "abracadabra" was once believed to cure fevers.

Floating Feat Victorian spiritualist Daniel Douglas Home could levitate! Many observers asserted that it was a trick although no one could explain how he did it.

Early Rapper The Fox family of Hydesville, near Rochester, New York, in December 1847 heard knocking coming from the walls of their cottage. They found out that the raps could answer questions, and Kate and Margaretta Fox started giving public demonstrations that led to the Spiritualist movement in America.

Dead Hands Patience Worth wrote novels 150 years after her death! In July 1913, Mrs. Curran received messages through a ouija board, and over the next 15 years the dead Patience Worth wrote four full-length novels and numerous poems through Mrs. Curan.

At two years old, Greg Sheldon Maxwell often would say "Old Nanna's here" and seemingly point at nothing in particular. When this photograph was developed, it was suggested that the haze in front of him was actually the ghost of his great-grandmother!

Termites Tell The Azande people of Africa use termites to answer questions about future events.

Blast from the Past Ghost gardeners, a man who disappeared, a lady sketching, and an 18th-century wedding were witnessed by two ladies, Charlotte Anne Moberley and Eleanor Jourdain, in the grounds of the Palace of Versailles, France, on August 10, 1901. Five months later they revisited the grounds but the places they had walked through did not exist. They had apparently somehow walked back in time and seen ghosts of the past.

The Spirits of Bull Henry Bull and his family regularly heard ghostly footsteps, a ringing bell, mysterious tapping, and strange voices when they lived at Borley Rectory in Essex, England. In 1892, when Henry Bull's son took over the house, an ethereal coach was seen in the drive and a headless man walked the garden. Later occupants saw scribbled messages appear on the walls.

Ghost Writer In 1998, three workers at a museum in Havana, Cuba, resigned after seeing the ghost of writer Ernest Hemingway.

This headless ghost of a dog was photographed in Buckinghamshire, England, in 1916. The detective inspector who took the photo did not recall seeing the apparition at the time!

BLOT ON THE FAMILY
£50,000 ($27,000) was paid by the Muret family of Thionville, France, to a magician to ensure their son's success on his exams. The family were instructed to take part in obscure activities, including drinking ink and balancing eggs on their heads—but the spell failed and the boy came last in the exam results!

Return Flight from Beyond Captain Bob Loft and Second Officer Don Repo were both seen by other pilots in other airplanes after their deaths on December 29, 1972, when they crashed in the Florida Everglades.

Killer Lemons Lemons were used by witches to kill people. The name of your enemy was written on a piece of paper pinned to a lemon. This resulted in him or her becoming ill, going mad, or even dying.

Rough Justice Women in the 17th century were often drowned to prove they were not witches. A suspected witch was bound and thrown into water. If she floated she was deemed to be a witch but if she sank she was innocent —many drowned in the process.

FORTUNE TELLING

- Moleosophy—discovering a person's destiny by "reading" the moles on their body

- Geomancy—using a handful of earth or random dots to tell someone's fate

- Axinomancy—fortune-telling with an ax

- Pessomancy—reading signs created out of patterns of pebbles

- Scapulomancy—using bones to determine someone's destiny

Fading Husband Seven people saw Captain Towns in his home near Sydney, Australia, in May 1873. However, the Captain had died six weeks before. When Mrs. Towns approached the apparition, it vanished and was never seen again.

Well-dressed Ghost The ghost of an 18th-century dandy seen by the author Baroness Orczy on a London Underground station, inspired her to write her stories about the Scarlet Pimpernel.

FIT TO BE WITCHES

In December 1691, seven young girls of Salem, Massachusetts, were thrown into violent fits when they played with an "oracle". Later they began seeing "spectral figures" that hit and scratched them. The girls blamed three local women for their ills and this started off the most famous witch hunt trial in American history.

Screaming Skull Ghostly groans and other terrifying noises were heard in Burton Agnes Hall, Bridlington, England, following the death of its 17th-century owner, Anne Griffith. She had asked for her head to be kept in the house but her wish was ignored. When the noises became unbearable, Anne's coffin was opened and it was found that the head was already severed from the body. The skull was taken to the hall and the noises stopped!

Haunted Island Britain has more ghosts per square mile than anywhere else in the world!

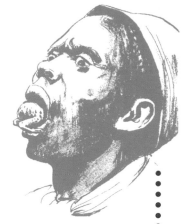

A native, accused of witchcraft in Kenya, Africa, was forced to hold a live frog in his mouth. If it slid down his throat, he was guilty. If not, he was innocent.

Aleister Crowley was dubbed "The World's Wickedest Man" because he claimed he had sold his soul to the Devil. Crowley liked to be known as "The Beast of the Apocalypse" and admitted to taking part in occult rituals and studying the secret powers of nature.

Magic in a Box

David Blaine from New York has become something of a modern-day phenomenon as an illusionist and close-up magician.

He first gained acclaim when he roamed the streets of various cities in the U.S.A., performing amazing, televised, close-up magic for random individuals. He has since attempted and succeeded in such endeavours as standing in a block of ice for hours on end, being suspended in a box, and being buried alive for one week. However, his phenomenal skills as a magician have led people to believe that these feats are purely illusionary!

In 2002, David Blaine stood on the 80-ft (24-m) pole in Bryant Park, New York City, for 35 hours straight! After being subjected to the wind, darkness of night, and the constant stares of the crowd from the ground below, he jumped into a pile of cardboard boxes that had been set up by his team beneath the pole.

In November 2000, David Blaine stood in the middle of Times Square, New York, surrounded by a 6-ton block of ice! He stood for more than 60 hours while spectators wandered round the ice, peering in at him. He emerged with swollen legs, but otherwise physically unharmed.

STREET MAGIC

David Blaine has astounded people all over the world with his street magic. He was seen pulling the head off a chicken before putting it back on, causing no apparent harm to the creature. During one trick he appeared to reach through ordinary glass to pull out a watch from a jewelry store display, and he once pulled a piece of string from his stomach!

" *Living on only water and under constant observation for 44 days straight* "

Doctor, Doctor At 16 years old, David Blaine levitated in front of his doctor, who took him in for immediate examination!

Magical Code *Mysterious Stranger*, David Blaine's book, is said to contain a code that, if read properly, can lead to hidden treasure!

Harry Houdini's original idea was the inspiration for David Blaine's New York feat in 1999. Blaine was lowered into the ground and buried alive in a glass box for one week, living on only four tablespoons of water a day.

Noah Kelly from England mimicked David Blaine's ice feat by covering himself in blocks of cheese in a shopping center in Weston-Super-Mare, England, for 48 hours!

David Blaine carried out another punishing feat of endurance in October 2003, when he spent 44 days in a glass box suspended from Tower Bridge, London, England. He was only allowed water during his time in the box, and was under constant observation from large crowds on the ground below. When he emerged from the box after 44 days, he had lost almost 55 lb (25 kg), and over the following weeks, was taken through a refeeding program in order to regain his health.

The Street of the Seven Devils in Jever, Germany, is so named because three men and four women living on it were executed for sorcery.

Suspended in Air In 1936, Subbayah Pullavar of India, levitated in front of 150 onlookers! Pullavar started by pouring water around a tent, which he then entered, hidden from the audience for several minutes. When the tent was removed, the audience were shocked to see him apparently in a trance and suspended horizontally about 3 ft (1 m) in the air. Some of the audience members waved objects underneath him but could find no evidence of support. Once the tent was placed around him again, he was seen by some onlookers descending back down to the ground, still horizontal!

Magical Name Welsh magician Richard Valentine Pitchford was a failure as "Valentine Professor Thomas" and "Val Raymond" but a huge success when billed as "Cardini"!

Devil Neighbor Near the Vatican in Rome, there is a museum devoted entirely to the Devil.

Walking Through Walls In 1986, American magician David Copperfield caused a sensation when, on a televised show, he walked through the solid mass of the Great Wall of China. However, his feat was not the first such event, as the English magician P.T. Selbit walked through a brick wall on stage back in 1914.

Witch's Craft Witches were once thought to be able to sail about in empty eggshells, which is probably why even today people often smash the shells after eating an egg.

This severed head may look very convincing, but is actually an illusion! It is created by vertically standing two mirrors under the table where the person's head is resting.

At the End of his Rope

In the Indian Rope Trick a *jaduwallah* (magician) throws a rope into the air, where it remains suspended. A small boy climbs up the rope and disappears. The magician orders the boy to descend and, receiving no response, climbs up the rope with a dagger between his teeth. He, too, vanishes! Loud screams are heard from the heavens and the dismembered body of the boy falls to the ground bit by bit. The magician reappears, shins down the rope, which then falls limp to the ground. The bits of the boy are gathered into a large sack and the boy emerges from the sack fully restored and none the worse for his dreadful experience. It is one of the most amazing feats in magic but very few people know how it is done!

Karachi and his son Khydar demonstrated their version of the Indian Rope Trick in 1935.

Light Touch In 1995, a woman on the Isle of Wight, Britain, complained that a ghost had switched on the electrical appliances in her holiday cottage! The electricity board said it was the first time a high bill had been blamed on a ghost!

Patience of a Saint St. Kevin, a 6th-century Irish saint, was canonized for tolerating the ghost of a woman he had murdered!

Burning Stakes Between 1621 and 1640, 30,000 women were accused of witchcraft and burned at the stake.

No Comforter Mrs. Dora Monroe moved into a house in Wisconsin in 1972 and found a haunted quilt! People who slept under it said that it talked to them, tugged itself off the bed, and even crawled under furniture!

GHOST TOWN, U.K.

The village of Pluckley is reputed to be the most haunted village in Britain. It has at least 11 ghosts:

- The 12th-century Lady Dering haunts the graveyard

- A screaming worker who was smothered by clay that fell from a container at a brickworks

- A highwayman who was attacked and speared to a tree at Fright Corner

- A mysterious lady in white

- A ghostly monk who haunts the grounds of a house

- A phantom coach drawn by four ghostly horses

- The black ghost of the old ruined mill

- A gypsy woman who was burned to death

- A lady who killed herself by drinking the juice of poisonous berries

- A schoolmaster who hanged himself in the village

- A colonel who hanged himself in the woods

"Man's figure appears in 'empty church' photograph"

Eddie Coxon took this photograph during a flower festival in a church in Staffordshire, England. He was sure that no one was in front of the camera, yet this ghostly figure appears in the photograph!

Lesson in History Coleen Butterbaugh in October 1963 in a room at Nebraska Wesleyan University, saw a woman vanish! When she described the incident to officials, she was shown a photo of the lady she had seen—Clarissa Mills, who had died in that room in 1936.

LINCOLN STALKS THE WHITE HOUSE

When Franklin D. Roosevelt was president, Queen Wilhelmina of the Netherlands reported seeing the ghost of Abraham Lincoln in the White House. President Theodore Roosevelt, Lady Bird Johnson, President Harry S Truman, and President Dwight Eisenhower also claimed to have seen this ghost.

Grave-robbers' Curse

The archeologists who were present when Tutankhamun's tomb was opened for the first time in 3,000 years, on February 17, 1923, ignored the warning inscribed above the tomb entrance to warn off intruders:

"Death will come to those who disturb the sleep of the pharaohs"

Howard Carter and his team of archeologists opened Tutankhamun's tomb in Egypt in 1922, oblivious to the death warning inscribed above the tomb's entrance.

PREDICTIONS OF NOSTRADAMUS

- The Parliament of London will put their king to death—Charles I was executed in London in 1649

- London to be burned by fire in three times twenty plus six—Great Fire of London 1666

- An emperor will be born near Italy and for 14 years he will hold the tyranny—Napoleon was born in Corsica, an island near Italy, and was in power from 1799 to 1814

- The dreadful war is prepared in the West, the following year the pestilence will come—World War I was followed by worldwide influenza

- For not wanting to consent to divorce the king of the islands will be forced to flee—King Edward VIII was forced to abdicate when he insisted on marrying the divorced Mrs. Simpson

Lord Carnarvon, the sponsor of the expedition, died 47 days after entering the tomb and various other expedition members died shortly after their return to England. Six years later, 12 of the expedition members were dead, and after a further seven years, only two of the excavators survived. From the original team, only Howard Carter lived into old age.

Novel Story When actor Antony Hopkins was offered the leading role in the 1974 movie *The Girl from Petrovka,* he searched in vain for a copy of the George Feifer novel on which the movie was based. While waiting for his train home he spotted a book lying on a bench. It was a copy of *The Girl from Petrovka.* During the filming in Vienna the actor was introduced to the novelist. It transpired that Feifer had lent his personal copy to a friend who had lost it in London. Hopkins showed Feifer the book he had found. It was Feifer's own copy!

A NUMBER OF PROBABILITIES

Did you know that in any group of 23 people, there is about a 50 percent chance that two of them will share the same birthday? It's nothing at all to do with coincidence, but everything to do with statistics.

PLUM OCCASIONS

The French poet Emile Deschamps once shared a table with a Monsieur de Fortgibu who was fond of plum pudding, and persuaded the poet to try some. Years later, Deschamps saw a plum pudding in a restaurant and requested a slice but was told it was reserved for another customer. This was his old friend Monsieur de Fortgibu! Several years after, Descamps attended a dinner party where one of the dishes was plum pudding. He told the story of the strange coincidence and everyone joked that Fortgibu might arrive. And he did. He had been invited to a dinner nearby but had got lost! "Three times in my life I have eaten plum pudding," said Deschamps "And three times have I seen Monsieur de Fortgibu."

Words out of Place Just prior to the Normandy landings of World War II, crosswords in the English newspaper *The Daily Telegraph* included the answers Omaha, Utah, Mulberry, and Neptune. They were all secret code names for the landings. The answer to another clue was Overlord, the code name for the operation itself. The crossword compiler, schoolteacher Leonard Dawe, was very quickly investigated by intelligence officers, but it turned out to be an astonishing coincidence.

Fall Guy Joseph Figlock was walking past a 14-story building in Detroit in 1975, when a baby fell from the building and landed on him. A year later another baby fell from the same building and survived the drop by falling on—Joseph Figlock!

David Mandell claims to have had premonitions in his dreams, which he sketched afterwards. He is seen here with some of the drawings, which bear a striking resemblance to events that happened shortly after his dreams.

Room Service In 1953 American journalist Irving Kupcinet traveled to Britain from Paris. In his hotel room he found some personal belongings of his friend, basketball player Harry Hannin. Two days later Kupcinet received a letter from Hannin in Paris, which said: "You'll never believe this, but I've just found a tie with your name on it in my hotel room."

Cradle to the Altar Alan Redgrave and Melanie Somerville had an instant rapport when they first met in a supermarket. They soon discovered that they had both been born on the same day, in the same hospital, and that their cots were placed together in the ward. Alan and Melanie married one another in 2003.

Bee Congregation Mrs. Margaret Bell, a well-known beekeeper in the English town of Ludlow, died in June 1994. For an hour during Mrs. Bell's funeral a swarm of bees settled on a building in Bell Lane!

An astrologer once assured William the Conqueror that he would invade England with 900 ships and in that vast armada, only one man would die. Only one man failed to survive the voyage—the astrologer!

Hanging Together Three men were hanged in London for murdering a man at a place called Greenberry Hill. The surnames of the murderers were Green, Berry, and Hill!

Copper-plated Katie

A psychic, named Katie, displayed the ability to grow copper on her skin! Katie had various psychic abilities, such as the ability to levitate objects, bend metal, and write medieval French while in a trance.

Psychic researcher Dr. Berthold E. Schwarz from Florida, studied Katie for some time and would watch her during her trances, as the copper appeared. It was also discovered that copper could be grown on objects that she carried, or people whom she touched. The copper was examined and found to contain 98 percent copper traces and two percent zinc. Examinations carried out on Katie led people to believe that she was exhibiting psychic side-effects, similar to the ectoplasm that mediums are said to be able to create from their mouths during states of trance.

Before she entered a trance, Dr. Schwarz would examine Katie closely and find no traces of copper, but it would often appear on her face, neck, hands, and back shortly after entering the trance. Peeling away the copper would often cause Katie some discomfort.

TELEPATHIC ESCAPE

In 1942, telepathy saved the life of British prime minister Sir Winston Churchill. He was scheduled to attend a military exercise on April 13, but, after a premonition, decided not to go. During the exercise 27 people were accidentally shot dead and 68 were seriously wounded. Brigadier Grant Taylor, who stood in for Churchill on that fateful day, was killed. Had Churchill attended as originally planned, the entire course of British history might have changed.

College Test The first scientific examination of ESP was undertaken by Professor Rhine at Duke University, North Carolina. Over 40 years, numerous people were tested and Rhine came to the conclusion that extra sensory perception or some form of telepathic communication does exist.

Water Diviner In 1952 Colonel Harry Grattan of the Royal Engineers was employed by the British Army to locate water sources in Germany. As a dowser (water locater) with years of experience, he successfully located many sites that produced water.

Swinging for Oil Ace Gotowski was called upon by the Fox Brewing Company of Chicago to search for oil in 1943. Using a pendulum Gotowski identified a suitable site; when the company drilled where he had indicated, it was discovered that he had located the largest oil field at that time.

It would appear that some people have magnetic abilities. In 1994, Edward Naumov from Moscow, Russia, displayed his ability to pin metal objects to someone. The subject found that no matter how hard he tried to resist the objects, Naumov's "energy" pinned them to him with no signs of touching or trickery!

Reading on the Radio Sydney and Lesley Piddington baffled British radio listeners with their thought-reading feats in 1949. They claim to have sent messages from the BBC to an underwater diving bell, using telepathy.

Long Distance Telepathy As part of a number of scientific tests in Russia in 1966, Karl Nikolatev was handed a sealed package chosen at random from a series of identical boxes. Nikolatev's friend, Yuri Kamensky, was 1,800 mi (2,900 km) away. While Nikolatev opened the box, Kamensky described the contents accurately. Both men were supervized by scientific teams to ensure that there was no trickery.

Tragedy Foreseen On October 20, 1966, a woman in Plymouth, England, told people in her church congregation that she had received a vision of an avalanche of coal in South Wales. The following day a mass of coal slid down from a coal tip onto the Welsh village of Aberfan, killing over 100 children and many adults.

Safe Return In 1960 the daughter of an American professor had went missing. After two months, in desperation the professor telephoned the Dutch clairvoyant Gerard Croiset, who was famous for helping in several police cases. Croiset told the father that he would hear from his daughter in six days. Six days later the professor went downstairs for breakfast and found his daughter sitting in the living room, completely safe!

Mental Moves Nelya Mikhaileva moved objects with her mind! In 1968 Russian scientists filmed her as she made a piece of bread and a glass tumbler move, and stopped and started a clock pendulum without touching anything.

Uri Geller, the Israeli psychic, explained his power to bend keys at a distance while taking part in a British radio call-in program in 1973. Minutes later the switchboard was lit up with calls reporting that keys, forks, spoons, and nails had bent spontaneously, and that watches and clocks that had not run for years had started to work again.

Putting Feet to the Fire

As part of their religious practices, people in Fiji, Asia, and India walk through red-hot coals without any apparent injury. In Fiji, the ceremony once held for religious reasons, is performed regularly for tourists. In India and other parts of Asia, the ceremony is still performed for religious reasons, and participants are required to prepare themselves spiritually before the ceremony. Many western people have tried fire walking without problems, even though the coals are hot enough to cause wood to burst into flame immediately. The ability to avoid injury seems to be because people walk on hot ashes, not on the flaming coals or wood, and because the heat vaporizes water in the skin and produces a protective film.

Fire walking is a feature at the annual Vegetarian Festival in Phuket, southern Thailand. The Buddhist devotees perform rituals to evoke good luck and purge their bodies of any evil.

Bursting into Flames

The charred remains of Dr. Bentley of Coudersport, Pennsylvania, baffled those who found him in his bathroom on December 5, 1966.

There have been many reports of people bursting into flames (spontaneous human combustion), and it is a phenomenon for which there appears to be no logical explanation. Frequently, the body is found partly consumed in a sealed room that is filled with soot and greasy particles. A common feature is that only part of the body is consumed and often combustible material nearby is completely unharmed. It was once believed that spontaneous combustion was a highly extreme reaction to drinking too much brandy or being too angry! What is most baffling is that even in a crematorium, where temperatures can reach up to 1,800°F (1,000°C), bones are not completely burned as they can be in cases of spontaneous combustion.

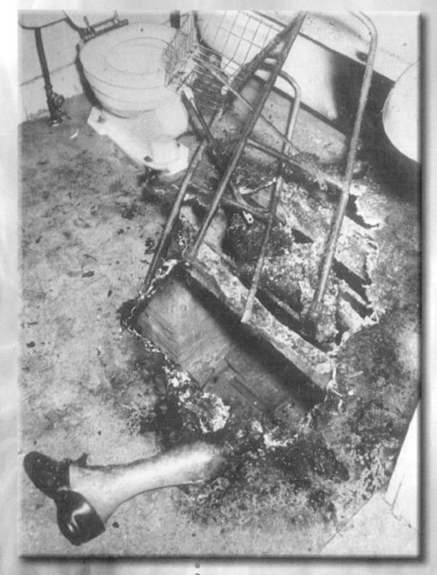

A pile of ashes and half a leg were all that was left of Dr. Bentley. An intense heat had consumed his body, but apart from the burned-through hole in the floor, little else had been damaged.

GONE IN A FLASH

- **Mrs. Mary Reezer—Florida, 1951.** The wall behind her chair and a pile of newspapers nearby had not been burned

- **Billy Peterson—Detroit, 1959.** The heat inside the car was so great that part of the dashboard melted, but Billy's clothes were unharmed!

- **Paul Hayes—London, 1985.** A fire engulfed him as he was walking in Stepney Green. The flames disappeared just as suddenly

Shocked Audience In 1880 an eminent physician, Dr. B.H. Hartwell, and several other people witnessed the death of a woman in Massachusetts, who burst into flames.

Closed in a Car In 1988, in Sydney, Australia, an elderly lady was sitting in a parked car. Minutes later, people noticed smoke coming from the vehicle, followed by an explosion. The victim was pulled out alive, but died a week later. Investigators found no trace of gas, electrical problems, or wiring faults—the case remains a mystery.

Barn Untouched In 1888 the body of an old laborer was found in a hayloft in Aberdeen, Scotland. He had burned to death but his face showed no signs of pain. The beam on which he was lying was unharmed, and nearby bales of hay had not burned.

Clue to the Triangle?

The sea between Bermuda, Florida, and Puerto Rico is reputed to have secret powers that have caused the disappearance of numerous ships and aircraft. Stories about the Bermuda Triangle began when five Avenger bombers vanished within five hours of taking off from Fort Lauderdale Naval Air Station on December 5, 1945. An interesting possible explanation was found in 2000, when a 72-ft (22-m) steel-hulled fishing trawler was found resting almost undamaged in a large crater on the bed of the North Sea, 93 mi (150 km) east of Scotland. The crater could have been caused by the release of a huge bubble of methane gas. Investigation found that the seabed in this area contained large deposits of an ice-like substance called methane hydrate, which is capable of suddenly releasing huge amounts of methane gas, which could have created a huge gas bubble to rise to the surface, causing a large ship to sink suddenly. This could also be the explanation for such disappearances in the Bermuda Triangle.

MISSING CRAFT

- *Bomber flight 19*—1945
- *Martin Mariner*—1945
- *City Belle*—1946
- *Superfortress*—1947
- *DC-3*—1948
- *Star Ariel*—1949
- *Revonoc*—1958
- *Witchcraft*—1967

Ghost on Ice While crossing a frozen lake in Canada, explorer James Alan Rennie saw tracks being formed in the ice with no visible explanation. As the tracks approached "I stood stock still, filled with reasonless panic. The tracks came within 50 yd [45 m] of me, then 20, then ten—then smack!
I shouted as a large blob of water hit me in the face. I swung round, brushing the water from my eyes, and saw the tracks continuing across the lake."

Wounded In September 1983, an Argentinean housewife had a vision of the Virgin Mary, and heard the first of 1,800 religious messages. A year later, mysterious red sores broke out on her wrists, feet, and forehead, representing the wounds suffered by Christ in his crucifixion.

Stigmata have appeared over the centuries on many highly religious people, and are often associated with "miracle cures." Italian Giorgio Bongiovanni is an unusual stigmatic in that he is not a religious person, yet he claims that in 1989 the Blessed Virgin Mary came to him in a vision and told him to travel to Fatima, Portugal. Six months after he did so, he received the first signs of the stigmata, the wounds in the palms of his hands. Since, he has also received wounds in his feet, side, and forehead. These wounds bleed daily and doctors can find no explanation for them.

Water Finders Many people seem to possess a mysterious ability to find hidden water. The dowser (person who locates water underground) holds a Y-shaped twig, traditionally of hazel, which moves violently when underground water is located. Mineral deposits and even underground cables have been located using this and similar methods, but no one seems to know exactly how or why it works.

GLOBSTER INVASION

In 1960, two Australian ranch hands found a gigantic carcass washed up on a remote beach in Tasmania. It was more than 20 ft (6 m) long, and 18 ft (5.5 m) wide. It was shaped like a turtle, and covered by greasy hair. Dubbed a "globster," a larger, similar creature was found in New Zealand in 1965, and another in Tasmania in 1970. Some have identified these creatures as blubber from dead whales, while others say they remain a mystery.

Ring of Misfortune Silent movie star Rudolph Valentino bought a ring that was supposed to be unlucky. When he wore it, his movies were flops. Several people who obtained the ring after Valentino's death fell ill or were killed.

Fishy Rain Bass and shad fell to the ground Marksville, Louisiana, on October 23, 1947. A shower of small fish, including smelts and flounder, fell from the skies in the garden of Ron Langton in West Ham, London, on May 27, 1984. The following year, a shower of fish fell in the backyard of Louis Castoreno in Fort Worth, Texas, on May 8, 1985.

Flop Jelly Rowland Moody of Southampton, England, was in his conservatory during a heavy snowstorm on February 12, 1979, when he heard something hit the roof of his house and bounce down to the ground. When he went outside to investigate, he found that his garden and those of his neighbors were covered with cress seeds (plant eaten in salads) coated in a sticky jelly.

On a dried-up lake in Death Valley, California, can be found the moving stones! These stones travel large distances, creating a variety of tracks, from straight, to curved or zig-zagged, without any apparent help. Some geologists attribute the phenomenon to strong winds, but others believe that there are stranger forces at work!

Signs in the Cornfields

Mysterious, huge patterns in standing corn, sometimes hundreds of feet across, began appearing in the 1970s in southern England. They consisted of huge circles where the corn had been pressed down, with all the stems facing in the same direction. Soon the crop circle designs became more elaborate, and spread to other parts of the world. Were they messages from aliens, or were they caused by some mysterious "ion plasma vortices"—a new scientific term invented by the self-styled cereologists who studied the phenomenon? Or are they just a new form of graffiti art carried out by hoaxers?

The Hopi Indians of Arizona believed that crop circles were signs that the world would soon end.

" Messages from aliens "

CROP SHOCKS

- Crop circles were reported as early as AD 815 in Lyon, France
- In the 16th century, a woodcut illustration shows the devil mowing patterns in a field
- More than 5,000 cases have been reported over the past 20 years
- Markings were once found in the snow in Afghanistan at an altitude of 20,000 ft (6,100 m)
- A pattern was once found underwater in a paddy field in Japan

Beasts Stalk England

One morning in 1994, actress Sarah Miles saw something unusual near her house in West Sussex. It was a huge, black cat, as big as a mastiff, and mysterious in appearance! From this sighting grew the legend of the Beast of Bodmin Moor.

Since the 1960s, there have been similar reports of large cats prowling the wild parts of Britain, and sometimes straying into built-up areas. Searches have failed to reveal them, though photographs have been taken, and livestock has been found that appears to have been killed by a large animal. However, some wild cats have been shot by farmers or run over, and among the corpses have been pumas and lynxes, as well as smaller types of jungle cat, which have been subsequently been blamed for the attacks.

This mould was made to show the size of a paw print that was discovered in West Sussex, England, said to be similar to the legendary Beast of Bodmin Moor.

This image was caught on camera by Rosie Rhodes in 1995, and is believed to be the Beast of Bodmin Moor. It was apparently far too large to be a domestic animal.

MYSTERY CREATURES

- Almas—Russia
- Orang Pendek—Sumatra
- Sasquatch—North America
- Wild Man of Hubei—southern China
- Yeti—Himalayas
- Yowie—Australia

1:37
4 12 1994

The Tracks of Bigfoot

There have been many reported sightings of a large, hairy, man-like creature—the Sasquatch—in Canada and the United States. The Sasquatch is popularly known as Bigfoot because most of the evidence of its existence is in the form of large footprints. The most impressive of these were found at Bossburgh, Washington State, in October 1969. Each footprint measured about 18 in (46 cm) long and the tracks covered about 0.5 mi (0.8 km).

A Forest Patrol officer took this photograph of "Bigfoot" in 1995, near Mount Rainier in Washington State. However, many believe it is a hoax photograph.

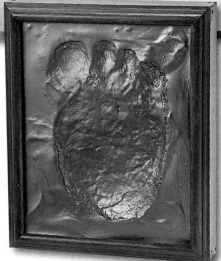

Ripley's ®

YETI FOOTPRINT
EXHIBIT NO: 22449
NEGATIVE CASTING OF A YETI
FOOTPRINT, CREATED IN TIBET IN
THE 1950s

Solid Curse A stone in the American city of Augusta, Georgia, was the cause of many deaths. It originally stood in the old slave market and rebellious slaves were tied to it and flogged. A curse was placed on the stone by the mother of a man who was killed by such a flogging. It is said that the stone has been the cause of numerous deaths every time someone has tried to move it.

Lost Civilization Atlantis, according to the Greek philosopher Plato, was an island civilization destroyed by earthquakes and swallowed up by the sea. Many attempts have been made to discover the location of this island, but without success.

LAKE MONSTERS

- Lake Champlain, U.S.A. (Champ)
- Lake Chini, Malaysia
- Lake Khaiyr, Russia
- Lake Nahuel Huapi, Argentina
- Lake Okanagan, Canada
- Loch Ness, Scotland (Nessie)
- Lough Rea, Ireland
- Tianchitianchi Lake, China

Deadly Gold No one who has seen the Lost Dutchman Mine of Superstition Mountain in Arizona has lived to tell the tale. According to local legend the mine is overflowing with gold, but every man who found it was killed by Apache Indians who were angry at the desecration of their land.

Flying Dutchman Stories of phantom ships abound, but the most famous is of the *Flying Dutchman*, which is condemned to sail around the Cape of Good Hope forever.

Snuff of That! Gold prospector Albert Ostmann was kidnapped by a family of Sasquatch in 1924 and only escaped when the male became ill after eating a box of snuff!

This Australian wildlife ranger stands with his sketch of the Yowie, which he drew shortly after apparently seeing the mysterious creature in south-east Queensland, Australia.

Atlantis West The Pacific Ocean version of Atlantis is the Great Empire of Mu. It was believed that Mu was the cradle of civilization, which sank beneath the waters of the Pacific over 12,000 years ago. No one knows its location.

CHUPACABRA FOOTPRINT
EXHIBIT NO: 22451
POSITIVE CASTING OF A CHUPACABRA
FOOTPRINT, CREATED IN PUERTO RICO
IN THE LATE 1990s

In 1995 in Puerto Rico, a strange creature was accused of attacking domestic animals and draining their blood through a single puncture wound. Eye-witnesses said that it resembled a kangaroo, with sharp fangs, red, lidless eyes, and bat wings, with spikes running down its back. The locals called the creature El Chupacabras, which means "goatsucker."

This kitten, found in Manchester, England, had a broad flat tail and "wings." The 11 in (28 cm) "wings" grew from the shoulder bone.

Vanishing Colony When John White returned from England to the island of Roanoke in Virginia, all the colonists he had left four years earlier had disappeared without a trace. No one knows what fate befell them.

Fatal Tune The song "Gloomy Sunday" was banned by Britain's BBC because it has caused too many deaths. Written in 1935 by Lazzlo Javor, a Hungarian poet, the song was associated with over 200 deaths around the world.

Path to Atlantis? American psychic Edgar Cayce predicted that remains of the temples of Atlantis would be discovered in the sea near the island of Bimini in the Bahamas in 1968 or 1969. A long "pavement" of symmetrically shaped stones was discovered on the seabed there in 1968!

Nessie's Getting Old Sightings of the creature said to inhabit Loch Ness in Scotland have been reported regularly since the 6th century. In modern times, photographs have been taken purporting to show the monster but, so far, in spite of repeated scientific expeditions, no physical evidence has been found.

LEAPING LEGEND
Victorian England was terrorized by a creature that attacked people, jumped over houses, and was impervious to bullets! Wearing a metallic-like suit and a glass and metal helmet, with talons projecting from its sleeves, it was nicknamed Spring-Heeled Jack because of its remarkable ability to jump over houses. For a period of 66 years from 1838, Jack spread panic throughout the land. But after a spectacular appearance in Liverpool in 1904 he was never seen again—and to this day no one knows who, or what, it was.

Ghostly Drumbeat A drum owned by Sir Francis Drake, England's heroic 16th-century admiral, is reported to have sounded without human hands to mark the outbreak of World War I.

Allegedly this is the hand of a yeti discovered at an altitude of 20,000 ft (6,100 m) in the Himalayas, on the border between Tibet and Nepal. In 1951, Eric Shipton photographed a long trail of huge man-like footprints. Two years later, Sir Edmund Hillary saw similar tracks during the first ascent of Mount Everest. They were believed to be the tracks of the Yeti or Abominable Snowman. The creature seems to exist, but no one knows what it is. Some people think that it is a bear, or an unknown great ape, or even a primitive form of human.

Haunting Puzzle

Sarah Winchester, of California, designed what may be the most puzzling house ever—and then spent 38 years trying to build it.

Doors that open onto blank walls, stairs that lead nowhere, trapdoors beneath which there are no openings, and balconies with no entrances are just some of the fascinating features Sarah built into her strange house in San Jose in Santa Clara Valley, California. From 1884 to 1922, builders and carpenters were kept busy building every day until Sarah died. During her life, Mrs. Winchester allowed no one inside the house except the workmen and a few maids. Today it is believed that the Winchester Mystery House is haunted by the ghosts of Sarah's husband and daughter.

Among the many strange and fascinating features of the house are a number of staircases that lead nowhere.

Built in San Jose, California, Sarah Winchester's house was originally built seven stories high! It was reduced to four stories in 1906, after damage caused by the famous San Francisco earthquake.

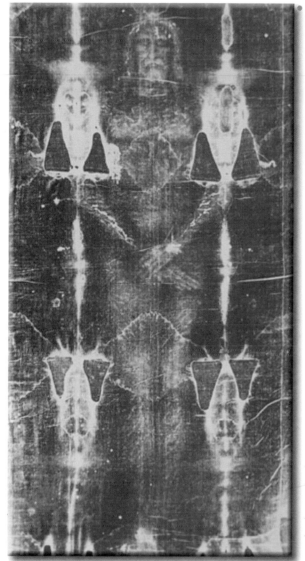

Despite attempts to prove the date of origin of the Turin Shroud by analysis, such as carbon dating, the shroud remains a mystery. Many believe that it is the shroud that Christ was covered with at his burial, while others believe it is a medieval forgery.

OPTICAL ILLUSION

IS IT A DUCK OR A RABBIT?

To see the duck, you need to rotate the image counter-clockwise. To see the rabbit, look at it from the right.

Men They Couldn't Hang

No matter how hard prison authorities tried, they could not hang John Lee. In 1885, 19-year-old Lee was sentenced to death for killing his employer. Several unsuccessful attempts were made to hang him and he was eventually reprieved.

Chaos in the Crypt

Coffins were thrown around a family vault in Bridgetown, Barbados, even though the vault was sealed! Over the next eight years, every time the vault was reopened to inter a family member, the coffins had been disturbed—but there was no sign of entry to the tomb!

Which is greater? The height of the hat or the width of the brim?

Neither! They are both the same size.

Priest Preserved

When the body of Reverend Father Paul of Moll was exhumed on July 24, 1899, it was found to be perfectly preserved. The Belgian priest had died three years previously.

Body Survives

In 1921, when the body of Julia Buccola Petta was exhumed seven years after her death during childbirth, her body was found to be in perfect condition.

Mountaintop Theater

There are over 200 stone blocks grouped to form what appears to be an amphitheater on the 2-mi (3-km) long plateau of El Enladrillado, in Chile. Archeologists do not know what the site is for, who prepared the giant blocks, or how they were transported to the site, which can only be reached by a three-hour journey on horseback.

The plain of Nazca, Peru, is covered with strange lines, some of which form patterns and others the shapes of animals. They can only be seen properly from the air—but the Inca people who made them had no knowledge of flight.

Babes in the Cosmos

HOME TRUTHS

- The amount of water on Earth never changes. Water is continually recycled—it just changes its location

- The Earth's surface area is almost 200 million sq mi (321 million sq km)

- The weight of the Earth increases by about 3,000 tons every year—this is caused by meteorites crashing into Earth

- If the Sun stopped shining, no one on Earth would know for 8 minutes

- New York is closer to the center of the Earth than it is to Honolulu

- The Earth's crust, its hard outer layer, is less than 3 mi (5 km) thick in places

Life appeared on Earth some 3.8 billion years ago, but humans have only been around for about 600,000 years.

If the history of the universe could be compressed into 24 hours, Earth began to be formed out of cosmic dust at around 9.40 a.m. Life appeared on Earth by 4 p.m. The first people walked on the face of our planet at only 11.59 p.m!

Our planet is about a third as old as the universe: Earth is between 4.3 and 4.55 billion years old, and the universe is approximately 11.2 billion years old.

Leveling of Lisbon One of Europe's worst earthquakes was in Lisbon, Portugal, in 1755. The city was wrecked and up to 60,000 people died. The opera singer Antonio Morelli (1739–1814), was buried alive under the rubble of a church destroyed in the quake. His hair had turned white.

High Speed Shock The shock waves forming an earthquake can travel at 5 mi (8 km) a second.

Ripling Rock In Holl Loch cave, Switzerland, two large stalactites hanging on a cave wall resemble flags flying in the wind.

Unshaken The Antarctic has active volcanoes and young mountain ranges, but it is the only part of the Earth that never experiences earthquakes.

Deep Tones A pipe organ was built in the Luray Caverns, in Virginia, using stalactites.

The Cave of the Swallows This deep, vertical cavern is named for the tens of thousands of swallows that live in it. Adventurers reach the floor of the huge cave, which is tall enough to hold the Empire State Building, by rappelling or parachuting—trying not to catch a swallow on the way down.

"Gosses Bluff, asteroid... 3,300 ft in diameter"

Gosses Bluff, a crater in Australia's Northern Territory, seen from space. The asteroid or comet that caused it was probably 0.6 mi (1 km) in diameter and it crashed into Earth about 142 million years ago, creating a ring of hills about 2.8 mi (4.5 km) wide.

Biggest in U.S. A man drilling for water at Manson, Iowa, in 1912 found an unusual rock at the bottom of a well shaft. It was created by the impact of an asteroid 70 million years ago. The huge rock from space, which was 1.5 mi (2.5 km) wide, was the largest known meteorite ever to have hit the U.S. mainland. It made a crater 3 mi (5 km) deep.

Two Miles Down The East Rand Mine, a working gold mine in South Africa, is 11,760 ft (3,585 m) deep.

Professors Giuseppe Geraci and Bruno D'Argenio from Naples found signs of life snuggled inside meteorites from outer space. Seen here showing their find, they discovered that once the micro-oganisms were revived they began to move and reproduce rapidly!

Blast From Space

On June 30, 1908, reindeer herders in the Tunguska region of Siberia were sent flying into the air by a huge explosion. They had been sleeping in their tents unaware that a meteorite, or a small asteroid, was heading toward them. About 4 mi (6.5 km) up in the atmosphere, the intruder from space exploded. The reindeer herders were thrown into the air and knocked unconscious. One man was killed. The mysterious object in the sky appeared to the men on the ground as if it were a great fireball. On the ground, trees caught fire. After the strange event, dust and smoke were all that remained of 40 sq mi (104 sq km) of forest.

Steady Pounding Around 20 substantial meteorites hit our planet annually. Wethersfield, Connecticut, is the only place to be struck twice by large meteorites—once in April 1971 and again in November 1982.

Well to Hell In a remote region of Russia, near the border with Finland, scientists have dug a hole 8 mi (13 km) deep. Called the Kola Well, it is the deepest hole in the world. Drilling began in 1970 and stopped in 1994. At the bottom of the hole, nicknamed the Well to Hell, scientists found rocks 2.7 billion years old.

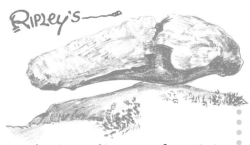

The giant rocking stone of Mt. Cimino, Italy, is 28 ft (9 m) long and weighs 385 tons, yet it rocks to and fro on its base without falling off!

Cool Cave Dwellers

The 4,000 residents of Coober Pedy, in the Australian outback, live underground to escape the blistering surface heat.

Above ground it reaches 120°F (49°C), while below ground it is a more comfortable 70°F (21°C). Almost all the population of this outback opal-mining community live below ground, where houses, churches, offices, shops, and hotels have been built. A new five-room house can be constructed with a tunnelling machine for a modest $25,000 (£14,000). The extremely harsh lunar-like landscape of this town also contains a grassless golf course where players carry around a small square of artificial turf from which they tee off!

"Crocodile Harry," a former crocodile hunter, stands in front of the walls of his underground home, which are littered with messages left by tourists who visit this subterranean mining town. Harry's house was featured in the film Mad Max: Beyond Thunderdome *(Aus 1985).*

The minister of the local church stands at the rear of the Coober Pedy underground catacomb church.

TOP FIVE
MOST DEVASTATING EARTHQUAKES

1 1,100,000 deaths, Eastern Mediterranean region—July 1201

2 830,000 deaths, Shanxi province, China— February 2, 1556

3 300,000 deaths, Calcutta, India— October 11, 1737

4 242,000 deaths, Tangshan, China— July 27, 1976

5 180,000 deaths, Gansu province, China— December 16, 1920

Since the San Andreas fault line came into being about 15 to 20 million years ago, the two sides have slid, like two lines of a highway, about 150 mi (240 km) in different directions! The fault line extends for more than 800 mi (1,300 km) and at least 10 mi (16 km) within the Earth.

Tunnel Vision Some caves are more difficult to explore than others. U.S. spelunker Mike Madden knows this better than most: in 1987, he led an expedition 25 mi (39 km) through an underwater cave in the Nohoch Nah Chuch cave system in Mexico.

Carved by Monks The Caves of a Thousand Buddhas, near Tunhwang, China, are ten storys high and 1 mi (1.5 km) long. The 500 caves in the system were carved from rock by Buddhist monks over a period of 1,000 years.

Crusty Plates The Earth's crust is not as solid as it may appear: this is because it is divided into seven large plates and nine smaller ones that move over the molten layers below. Hawaii is moving westward by around 3 in (8 cm) a year.

Justo Rosito of Lino Bueno, Spain, spent 25 years (1907–32) carving himself a home out of solid rock, using only a common pick ax. His seven-room house even includes shelves, benches, a fireplace, and a kitchen, all carved into the walls. The Spanish government was so impressed with his building that they gave him 5 acres (2 ha) of land, a medal, and a lifetime pension of 1 peseta a day!

Champion Chamber Deep below the Mulu Mountains of Sarawak, Malaysia, is the Sarawak Chamber—the largest cave in the world. It is so large that it could hold the White House, the Capitol, and Washington's National Mall. Every night at dusk three million bats emerge from the mouth of Deer Cave, one of the three other huge caves in the area.

Miles of Darkness The Mammoth Cave system in Kentucky is more than 1,000 mi (1,600 km) long. If the cave tunnels were joined in a straight line, they would stretch from Detroit to New York City.

Josefsberg, a village in South Tyrol, Italy, is in perpetual shadow for 91 days of the year. The mountains cut off the Sun from November 3 until February 2.

Overnight Success Vulcan Island, in Rabaul harbor, Papua New Guinea, rose from the ocean floor in a single night in 1870. Within a few years, the volcano had grown to become a 600 ft (180 m) peak. Cooled lava eventually joined Vulcan to the mainland.

Molten Gold When Mount Erebus, Antarctica, erupts, it throws out pieces of pure gold in its volcanic lava.

Bridge Builder Mount Sakurajima in Japan was an island until 1914, when it erupted so violently that its lava filled a strait 1,000 ft (300 m) wide and 300 ft (90 m) deep, making the island part of the mainland.

At approximately 4 a.m. on August 24, AD79 Mount Vesuvius erupted and killed the inhabitants of Pompeii, burying them under a fine ash that petrified and solidified over time. The flesh and organs decomposed leaving behind the shape of those that had died.

Surprise Crop Mexican farmer Dominic Pulido witnessed the birth of a volcano in 1943. Working in his fields, he saw a hole open in the ground, from which smoke and dust emerged as well as sulphurous materials. Slowly, a tiny volcanic cone formed. Now called Paricutin, the volcano had reached a height of 1,391 ft (424 m) by the time it became dormant in 1952. Robert Ripley tried to buy this volcano!

Lassen Volcanic National Park, northern California, attracts many tourists who want to stand on "California's Hot Rock." The rock remained hot for three weeks after being blown 3 mi (5 km) from the crater of Mt. Lassen when it erupted in 1915.

Explosive Exit Krakatoa, a volcano in Indonesia, completely disappeared on August 26, 1883. The island volcano was ripped apart by an eruption and the whole island was destroyed. The explosion was heard over 10 percent of the globe. Near the volcano, the Sun was blocked out, and dust was still falling 10 days later.

People frequently immerse themselves in the supposedly therapeutic hot mud that fills the crater within Totumo volcano, in Colombia.

"Totumo volcano in Colombia spurts mud 50 ft in the air"

Deep Sea Fire A volcano 39,000 ft (12,000 m) below the waters of the Bismarck Sea, off Papua New Guinea, emits tiny amounts of molten silver and gold when it erupts.

Sole Survivor Only one person escaped the eruption of Mont Pelée, on the Caribbean island of Martinique, in 1902. Everyone in the town of St. Pierre, at the foot of the volcano, perished, except a prisoner being held in a thick-walled cell.

Afterglow After the eruption of Mont Pelée, the tower of lava it threw up glowed so much that it lit up the night sky above for months.

Now You See It, Now You Don't Giulia Ferdinanda, a tiny volcanic island off the coast of Sicily, Italy, regularly emerges from, and disappears under, the waves of the Mediterranean Sea.

Growing in Peak Season Showa Shinzan in Japan is the fastest-growing young volcano. The cone appeared on December 28, 1943 and erupted the following year, by which time it had reached a height of 656 ft (200 m). It has now reached a height of 2,400 ft (732 m)—and is still growing!

Driven Inland The eruption of Krakatoa unleashed a tidal wave that washed the Dutch ship *Berouw* some 2 mi (3 km) up onto the shore.

TOP FIVE
DEVASTATING VOLCANIC ERUPTIONS

1 **Unnamed volcano— New Zealand—c. AD 130.** Huge crater now filled by Lake Taupo, created by massive explosion that threw out 30 million tons of ash

2 **Santorini (Thera)— Greece, c. 1550 BC.** Volcanic explosion caused a tidal wave that may have wiped out the ancient Minoan civilization in Crete

3 **Krakatoa—Indonesia, 1883.** The volcanic eruption threw material 34 mi (55 km) in the air

4 **Tambora—Indonesia, 1815.** Top of the volcanic cone was lowered by about 4,000 ft (1,219 m) in seconds by the force of the eruption

5 **Vesuvius—Italy, AD 79.** The Roman towns of Pompeii, Hercolanium, and Stabiae were buried under ash clouds of gas

Mounting Everest The height of Mount Everest increased by 6 ft (2 m) in 1999. The official height was changed as a result of using the satellite-based technology of the Global Positioning System (GPS).

Shell Shock Fossils of creatures that once lived in the sea have been found near the summit of Everest.

Fast Climb Sherpa Lhakpa Gelu conquered Everest in record time— 10 hours 56 minutes in May 2003.

Summit to Brag About Earth is not a perfect ball shape, so the summit of the Andean peak Chimorazo— 20,561 ft (6,267 m) high—is farther from the Earth's center than the summit of the highest peak—Mount Everest 29,035 ft (8,850 m) high.

Highly Mistaken Pico de Teide, in the Canary Islands, was once thought to be the world's highest mountain, but poor measurement had overestimated its height by several thousand feet.

Erik Weihenmayer, seen here about to cross a ravine, became the first blind person to climb to the summit of Mount Everest in 2001. He has also conquered the seven tallest summits of the world's seven continents as well as the Polar Circus, a 3,000 ft (900 m) ice waterfall in Alberta.

HIGH LIFE

- Sherpa Apa has climbed Mt. Everest 13 times!

- American Gary Guller was the first one-armed person to climb Mt. Everest in 2003

- In 2001 Marco Siffredi descended from the summit of Mt. Everest on his snowboard

- Davo Karnicar in 2000 came down Mt. Everest on skis

- The only person to have slept on the summit of Mt. Everest was Sherpa Babu, who spent over 21 hours there in 1999

Running on Thin Air Italian mountaineer Rheinhold Meissner was the first person to climb the world's 14 highest mountains—all the peaks above 26,250 ft (8,000 m)—without using oxygen.

At the age of 70 years, 222 days Japanese professional skier Yuichiro Miura (left) and his son display their flag at the summit of Everest. He broke the record for the oldest person to climb the peak in May 2002.

Over 1,100 climbers have reached the top of Mount Everest and at least 170 have died in the attempt.

"Over 1,100 have reached the top of Everest"

Talking Mountain The roaring mountain of Fallon, Nevada, is composed of sharp, fine, white sand. At times the sound of it rumbling and roaring can be heard for miles.

Climb on a Bus The highest point of the world's lowest-lying nation—the Maldives—is about the same height as a school bus.

Equatorial Snow Mount Kenya is situated on the Equator in tropical Africa, but despite this it is always covered with snow.

Sea for Miles Vatnajökull, in Iceland, can be seen from the Faroe Islands, 340 mi (547 km) away—the world's longest view between mountains.

Vanishing Peak In 1991, the top 33 ft (10 m) of New Zealand's Mount Cook, (the country's highest mountain) fell off in an avalanche. The peak now measures 12,316 ft (3,754 m).

Ocean Views Standing atop Costa Rica's Mount Izaru, which rises to 11,200 ft (3,414 m), a person can see both the Pacific and Atlantic oceans.

Undersea Mountains The world's longest mountain chain is under the sea. The Mid-Ocean Ridge snakes beneath the waters of the Pacific, Arctic, Atlantic, and Indian oceans for about 52,080 mi (83,812 km). This submarine mountain chain is almost 11 times longer than the Andes, the longest range of mountains on land.

Silbury Hill in Wiltshire, England, is very strange. It is a mound containing 1,250,000 tons of earth built by prehistoric man for no apparent reason!

Tabletops The flat mountain tablelands of Venezuela—called tepuis—are among the most unusual mountains in the world. The largest tepui is called Roraima, a 44 sq mi (113 sq km) tableland that rises in sheer cliffs some 9,200 ft (2,804 m) high. On this isolated tableland, all of the plant species are native, and are not found anywhere else in the world.

Lightning Strikes Seven Times!

Roy Sullivan, a park ranger in Yosemite National Park, California, survived seven lightning strikes during his life. The first strike in 1969 singed his eyebrows.

The next year he suffered burns to his left shoulder. Three more strikes followed in 1972 and 1973. The first set light to his hair—he extinguished the flames by throwing a bucket of water over his head. Just as his hair had grown back, another bolt ripped through his hat and struck his head, setting his hair on fire again. The third bolt caused an injury to his ankle. Four years later, lightning burned his chest and stomach. Finally, he survived a lightning strike that brought power lines crashing into the cabin where he was living.

BOLTS FROM THE BLUE

- A lightning bolt, on average, is 2 mi (3 km) long and 3 in (8 cm) wide
- 84 percent of people struck by lightning are male
- The temperature of a lightning bolt can reach 540,000°F (300,000 °C)—about six times hotter than the surface of the Sun
- At any given moment, there are about 1800 thunderstorms raging around the world, generating 50 to 100 sky to ground lightning strikes each minute
- Lightning can travel through the air at about 90,000 mi (145,000 km) a second—nearly half the speed of light

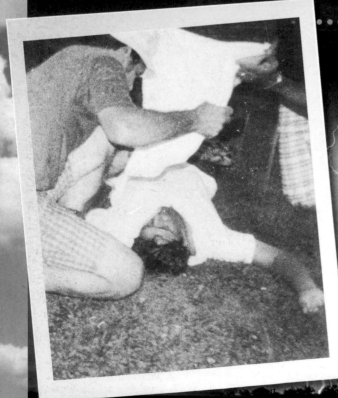

Lee Trevino was one of four golfers to be struck by lightning during the Western Open tournament held in Chicago in 1975. The bolt threw him 18 in (46 cm) into the air and knocked him unconscious.

One Hot Town Residents of Bremanger on the Norwegian coast blame a nearby power line for attracting lightning bolts that have struck all 11 houses in the village at least once in the last 35 years. One house, belonging to Klara and Kare Svarstad, was struck by lightning four times in 1999.

JUMPING THE GUN

In June 1987, lightning triggered the launch mechanisms of three rockets at NASA's Wallops Island, Virginia, launchpad. Ironically, the rockets were fitted with instruments designed to investigate lightning. "We were hoping for lightning. We just had it a little closer than we would like," said Warren Gurkin, head of NASA's sounding rocket projects branch.

Homes Blown In May 1951, lightning set fire to two houses in Marianna, Florida—one belonging to C.N. Horne of North Green Street, and the other to S. H. Horne of South Green Street.

On June 22, 1918, 504 sheep were killed by a single lightning strike in the Wasatch National Forest, Utah.

Nine years after being blinded in an accident, Edwin Robinson of Falmouth, Maine, recovered his sight after being struck by lightning on June 4, 1980.

Bolt Triggers Disaster During a thunderstorm on November 2, 1994 a bolt of lightning derailed a train carrying fuel oil through the southern Egyptian town of Drunka. The lightning ignited the oil, which in turn set fire to an oil depot close to the crash site. The blazing oil was carried through the town by the torrential rainwater, killing an estimated 500 people.

Heavenly Message In July 1984 three days after a bishop with controversial views was consecrated in York Minster, a thunderbolt struck the cathedral, causing more than £2 million ($ 3.5 million) damage.

Strokes of Luck If you have been struck by lightning and survived, you are eligible for membership of the Lightning Strike Survivors club with its motto "Join us if it strikes you."

High Toll A deadly lightning bolt struck a Boeing 707 in 1963, causing the plane to crash, killing 81 people.

Team Loss All 11 members of a soccer team were killed by lightning, during a match in the Democratic Republic of the Congo on October 25, 1998. The other team was untouched.

Winning Charge In 1910, Ray Caldwell, a baseball pitcher for the Cleveland Indians, was struck by lightning and knocked out, but went on to finish and win the game.

Scorched Earth In the Xinjian Uygur autonomous region of China, there is a 60-mi (100-km) long area where freak lightning storms regularly cause trees to burst into flames.

The Empire State Building in New York—and the Eiffel Tower in Paris—are struck by lightning an average of 20 to 30 times a year because lightning usually seeks out the highest object.

Whits Sands On January 6, 1913, 4 in (10 cm) of snow fell on Jabal Gargaf, Libya, in the Sahara Desert.

High Fall The deepest snow after one snowfall was appropriately at Mount Shasta Ski Bowl, California, from February 13 through February 19, 1959. This prolonged white-out resulted in 189 in (4.8 m) of snow.

Ski Polars Russian Dmitry Shparo and six members of his team, were the first to ski to the North Pole. Their 900 mi (1,448 km) journey took 77 days.

Cloaked in White The deepest snowfall ever recorded was 38 ft (11.5 m). This astonishing blanket of snow piled up during a single blizzard on March 11, 1911 in Tamarac, California.

Tusk, Tusk! In 1997, six elephants were killed by a single lightning bolt in Kruger National Park, South Africa.

Snowmobile Sojourn U.S. brothers Andre, Carl, and Denis Boucher—along with John Outzen in 1992—crossed the snow and ice of the North America polar cap, from the Pacific to the Atlantic, on snowmobiles. They took 56 days to cover the 10,250 mi (16,495 km) from Alaska to Nova Scotia.

Thomas the Tank Engine and his Friends were frozen in ice at the annual Japanese snow and ice sculpture festival in Sapporo, Japan. More than 3,000 people are needed to build the largest sculptures.

Holy Sign In August 2000, in Ontario, Canada, a lightning bolt ripped through a tree and set an empty three-bedroom cottage ablaze. In the ashes all that was left was a plaque of the Virgin Mary.

Frozen Funerals In the Russian city of Yakutsk, which lies deep in eastern Siberia, the ground is frozen so hard that graves can only be dug from March through September during the thaw. The citizens of Yakutsk must postpone the burial part of all funerals until summer.

COLORED SNOW

Red snow fell on part of the Swiss Alps on October 1775, and chocolate-colored snow fell on Mount Hotham, in Victoria, Australia, in July 1935. The red snowflakes were colored by sand dust blown north from the Sahara, while the chocolate snow held dust from Victoria's dry Mallée district.

In 1997, Norwegian explorer Boerge Ousland traveled solo across Antarctica in 64 days. He became the first person to journey unaided across the snowy southern continent.

Hailstones the size of tennis balls were collected by storm chasers after a hailstorm near Sitka, Kansas in 1999.

SNOW IN THE DESERT
The Gulf emirate of Dubai will have snow starting in 2006. A $277 (£153) million "ski dome" is being constructed in the desert to bring winter sports to the Arabian peninsula. The dome, which will be open to public skiing, will include a revolving ski slope through an artificial mountain.

Ice Blanket In August 1980, residents of Orient, Nebraska, were startled to see white drifts of hail blanketing their neighborhood. The hail had covered the ground to a depth of 6 ft 6 in (2 m).

Slow Thaw The amount of hail that fell on Adair and Union Counties, Texas, in August 1890, was so heavy that some stayed on the ground for six months.

Heavy! Hailstones that weighed more than 2 lb 3 oz (1 kg) fell on Gopalganj in Bangladesh in 1986.

Fatal Fall On July 19, 2002, hailstones the size of hen's eggs fell in Henan province, China. There were 25 fatalities, many people were hospitalized with head wounds, buildings were destroyed, and the windows of vehicles were smashed.

Handful of Hail A giant hailstone was found in Coffeyville, Kansas, on September 3, 1970. When scientist Nancy Knight held the hailstone in her hand, it was larger than her palm.

TOP FIVE
STRANGEST RAINS
We're not serious when we say it's raining cats and dogs, but history has recorded some unusual precipitation.

1 **Dead mice**—Bergen, Norway, 1578

2 **Live toads**—Lalain, France, 1794

3 **Live snakes**—Memphis, Tennessee, 1877

4 **Live mussels**—Paderborn, Germany, 1892

5 **Live maggots**—Acapulco, Mexico, 1968

"Hailstones the size of hen's eggs killed 25 people in China"

Hail Horror The deadliest hailstorm on record killed 246 people and more than 1,600 farm animals in Moradabad, India, on April 30, 1888.

Crossroads near Hitzacker in Germany, in 2002 were cut off by rising water levels, caused by the surging River Elbe overflowing its banks.

DON'T LOOK UP!

Frogs and toads showered down on the residents of Leicester, Massachusetts, on September 7, 1954. Tiny frogs fell from the sky in many parts of Gloucestershire, England, in October 1987; a shower of frogs occurred during a storm at Brignoles, France, on September 23, 1973, and Sylvia Mowday and her daughter were showered with tiny frogs in Birmingham, England, on June 12, 1954.

Rainfree No rain has fallen on parts of the Atacama Desert in northern Chile in recorded history.

Seeing Red On June 30, 1968, it rained blood in Britain. Upon closer examination it was found that the rain had been stained by red sand—which had come from the Sahara Desert, some 2,000 mi (3,200 km) away!

Wettest Places Every year, 467 in (12 m) of rain falls on Mawayram, India. The wettest place in the U.S. is Mount Waialeale, Hawaii, which gets 460 in (11.7 m) of rain a year.

Heaviest Rain In 1952, the heaviest single rainfall ever, dropped more than 7,500 tons of water on one acre (0.4 ha) of land on the Indian Ocean island of Réunion.

Greatest Gust The strongest wind ever recorded in the U. S.—and the highest wind speed at ground level ever recorded on Earth—was a gust of 231 mph (372 km/h) on Mount Washington, New Hampshire, on April 12, 1934.

Hold On! The world's windiest place is Commonwealth Bay, Antarctica, where gales regularly reach as much as 200 mph (322 km/h).

This mule, belonging to dairy farmer W.T. Perry of Jefferson County, Kentucky, climbed into a tree to escape a flood in January 1937.

The end of this house was carried away by a tornado, but the dishes in the pantry remained intact where they were!

Heavy Oil Deposit
A tornado that struck Bakersfield, California, in 1990 moved two 90-ton oil drums 3 mi (4.8 km), depositing them 600 ft (183 m) up the side of a mountain.

Fast Track
A tornado that swept through Wichita Falls, Texas, on April 2, 1958, traveled at a speed of 280 mph (451 km/h).

Tornado Festival
Between April 3 and 4, 1974, the U.S. experienced 148 tornadoes.

Off the Rails
On May 29, 1934, a tornado at Moorhead, Minnesota, lifted and carried an eight-car passenger train 80 ft (24 m) from the railroad tracks.

Flying Hound
In 1994, at Le Mars, Iowa, a tornado picked up a dog and its doghouse, depositing them both unharmed several blocks away.

Hot Shade
The highest temperature ever recorded was 136°F (58°C) in the shade at Al'Aziziyah, in Libya, on September 13, 1922.

Cold Out There!
The coldest temperature ever recorded on Earth was –128.6°F (–89°C) at Vostok base, Antarctica, on July 21, 1983.

On average, there are 140 tornadoes annually in the U.S.

Sunglass Cities
Sun-worshipers should head for either Yuma, Arizona, which has the highest annual average days of sunshine in the world, or St. Petersburg, Florida, where the Sun shone for 768 consecutive days from February 1967 through March 1969.

Flying Cow
In 1878, a tornado in Iowa carried a cow about 10 mi (16 km) through the air.

A Ball at the Falls

Jean Lussier, a 36-year-old from Massachusetts, made history by going over Niagara Falls in an inflatable rubber ball, rather than a wooden barrel or steel drum. He lived to tell the tale.

Lussier put his $1,500 (£800) life savings into building the 6-ft (1.8-m) diameter rubber ball, lined with 32 inner tubes to protect against shock, and an empty interior with an air cushion for protection. The ball had 150 lb (68 kg) of hard rubber ballast placed at the bottom to keep it stable, and contained enough oxygen to keep Lussier alive for 40 hours in case he was trapped under the water. On July 4, 1928, he rowed his ball out into the middle of the river, 2 mi (3 km) upstream of Horseshoe Falls. Cut free, the ballast immediately ripped from the bottom of the ball, before Lussier went over the edge at 3.35 p.m. Three of the inner tubes burst in the fall and the frame was badly damaged. However, at 4.23 p.m. the rubber ball and Lussier were picked up by the *Maid of the Mist*, a sightseeing tourist boat. Lussier survived and only suffered minor bruising!

After Lussier's successful descent of the falls, he sold off pieces of his rubber ball to tourists. When he sold out he reportedly began selling pieces of rubber that he had bought from a nearby tire store!

William Red Hill Snr. in his steel barrel in 1930 before his successful navigation of the lower rapids and whirlpool at Niagara Falls. In 1951, his son, Red Hill Jnr. repeated his father's stunt in a barrel made of rubber tubes—but died in the attempt.

DAREDEVILS

In October 1829, Sam Patch became the first person to leap over Niagara Falls. He jumped twice, with no protection. "No one ought ever do that again," said Annie Taylor, the first person and only woman to go over the falls, after she successfully plunged over Niagara Falls in a barrel in October 1901 at the age of 63. In July 1920, Englishman Charles Stevens went over the edge in a barrel with an anvil tied to his feet. All that was found of him was an arm attached to the barrel. Robert Overacker fell to his death in 1995 having attempted the jump on a jet ski and rocket backpack.

Deluge The biggest flood ever occurred about 7,500 years ago when water poured over a narrow lowland to the east of the Mediterranean, creating the Black Sea. This torrent drowned towns, villages, and farms, and may have been the flood in the Bible story of Noah.

Washed Away In the 1540s, the city of Ciudad Vieja in Guatemala was destroyed when a huge wave of water was released from beneath Mount Agua during an earthquake.

Call of the Falls In 1855, explorer David Livingstone became the first non-African to see the falls he named the Victoria Falls. However, he actually heard the roar of the falls when he was still 20 mi (32 km) away. The local name for the waterfall, Mosi-oa-tunya ("the waters that thunder"), could not be more appropriate.

When floods swept away crops and homes in Mozambique in 2000, Sophia Pedro was forced to take refuge from the rising waters in a tree. High in its branches, she gave birth to a baby, Rositha. An hour later, soldier Stewart Back was lowered from a South African military helicopter to rescue mother and baby.

Frozen Stiff On March 29, 1849 during extremely cold weather, an ice jam temporarily stopped the massive flow of water over Niagara Falls.

Falls Facts An amazing 370,000 tons of water pass over Niagara Falls every moment, but even at this rate, it would take more than 2 million years for all the water on Earth to flow over Niagara. The greatest waterfalls on Earth by volume, however, are the Buyoma Falls on the Congo River. Three times as much water plunges over Buyoma than the cascade over Niagara.

Highest The steepest waterfall is Angel Falls on the Carrao River in Venezuela. The falls drop a total of 3,212 ft (979 m), with the highest individual fall being 2,648 ft (807 m).

The Leukbach, a tributary of the Saar River in Germany, plunges over a fall as it races through a narrow street in Saarburg.

Fall Moon Cumberland Falls, Kentucky, is one of only two waterfalls on Earth that form a moonbow—a feature resembling a rainbow but seen by the light of the moon reflected on water. During a full moon, the colored moonbow is seen in the waters of the 150-ft (46-m) wide waterfall.

The Tonle Sap River, Cambodia, flows south in January, north from February to June, then changes back to south again for the rest of the year.

Ice Cliff A frozen waterfall has been discovered on the slopes of Mount Beardmore. More than 10,000 ft (3,084 m) of vertical ice now marks the former waterfall that was once 60 times the height of 160 ft (50 m) of Niagara Falls.

Rise and Fall Lake Wakatipu in New Zealand changes its level at least 320 times every day! The 52-mi (84-km) river rises and falls 3 in (7 cm) every five minutes.

Two-way Current The Baleswar River in India flows both north and south in the rainy season. It flows southward at the surface while its lower currents race in the opposite direction.

Deepest Valley Carved by a tumbling torrent, Tibet's Yarlung Zangbo is the deepest valley on Earth: its depth is equivalent to 22 times the height of the Statue of Liberty.

Tide Rules River water does not always flow to the sea: In the lowest section of the river the tide reverses the flow. The tidal wave that sweeps upstream on the Qiantong Jiang river in China is 25 ft (8 m) high.

Shortest River The world's shortest river, Montana's North Fork Roe River, is only 58 ft (17.7 m) long.

Hidden Falls Trümmelbach Cascade, a waterfall in Switzerland, is invisible for much of its height because it is inside the core of Mt. Jungfrau.

John-Paul Eatock and his Jack Russell, Part-Ex, brave swirling waters while white water swimming. This action dog also takes part in windsurfing, kayaking, rock jumping, and parachute jumping!

For half the year the water at The Trick Falls at Glacier National Park, Montana goes over the high falls, and for the other half it falls under the high falls! The reason for this is that underneath the rock precipice is a subterranean outlet for the waters of the river above. During the dry season this underground passage is large enough to hold the entire flow of the river and water goes under the falls (see bottom). During the wet season the falls increase so that the underground river is entirely hidden and the water cascades over the top falls (see top).

Deep Freeze The ground is frozen solid to a depth of 4,500 ft (1,400 m) beneath parts of Siberia—that's over three times the height of New York's Empire State Building!

Great Depression The basin that contains the Caspian Sea is so large that it could contain Missouri, Iowa, Illinois, New Hampshire, and Vermont. The Caspian lowland is the world's largest depression.

Lifeless Arab Plain Cover all of Texas with sand and you would have a desert the same size as Arabia's Empty Quarter (the Rub al-Khali), which is the world's largest expanse of sand. The Empty Quarter has no water and almost no life.

Dune of Oz The longest sand dunes are in Australia's Simpson Desert. They stretch in parallel lines a distance equal to from Washington D.C. to Philadelphia.

Dank Desert Around 90 percent of the sand in the Kara Kum Desert in Central Asia is black.

Color Map Trackers can find their way around the Namib Desert, along the coast of Namibia, southern Africa, by the color of the sand. The farther inland the sand, the older it is and the longer it has been baked rusty red in the Sun.

Singing Sands Winds blowing over the sand dunes in the Gobi Desert in Mongolia, cause a constant sound that varies from drum roll sounds to a deep chant.

A Desert is Born The world's newest desert appeared in 2001. The Hamoun, on the borders of Iran and Afghanistan, is normally a great wetland that varies in size between 400 and 800 sq mi (1,035 to 2,070 sq km). However, unreliable rainfall in the distant mountains that feed the rivers flowing toward the Hamoun, periodically turns the marsh and lake into a desert. From 1999 through 2001, these mountains experienced an extended period of drought. As a result, the Hamoun is now a salt desert. When the rivers flow again, it will fill with water.

TOP FIVE
DESERT EXPANSES

1 Sahara, North Africa— 3,250,000 sq mi (8,416,850 sq km)

2 Australian Desert, central Australia—600,000 sq mi (1,553,880 sq km)

3 Arabian Desert, Oman/ Saudi—500,000 sq mi (1,294,900 sq km)

4 Gobi Desert, Mongolia/China— 400,000 sq mi (1,035,920 sq km)

5 Kalahari Desert, Botswana— 200,000 sq mi (517,960 sq km)

The Aral Sea formerly was the world's fourth largest lake covering 26,250 sq mi (68,000 sq km), equal to the area of southern California. Today, it has decreased by 75 percent, the equivalent of draining Lake Ontario and Lake Erie. The sea level has fallen by 50 ft (16 m) leaving abandoned ships sitting on the sand.

Brutal, Dry, Run to a Hot Finish

The annual 105 mi (160 km) non-stop Desert Cup race across the arid desert of Jordan/Arabia requires the participants to carry their own equipment and supplies—apart from drinking water.

The maximum time allowed to complete the non-stop Desert Cup race is only 60 hours. Competitors race 25 mi (40 km) through mountains, then 35 mi (56 km) running over desert stones, and finally 45 mi (72 km) across sand. The frontrunners in the competition cross the Wadi Rum desert at night avoiding the intense heat, while those that follow have to run in sweltering 110°F (43°C) heat. The rules state that no runner is allowed to help any other if they get into trouble.

Leaving Petra at the start of their journey, competitors face two days of non-stop running across bleak, barren, desert terrain, stopping only briefly for a rest.

SAND BOWL

The semidesert north and east of Lake Chad in central Africa is the single most important source of dust in Earth's atmosphere. Dust is lifted off the desert's arid, dry surface by winter winds and dispersed through the planet's atmosphere.

Made in the Shade Humans have made 75 percent of the oases in the Sahara Desert. These artificial oases are irrigated valleys in which palm trees have been planted to provide shade from the Sun.

Dead Flat Australia's Nullabor Plain, a featureless, treeless expanse, is so flat that the railroad that crosses the plain runs completely straight for 300 mi (483 km).

Our Own Oasis The largest oasis in the Universe is 7,900 mi (12,713 km) in diameter. Planet Earth is the only known world where plants grow, water flows, and animals live.

Ice Trench The deepest point on land is the Bentley Trench, which lies under the ice of Antarctica. This depression is more than 8,320 ft (2,536 m) below sea level.

Lowland The deepest exposed depression on Earth surrounds the Dead Sea, between Israel and Jordan. The lakeshore is 1,310 ft (399 m) below sea level.

Over a period of 40 years the wind eroded the ground away leaving this pine tree stump in Tuscola County, Michigan, standing 6 ft (2 m) above the ground.

Dry Rot Over time, the advance of the Sahara Desert toward the Mediterranean Sea has buried some 600 Roman cities.

Wide Sahara The Sahara Desert is as large in area as the U.S.A.

A competitor in the 2003 Dakar Rally takes time out to do his ironing—on the roof of his car!

Great Grove! The largest palm grove oasis in the world, at Palm Canyon, California, stretches a distance of 15 mi (38 km) end to end.

Ships in the Sand Seals live in a desert where shipwrecks can be found. The Skeleton Coast of Namibia is a desert landscape where soaring dunes rise from beaches that are home to seal colonies and are littered with remains of craft that have floundered on the treacherous shore.

Hot Airmail The longest regular weekly mail delivery trip into a desert is a 1,625-mi (2,615-km) airplane mail run that sets off from Port Augusta, South Australia, every Saturday for Boulia in the hot dry interior.

Buried in Time Desert sands completely buried the city of Ubar, in Oman. This city was a flourishing trading center 1,700 years ago but it disappeared under the sands and was only rediscovered in 1974.

Last March An entire army disappeared in the desert without a trace. Sent by the Persian king Cambyses in 525 BC to reconquer ancient Egypt, the army was journeying to Siwa Oasis to destroy the temple of the god Amun. The oracle of the temple prophesized that the army would be defeated. It vanished in the Western Desert.

Just outside Tucson, Arizona, in the Sonora Desert, lies an airplane graveyard. Nearly 4,400 decommissioned airplanes and helicopters lie abandoned over 2,600 acres (1,050 ha) of land. The desert's climate stops the planes from deteriorating or corroding too quickly, and millions of dollars of spare parts are regularly salvaged from the planes. The FBI uses the site for rehearsing airplane hostage rescues.

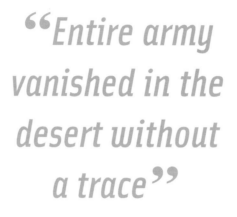

"Entire army vanished in the desert without a trace"

This tree growing in the middle of U.S. highway 60 near Fairland, Oklahoma, can never be cut down. The deed for the land for the highway was given to the state on the proviso that the tree never be disturbed. The elm was planted by a small boy in honor of his deceased father.

From Green to Grit Twenty thousand years ago, the Sahara Desert was actually covered in grasslands, rivers, lakes, and forests, when cool winds from Europe carried moisture to northern Africa.

A mirage seen in the sky over Ashland, Ohio, on March 12, 1890, appeared to be a reflection of another town some 30 mi (50 km) away.

O.00662

A Gem for the Gulf

The man-made island of Palm Jumeirah, in the Persian Gulf, will be the first man-made object to be visible from miles up in the air built since the Great Wall of China.

What will be the world's largest artificial island will form part of an enormous complex of islands and causeways, covering more than 3 sq mi (8 sq km) and measuring 4 mi (6.5 km) in length. The island will be part of a structure shaped like a palm tree, with a trunk nearly 1 mi (1.5 km) wide and 17 great leafy "fronds." The island will be the world's most luxurious beach resort with 35 mi (56 km) of artificial beaches, 50 luxury hotels, 4,500 apartments and villas, shopping complexes, cinemas, and the Middle East's first marine park.

This satellite image shows the giant palm-tree-shaped island of Jumeirah, off the coast of Dubai, jutting 3 mi (5 km) out into the blue sea.

TOP FIVE
SHORT COASTLINES

Some coutries have unbelievably short coastlines

1 **Monaco**—3 mi (5 km)

2 **Nauru**—12 mi (19 km)

3 **Bosnia-Herzegovina**— 13 mi (21 km)

4 **Jordan**—16 mi (26 km)

5 **Slovenia**—19 mi (31 km)

Delta Nation The largest delta in the world is a country—most of Bangladesh, which comprises some 55,600 sq mi (143,993 sq km). It is formed by the combined deltas of the Ganges and Brahmaputra rivers.

Ultrawave! The tallest wave ever to hit the shore was a monster of 1,720 ft (524 m) that battered Lituya Bay, Alaska, in July 1958.

Water Births The world's newest island was a surprise—and so is its name. Surprise Rock Island (Pulau Batu Hairan) off the state of Sabah, Malaysia, rose from the ocean floor in 1988. Several other tiny volcanic islets have appeared from the sea since then but, unlike Surprise Rock Island, they have either sunk back into the ocean or been washed away.

Stranded The longest involuntary stay on an island was that by the crew of the ship *Invercauld*, which was wrecked on sub-Antarctic Auckland Island in May 1864. Only three of the 19 crew were rescued alive 375 days later.

Largest Atoll Kwaljein, in the Pacific island nation of the Marshall Islands, is the world's largest atoll. The thin island bends round to enclose an area the size of Rhode Island.

Island Neighbors The island of Little Diomede, part of the U.S., sits in the Bering Strait between Siberia and Alaska. Two mi (3 km) west of Little Diomede is the island of Big Diomede, part of the former Soviet Union. The position of these two islands means that the former Soviet Union and the U.S. are only a couple of miles apart.

All at Sea The uninhabited bleak and icy island of Bouvet in the Southern Ocean is 1,050 mi (1,690 km) from the nearest land, about the same distance as from Omaha, Nebraska, to Salt Lake City, Utah.

Building Stones At Kotor in Montenegro, locals threw stones at Chisel Rock over a period of 150 years. Eventually, the small rock emerging from the waves was transformed into a more substantial islet, large enough for a church to be constructed on it.

Floridian Iceberg The farthest south an Arctic iceberg has been seen in the Atlantic Ocean was at latitude 28°22'— slightly farther south than Daytona Beach, Florida.

Divers in Egypt in 2001 made an unbelieveable discovery beneath the waves. A statue of the ancient Egyptian god, Hapi, was found at the sunken site of Heracleon.

A sheer rock pinnacle called Ball's Pyramid that rises 1,843 ft (562 m) out of the sea near Lord Howe Island, Australia is 2.5 times the height of the towers of San Francisco's Golden Gate Bridge.

This amazing Olympic torch enables a flame to exist even when submerged in water! It was carried by Wendy Craig Duncan during the preparation for the 2000 Sydney Olympic Games.

Kingdom on Stilts

Roy Bates claims that the "island-fort" he owns, which measures 430 x 120 ft (131 x 37 m), is the smallest state in the world. Eight miles off the eastern coast of England, the fort, a former World War II British Royal Navy fort, named Roughs Tower, stands on stilts above the North Sea.

SHIPWRECK ISLAND

In the Moroni River between Suriname and French Guiana, a wrecked ship has given birth to an island. The vessel slowed the water flow, allowing mud to be deposited. The ship filled with mud, and seeds carried by the water became lodged and germinated. Over a period of 36 years, the shipwreck was transformed into a tiny (nameless) island, sprouting trees.

In 1966, Bates and his wife Joan, declared the fort to be the kingdom of Sealand and themselves to be king and queen, despite never receiving official recognition of such. "King Roy" over time developed national treasures, such as the flag of the Principality of Sealand, a national anthem, gold and silver coins launched as Sealand dollars, stamps, and passports.

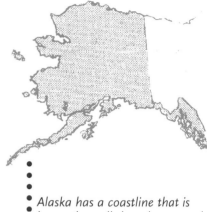

Alaska has a coastline that is larger than all the other coastal states in the U.S. combined.

Michael Bates is King Roy's heir apparent to Sealand (seen in the background), the fort they claim to be the smallest state in the world.

Surfing the River

An amazing natural tidal wave races each year up the River Severn in England.

This phenomenon travels up the Severn estuary, tumbling its way for a distance of 25 mi (40 km). The tidal wave, known as a bore, occurs when the volume of water entering the Bristol Channel from the Atlantic is forced into a narrow channel and rises in height by up to 50 ft (15 m). The speed of the water increases to an average of 10 mph (16 km/h). Dave Lawson holds the record for the longest river tidal wave to be ridden by a surfer—he traveled a distance of 5.7 mi (9.2 km) in 40 minutes.

MONSTER WAVE
The highest wave at sea verified in modern times was a 280-ft (85-m) wave that struck Japan's Ryukyu Islands in 1771. The wave was powerful enough to toss a huge rock, weighing over 75 tons, more than 1 mi (1.6 km) inland.

Deep Blue Sea The deepest point in the ocean bed is 1.25 times deeper than Mount Everest is tall! A staggering depth of 35,830 ft (10,921 m) has been recorded in the Marianas Trench in the Pacific Ocean.

Delving the Depths On January 23, 1960, the U.S. Navy bathysphere *Trieste* descended to a depth of 35,797 ft (10,911 m), the deepest point descended to in the Marianas Trench.

Clear as Glass The water of the Weddell sea off Antarctica is so clear that you can see small objects more than 260 ft (79 m) below the surface!

Undersea Jet The water coming from one underwater hot spring, 300 mi (483 km) off the U.S. West Coast, is 759°F (404°C).

Freshwater Ocean Beyond the mouth of the Amazon River, for between 100 and 160 mi (160 and 255 km) beyond the mouth of the Amazon River is water from the Atlantic.

An island in a lake on an island in a lake on an island! The surface of the lake in Taal Volcano on the Philippine Islands is below sea level.

A surfer rides the waves on the River Severn bore.

Bed of Mud Beyond the mouth of the Amazon River are deep deposits of mud and other sediments carried by the river. These deposits form a cone that is 425 mi (685 km) long and 160 mi (260 km) wide. The mud is 36,000 ft (11,000 m) deep, more than 6,000 ft (1,829 m) deeper than Mount Everest is high!

Pacific Jacuzzi Geologists have estimated that there might be as many as one million volcanoes on the floor of the Pacific Ocean. So far, more than 5,000 active sub-marine volcanoes have been discovered.

Mighty Amazon The amount of fresh water pouring from the mouth of the Amazon into the Atlantic Ocean in one day would be enough to satisfy the entire water needs of the U.S. for five months.

Flight from the Deep The deepest underwater escape was made by Roger Chapman and Roger Mallinson from a depth of 1,575 ft (480 m) off the coast of Ireland in 1973. Their vessel, *Pisces III*, had sunk and they remained trapped for 76 hours before escaping.

The highest waves regularly ridden by surfers are at Waimea Bay, Hawaii. The waves at this bay frequently rise to a staggering 30–35 ft (9–11 m).

High Deposits On the Hawaiian island of Lane there are sediments that were deposited by waves at a height of more than 1,200 ft (366 m) above the sea. Such huge waves could only be caused by a massive landfall underwater.

Tsunami Rider The greatest wave ever ridden by a surfer was a wall of water about 50 ft (15 m) high. It was probably a tsunami (a wave created by an earthquake). It was ridden in 1868 on the ocean off the Hawaiian island of Minole by a Hawaiian surfer who was caught by the wave.

Underwater Everest The tallest underwater mountain is nearly as tall as Mount Everest. A seamount between Samoa and New Zealand rises 28,500 ft (8,687 m).

Towering Wave A U.S. serviceman on board the USS *Ramapo* in the Pacific in 1933 recorded a wave 112 ft (34 m) high. This wave was nearly twice as high as the bust of Abraham Lincoln on Mount Rushmore.

Seabed and Breakfast A hotel beneath the waves is under construction off the coast of Dubai, in the United Arab Emirates. Access will be through a glass tube from the reception area onshore.

Running Water The strongest ocean current is the Antarctic Circumpolar Drift that flows at nearly 7 billion cu ft (2 billion cu m) per second in the confined passage between South America and Antarctica.

"A wave twice as high as the bust of Lincoln on Mount Rushmore"

Deep Salvage In 1992 a wreck 17,250 ft (5,258 m) below the waves was salvaged by the USS *Salvor*.

Room at the Bottom Richard Presley spent 69 days underwater in a module at Key Largo, Florida, in 1992.

Wandering Raft A raft called the *La Balta* drifted 8,600 mi (13,840 km) across the Pacific Ocean from Ecuador to Australia in 1973.

Six Months Adrift Maurice and Maralyn Bailey were adrift on a raft in the Pacific Ocean for 177 days after a whale sank their boat.

Surviving Alone Poon Lim, a British seaman, was adrift 133 days alone on a raft in 1943.

The Strokkur hot spring geyser in Iceland sends jets of boiling water and hot steam 115 ft (35 m) into the air every seven to ten minutes. Iceland has more than 700 geysers and hot springs.

European Record The hot water springs at Polichnitos, on the Greek island of Lesvos, are the hottest in Europe. The water bubbles from the ground at temperatures of between 169°F and 196°F (76°C and 91°C).

Snow Bathing Iccland's natural hot water feeds the Blue Lagoon, a pool whose waters look frosty blue. The water, however, averages 104°F (40°C) and its mineral-rich properties have medical powers. In winter, bathers enjoy the hot water while temperatures are way below zero and the pool is surrounded by snow.

Himalayan Heat Water gushes from the hot springs of Manikaran, in the Indian Himalayan foothills, at 201°F (94°C) for those able to stand the high temperature. Regular dips in the Manikaran spring—the world's hottest—are said to cure all kinds of skin diseases. Rice will cook in Manikaran spring water in 20 minutes.

ICELANDIC BANANAS
Hot water springs feed pipes that heat the buildings of the Iceland's capital, Reyjavik. Hot water pipes are also used to heat greenhouses that grow fruit and vegetables that could not survive in the open. A bunch of bananas grown in an Icelandic greenhouse heated in this way was once presented to British prime minister, Sir Winston Churchill.

Hot Water Much of the water in Norris Geyser Basin in America's Yellowstone National Park is hotter than the boiling point. A scientific drill digging at nearly 1,000 ft (325 m) below the surface measured a temperature of 459°F (237°C). Yellowstone contains more than 10,000 thermal features, including about 500 geysers—more than 60 percent of the world's geysers.

Tallest Geyser The tallest geyser in the world is Steamboat geyser, in Yellowstone National Park. The geyser throws water between 300 and 400 ft (100 and 135 m) in the air during eruptions. The problem for visitors is that it is temperamental. Its highest eruption was in the 1950s and Steamboat has not thrown a really high water spout since May 2000.

Roaring Tide

In a matter of hours, Canada's Bay of Fundy daily fills with water as high as a four-story building. Twice a day, the world's highest tides create a difference of between 24 and 54 ft (7 and 16 m) in the depth of the seawater—the average difference is 48 ft (14 m). At mid-tide, the currents in the bay give out a roar that is known locally as "the voice of the moon."

The low tide exposes a "flowerpot" rock in the Bay of Fundy, on which a lone tree grows.

Regular as Clockwork Yellowstone National Park's Old Faithful Geyser gets its name because of the regularity of its eruptions. It erupts every 63 to 75 minutes. Nearby Anemone geyser is even more predictable: it erupts every seven to ten minutes. Anemone's pools fill with water that splashes as it boils. When the water is thrown up 10 ft (3 m) in to the air, the pool drains completely.

Acidity Echinus Geyser in Yellowstone National Park is the highest acid-water geyser in the world. It erupts to a height of 40 to 60 ft (12 to 18 m).

In Hot Water Thermopolis, Wyoming, boasts the world's largest hot water spring. The first written account of the spring, in 1776, recorded that a rattlesnake had fallen in the hot water and been cooked. The main spring at Thermopolis gushes 18,600,00 gal (84,500 million l) of water a day.

"Chess pieces in hot water"

Chess boards and pieces are provided for bathers who dip into the hot springs in Budapest, Hungary!

Deep and Deadly Bite

The viperfish's teeth protrude far beyond its mouth and eyes. To scale, if your teeth were this big, they would stick out an amazing 12 in (30 cm)! It has the longest teeth, in proportion to its head, of any animal.

The viperfish has over 350 light organs on its body to attract fish in the dark depths where it hunts.

This monster fish is one of the fiercest predators of the deep. To attract its prey it has a long dorsal spine with a light-producing tip. It is thought that the viperfish approaches its victims at high speed, impaling them on its teeth, extending its hinged skull to swallow large prey.

TOP FIVE BRIGHTEST FISH

More than 1,500 kinds of fish glow or shine to lure prey and attract mates. Some can be seen from 98 ft (30 m) away.

1 **Flashlight fish**
2 **Lanternfish**
3 **Dragonfish**
4 **Slickhead**
5 **Midshipman**

Slimeball The world's slimiest animal must surely be the hagfish. It sheds a sticky substance from its skin that mixes with seawater to make a mass of slimy mucus ten times the volume of the fish itself.

Scavenger Hagfish have the slimiest habits too. They use their sucker-like mouths to bore into decaying carcasses, then live inside the dead animal as it rots away.

Flashdance A flashlight fish's light organs act like headlamps. By blocking off these lights and changing direction in the dark, it can confuse predators.

LIKE MOTHS TO A FLAME

Lanternfish use their bodily light (photophores) to attract both their prey, which comprises smaller fish, and also to attract a mate at breeding time. Some males and females have different patterns, allowing them to recognize each other in dark water.

Never seen Alive Beaked whales are champion divers, staying underwater for two hours or more. Most kinds are rare—Longman's beaked whale has never been seen alive and is known only from two washed-up skulls.

The giant squid can grow to a massive 66 ft (20 m)— that's almost as long as a tennis court! It has the world's biggest eyes. Larger than soccer balls, they help it to see flashes of light that are made by its prey of fish and smaller squid, at its favorite hunting depth of up to 3,000 ft (1,000 m).

At 65 ft (20 m) long and 60 tons in weight, the bull sperm whale is the world's biggest predator. One was found with an entire 4-ft (12-m) long giant squid in its stomach! This gigantic specimen was stranded and died on Roemoe Island in the North Sea in 1997.

COOL HEAD

As the sperm whale comes up from a dive, its head "melts"! The forehead contains about 25 bathtubfuls of the substance spermaceti. This turns hard and waxy in the cold depths, then expands and becomes more oily as the whale rises again.

Take a Breath When a whale breathes in, it sucks about 500 gal (2,000 l) of air within about 2 seconds!

BOTTOM FIVE
DEEPEST-DIVING MAMMALS

1 Sperm whale
9,900 ft (3,000 m) plus

2 Bottlenose whale
6,500 ft (2,000 m)

3 Killer whale
3,300 ft (1,000 m)

4 Elephant seal
2,300 ft (700 m)

5 Weddell seal
1,970 ft (600 m)

"swallows prey weighing ten times more than itself"

SICKENING TRICK

Sea-cucumbers are relatives of starfish and sea urchins. They live in deep waters and tidal pools and sift mud for edible scraps. In some regions they are the most common dwellers of the ocean floor. If disturbed, they throw up —ejecting not only feces, but also particles of decayed food and mud over their attacker. The slimy discharge contains much of their guts, which look like pale threads.

The largest animal mouth, compared to body size, belongs to the gulper eel (pelican eel). This weird fish, 24 in (60 cm) long, extends its jaws to swallow prey weighing ten times more than itself.

In Pieces A type of sponge, called the red sponge, incredibly can break into thousands of pieces—without dying! The broken pieces of the animal reform until it is whole again.

KISS OF LIFE

In the vast black ocean depths it can take time to find a breeding partner. When the tiny male deep-sea anglerfish mates, he grabs the larger female with his mouth, hangs on, and gradually joins or fuses with her body so that he can never leave. He even shares her food via her blood supply, and, in return, fertilizes her eggs.

Back in the Swim Again The 5 ft (1.5 m) fish, the coelacanth, thought to have died out with the dinosaurs, caused a sensation when discovered alive and well by scientists off southeast Africa in 1938. Exactly 60 years later the same thing happened in Indonesia, when another, different species of coelacanth was found.

Longest Survivor The title "greatest living fossil" goes to the lampshell or lingula. It looks like a clam but is a separate animal group that has survived for more than 450 million years.

Octopuses can learn to count to five and even distinguish different shapes! Apart from dolphins, they are the cleverest sea creatures—this octopus has been taught to open closed jars in order to grab hold of the small crabs inside.

Killer Shark

The huge, serrated, triangular teeth of the great white shark are amazingly adapted for tearing into flesh! It often swims along with teeth bared, just to warn other sharks to keep away from its territory.

TOP FIVE
DEADLIEST SHARKS

Each year 50 to 100 serious shark attacks are reported worldwide, with usually less than ten fatalities. But that's just the reported ones...

1 Great white shark
2 Tiger shark
3 Bull shark
4 Sand shark
5 Hammerhead shark

Great whites are fast learners, and some develop the habit of cruising just off beaches, waiting for unwary swimmers. A "small" great white caught off Japan in 1954 had swallowed a 13-year-old boy—whole!

The great white attacks ferociously, retreats while the injured prey becomes weaker, and then returns to gorge on the flesh!

The movie Jaws (U.S. 1975) was based on a rogue shark that terrorized beaches on Long Island, and killed at least five people in the summer of 1916. The most likely culprit, which had the shin of a boy in its stomach when caught, was probably not a great white but a bull shark.

Bitten in Half

Australian diver and shark expert Rodney Fox needed 462 stitches during a four-hour operation after a shark attack. He was nearly bitten in half, and his abdomen was fully exposed with all his ribs broken on the left-hand side of his body. He was rushed to hospital—only held together by his wet suit! Just three months later, he was back in the water with his own personal memento—a great white tooth embedded in his wrist.

Rodney Fox was ferociously attacked in 1963 by a great white shark during a spear-fishing tournament off Aldinga Beach, Australia—and survived to tell the tale!

Dangerous Waters In South America, people swimming or even doing their washing have been bitten and killed by bull sharks that have swum up the Amazon, 1,500 mi (2,500 km) inland.

EATEN ALIVE

Sharks attacked and killed more than 500 men in 1942 during World War II. A German submarine torpedoed a British ship carrying Italian prisoners-of-war off the coast of South Africa—all the men on board either drowned or were killed by the sharks.

The whale shark is the world's biggest fish, weighing in at more than 15 tons. Although five adults could fit into its cavernous mouth, fortunately it only eats minute plankton.

Not Fussy The tiger shark is called the "dustbin shark" because it bites and swallows almost anything— edible or not. Tiger sharks have been cut open to reveal swallowed fuel cans, bicycle tires, lumps of wood, parts of a dead dog and in one, a tom-tom drum bigger than a soccer ball.

Largest Fish Ever Caught! A whale shark measuring 45 ft (14 m) in length, 23 ft 9 in (7 m) round its girth, and weighing 30,000 lb (13,600 kg) was captured after a fight lasting 39 hours at Knights Key, Florida, on June 1, 1912.

Pet Monster Hawaiian Tom K. Maunupau from Honolulu rode a 6-ft (2-m) shark that he kept as a pet!

Back to the Sea A dead shark sinks so slowly that its body is almost completely dissolved by the salt water before it reaches the bottom of the sea. The only part of the shark that is impervious to the action of the salt is its teeth.

Baby Teeth The tiger shark bears live young and may give birth to as many as 27 infant sharks, all perfectly formed and equipped with teeth.

Growing Smaller The paradoxical frog ouf South America grows up to 10 in (25 cm) as a tadpole but shrinks to about 3 in (7 cm) long when adult!

Water Filter Basking sharks take in 400,000 gal (1,500,000 l) of water through their mouths every hour.

Give us a Wink The shark is the only fish that can blink its eyes.

Blubber Lips The megamouth shark has bathtub-sized lips that could suck you in whole. But this shark, which grows to 16 ft (5 m) long and almost 1 ton in weight, feeds on tiny creatures hundreds of feet down. It was once thought to have glow-in-the-dark lips, but this has not been proved!

Large moray eels dart out from cracks and inflict lightning bites with their needle-like teeth. Its mouth is home to more than 100 kinds of deadly germ!

Sea Floor Builders Lamprey eels build nests 3 ft (10 m) high and 4 ft (1 m) wide on the bottom of the sea—both parents work together to carry heavy stones that make the nest.

Full of Air To ward off attackers, the globe-fish can inflate its body to three times its normal size by filling an air bladder inside its body.

Dangerous Jolts! The 220-lb (100-kg) Atlantic torpedo or electric ray sends out shocks of 200 volts, which could kill a person. In freshwater, the meter-long electric catfish generates 400 volts, while the electric eel delivers 500-plus volts, enough to knock out a horse.

Slippery Trip In New Zealand, blackwater rafting has become increasingly popular. The pastime involves riding inner tubes through dark, underground cave rivers that can be teeming with eels.

WAR IN THE WOMB!
The sand tiger shark grows its young in a womb-like part inside the body. The babies bite and fight inside the womb until the strongest one—usually the one that reaches a length of 2.5 in (60 mm) first—is left, having eaten the other babies. Some people have cut open pregnant sand tigers and had their fingers bitten by the unborn babies.

Ripley's
MEGALODON SHARK JAWS
EXHIBIT NO: 17583
JAWS BIG ENOUGH TO
SWALLOW A CAR

Ripley broadcasted a live radio show from the bottom of the shark tank at St. Augustine, Florida, on February 23, 1940.

Killer whales can weigh up to 10 tons and grow to 33 ft (10 m) in length—that's as big as a three-story building! There are only a few recorded attacks by killer whales on humans. They have at least 25 methods of hunting victims, including tipping penguins off ice floes. They also ride waves onto the shore and hurl themselves from the foam up the beach to grab an unwary seal. Then they wriggle around back into the water.

TOP FIVE
WHALE PARASITES

Who'd be a whale? Many are infested with strange parasites that live on no other animal.

1 **Tapeworms** 98 ft (30 m) long in a sperm whale

2 **Lungworms** the size of a banana

3 **Lip lice** thumb-sized, not real lice (insect) but crab relatives

4 **Sinus flukes** leech-shaped, hand-sized animals in the sinus airways, occasionally burrow into the brain

5 **Barnacles** up to fist-sized, mainly on the head

Sonic Attack Whale grunts are measured at 180 decibels. They are the loudest sounds made by any animal—about as loud as a rocket taking off. Sperm whales use their loud grunts to knock out prey.

Tune that Carries Humpback whales can sing for more than 20 hours non-stop. Their eerie moaning songs have been detected by underwater microphones from over 62 mi (100 km) away.

Hum Bug The 72-ft (22-m) fin whale's communication "song" is an immensely loud, low hum that has such a constant pitch that it has often been mistaken for throbbing ship engines. In 1964 a fin whale nearly caused a nuclear incident— U.S. sailors thought they heard a Russian attack submarine creeping into American waters.

ANTARCTIC PERIL

The first recorded fatality due to a leopard seal was in Antarctica in 2003 when a research scientist was attacked while snorkeling near the shore. The seal pulled the scientist under and she drowned. Leopard seals are big, fast, and fierce—over 13 ft (4 m) long and weighting in at half a ton.

The bowhead whale has the biggest head of any animal—one-third of its total body length! This whale was 53 ft (16 m) long with an 18-ft (5-m) long skull. Each lip measured over 33 ft (10 m) around the curve.

Waterproof In the days of mass whaling, sailors cut off the foreskins of male great whales and used them as poncho-like raincoats.

Poison in the Pool

The blue-ringed octopus may have a body that is only a little larger than a tennis ball, but it has a deadly bite, packing enough venom to kill at least seven people.

The blue-ringed octopus is usually dark brown. However, when it becomes agitated it turns a vivid yellow with electric blue rings.

In 1967 a man paddling in a rock pool in Australia lived only 90 minutes after being bitten. The blue-ringed octopus lurks in rock pools on the the coasts of the Indian and Pacific Oceans and bites people as they wander in the shallows. The bite itself may not be felt, but within five minutes or so the victim will become dizzy and have difficulty breathing.

Disarming The female nautilus, a deep-sea creature related to the octopus and squid, has about 90 arms.

All Eyes The deep-sea benthal octopus has eyes that are one-third the size of its entire body.

SALVAGE TOOL
A cargo of porcelain in a ship at the bottom of Japan's inland sea was recovered a century after the sinking. Octopuses like to curl up in confined spaces, so they were lowered into the wreckage and clung firmly to porcelain bowls and vases allowing them to be hauled safely back to the surface.

Struggle to Survive The female octopus gives birth to 200,000 offspring—but only one or two will reach maturity and reproduce themselves.

Fast Gain An octopus can increase its body weight by 2 percent a day.

Slow Loss In many species of octopus, the female is able to breed before she turns three years old, but she does so only once, dying soon after!

Land Grabs Some octopuses occasionally leave the water and crawl onto land to hunt for food. They can climb out of the water and up over rocks, or even walls.

Poor Crabs Octopuses have been known to climb over the edge of fishing boats and open up a hold full of crabs.

SUCKER FACTS

- An octopus has no skeleton and can "ooze" through an opening no bigger than its eyeball
- The octopus has three hearts, blue blood, and permanent high blood pressure
- The blue-ringed octopus usually only lives for two years
- Each octopus sucker can have up to 10,000 neurons (nerve cells) to help it touch and taste
- The pygmy octopus can live in one half of an empty clamshell, pulling the other half of the shell shut with its suckers
- Octopuses pass food from sucker to sucker into the hard beak within their mouth

SEA FACTS

- Many fish can change their sex
- Vampire snails crawl from the seabed at night to suck sharks' blood
- The Australian glass eel is so transparent that if you held it in front of these words you could easily read them
- Starfish feed by turning their stomach inside out through their mouth
- The giant ocean sunfish grows from the size of a pinhead to weigh more than 2 tons!

Sex flee Oysters are able to change from male to female and back again, depending on which is best for mating!

Suicide fish The porcupine fish is so poisonous that it is often eaten in Japan as a means of committing suicide.

Seasonal Dish The Chinese fish of Australia is edible for nine months of the year, but poisonous in June, July, and August!

Deadly Beauty With a dark blue body and red teeth the trigger fish of Hawaii can be eaten safely, but when it is pale blue it is violently poisonous!

Laff fish Stepping on the hollow spines of the laff fish's back can cause an extremely painful death to humans!

Quiet life It is thought that some species of clams have lived for over 100 years.

Killer jellies In Australia a young boy died in less than five minutes after swimming into a swarm of jellyfish, called sea-wasps or box-jellies. He was allergic to the stings and his body couldn't cope with the poison.

The giant clam can weigh up to 500 lb (225 kg)—more than three average-size people! The shell opens and closes very slowly, and stories have been told of human-beings becoming trapped within its jaws!

If a starfish loses an arm, it will grow another! Indonesian fishermen caught and chopped up starfish that were eating and ruining their shellfish beds. They threw the bits back into the water—and the starfish population rocketed because each of the arm parts grew into a new starfish.

TOP FIVE
STINGERS

These innocent-looking creatures can cause you intense pain if they sting you.

1 **Jellyfish** box-jellies and sea-wasps
2 **Sea urchins**
3 **Fire corals**
4 **Weever fish**
5 **Stonefish, lionfish**

Christmas Road Kill

A staggering 120 million red crabs crawl out of their burrows from the forest on Christmas Island and start their annual mating migration to the seashore. The route takes them through towns, highways, railroads, and cliffs to the sea.

About one million red crabs are killed every year crossing streets and railroad tracks on Christmas Island.

Revenge Ten times more people are stung by lionfish that are captive in aquariums, than by those in the wild. The sharp spines inject a poison causing an unbearable stinging pain.

LAND LOVER

The tree-climbing crab, which is commonly known as the robber or coconut crab, can grow to a width of 40 in (1 m) and weighs about 37 lb (17 kg). It lives mostly on land and, if submerged beneath the water for more than a few minutes, will drown.

Watery End The candiru, a parasitic fish of the Amazon, enters the body through the urethra and lodges itself in the bladder. It is fatal unless surgically removed quickly.

Deadly Spines The stonefish is said to have the most powerful poison of any sea animal and it can kill in 15 minutes. More than 50 deaths per year have been reported along coasts from India to Australia. The poison is injected by spines on the fish's back, as it lies camouflaged on a rock or is part-buried in sand.

Afterlife Men o'war and box-jellies can sting for many hours after being washed-up dead on the beach.

"bulls weigh up to five tons"

Elephant seals are as big as real elephants—the males weigh up to 5 tons. At breeding time they rear up and roar, and bite deep wounds in their rivals. They are so heavy that sometimes they trample or crush their own partners and offspring.

Mixed Family Female tortoises mate with several males at sea. One nest, therefore, can contain hatchlings that have different fathers.

TOP FIVE

SURVIVAL OF THE FITTEST

Some sea animals can survive on land an amazingly long time.

1 Robber crab
2 Climbing perch
3 Common eel
4 Mudskipper
5 Ghost crab

Oily Resource Although a male elephant seal's blubber is just 7 in (18 cm) thick, it can yield as much as 210 gal (800 l) of oil!

Boring Shellfish The piddock shellfish slowly drills itself into solid rock by twisting its rough-surfaced shell to and fro. As it burrows it grows, so that it can never escape its stony prison. It feeds on tiny particles filtered from seawater.

Attack from the Rear One of the nastiest parasites on Earth is the parasitic barnacle. It lodges itself directly under a crab's tail and grows tentacles from its bag-like body into its host. It sucks out all the nutrients, eventually killing the crab!

Misleading Frills The king ragworm, up to 1.5 ft (0.5 m) long, has a frilly-edged body and looks harmless. Unlike most worms, it has a powerful bite and can easily draw blood.

WORLD'S LONGEST ANIMAL?
The longest creature is not a snake or even a whale—it's the bootlace-worm (ribbon-worm or nemertean), which lives on the seashore. Some estimates put its length at more than 98 ft (30 m), but it's only as thick as a little finger. This wriggling predator loops and coils itself under stones, and it can turn its guts inside out in self-defense.

Water Pistols Sea-squirts are simple creatures with leathery, bag-like bodies that stick to rocks and filter water for food. They have no proper eyes, brain, or limbs. Yet they are probably the ancestors of all vertebrate (back-boned) animals, from fish to humans. If prodded when the tide is out they squirt out water.

Bags of Water Jellyfish consist of more than 95 percent water. They have no bones, heart, brain, or real eyes.

Slow Assassin The deadly snail inside a coneshell can jab a small venom-loaded "dart" into your skin. The pain has been described as "red-hot needles being twisted through the veins."

Mudskippers prefer to swim with their 360° swivelling eyes above water. On land they keep them moist by retracting them into water that is stored at the bottom of the eye sockets.

Skipping a Breath
Mudskippers can stay out of water for a day or more, by breathing in three different ways. They carry a small "personal pond" of water inside their large neck gill chambers, from which they absorb oxygen as usual, and which is "refreshed" by dipping into a puddle now and then. They also take in oxygen through their tough, slimy skin. And last, the mouth gapes to absorb oxygen through its blood-rich lining. Mudskippers skip along using their pectoral (front) fins as stumpy legs, and with a tail-flick they can leap a distance of 3 ft (1 m) or more.

Vampire bats make small cuts with their sharp teeth, sucking blood from victims while they are asleep. Special chemicals in their saliva stops the blood from clotting.

Rocky Horrors

As many as ten million bats hang from the roofs of single caves in North America and Indonesia during daylight hours. Their droppings form huge, stinking, slimy mounds of guano, which feeds birds, insects, and other swarming life forms that share the almost total darkness.

BOTTOM FIVE
CAVE DWELLERS

Some animals live deep below the surface of the Earth, depending on water on the cave walls to wash down food from lakes on the surface.

1 **Eyeless shrimps and crayfish**

2 **Blind cave-fish**

3 **Cave crickets**

4 **Cavern salamanders**

5 **White wingless beetles and crickets**

This amazing two-headed American rat snake hatched at an animal park in Tilburg, the Netherlands, in 2002.

Spittle for the Soup

Cave swiftlets of Southeast Asia nest in the ceilings of great caverns. They make their nests from their own saliva, or spit, which dries as a glassy solidified goo, glued to the cavern rock. People use ladders to reach and collect the nests, which are made into the culinary delicacy bird's nest soup. The essence of this dish is therefore swiftlet spit!

Collecting nests for bird's nest soup in Payanak Cave, on Ko Phi Phi Island, Thailand.

Dribble Trap Fungus-gnat grubs in New Zealand cave roofs dribble slime as sticky threads that hang down, then light up their bodies like glow-worms. Small flies are drawn to the light, get trapped in the slimy "web," and the grub hauls them in to eat.

The large African bullfrog can remain underground for a long time, sometimes as long as several years, in the absence of heavy rain. When underground it forms a cocoon that helps to stop water loss. It feeds on other frogs as well as insects and worms.

Roach Hotel The cave cockroach lives its entire life on and in guano—bat droppings on the cavern floor. The cockroaches mate and lay their eggs there, feeding solely on the guano.

Feeling its Way Some kinds of cave cricket have antennae (feelers) ten times longer than their body. The antennae are used not only for touch, but taste and smell too. The cave cricket has no eyes, so if the antennae are damaged, it is doomed.

Hard to Swallow The world's biggest earthworms live in South Africa and Southern Australia. These giants are more than 16 ft (5 m) long when extended and as thick as a wrist when contracted. Their tunnels are so big and slimy that as the worms slide through them, they make gurgling noises audible 300 ft (100 m) away. Toads and birds that try to eat these worms partly swallow one end, and then choke and die as the worm wriggles away unharmed.

Dropping Clues In Australia, a wombat's tunnel entrance can be recognized by its large size, and also by its distinctive droppings nearby, which are cube- or brick-shaped.

Dark Lives Cave fish live their whole life in caves. Because of this they are pale and blind—some have no eyes at all!

Lurking in the Swamps

The huge, saltwater crocodile is the biggest and deadliest reptile, possibly killing as many as ten people each year. Exact numbers of victims are not known since some bodies are never recovered.

Saltwater crocodiles grow to over 23 ft (7 m) long and weight over 1 ton! On hot days they bask on the bank of rivers with their mouths wide open. This stops them from overheating and allows birds to remove parasites and bits of food stuck in their teeth.

SWAMPY FACTS

- Prehistoric crocodiles grew to over 50 ft (15 m) long
- The teeth of alligators amazingly have no roots!
- Alligators, like all reptiles, drown if they are held under water
- Alligators can go without food for up to a year

The saltwater crocodile's varied diet consists of fish, turtles, snakes, birds, buffalo, wild boar, and even monkeys!

CROC SHUTS DOWN MOTORS

In the 1970s in northern Australia, an 18 ft (5.5 m) saltwater croc nicknamed Sweetheart attacked boats and chewed up more than 20 outboard motors—but no people. Its stuffed body is displayed in Darwin Museum.

One in the Eye On Ossabaw Island, Georgia, a biologist was making alligator grunts and splashing his hand in the water, when a huge alligator reared up right in front of him and grabbed his arm. He poked its eye with his other hand and escaped with minor injuries.

Baby white alligators are rare and often suffer from sunburn in the wild.

River Tusker

The male hippo has massive, tusk-like lower canine teeth that can grow to more than 16 in (40 cm) long. When two of these 1.5-ton monsters battle for control of a stretch of river, they can inflict terrible, and even fatal, wounds or may lunge at nearby boats and tip them over.

A hippo's skin sweats an oily red fluid to keep the skin healthy. People used to think that hippos sweated blood!

Low Toll Down Under In Australia you are as likely to be killed by a crocodile as by a shark—about one death yearly, compared to two from lightning, 300 from drowning, and nearly 1,000 from road accidents.

Mugged at Water's Edge The Indian crocodile called the mugger is now feared more than the tiger in some places. It swims into drainage ditches and channels, and grabs people as they come to fill water buckets for their farm animals.

People make me Sick! In 1956 a man near Manaus, Brazil, told how he came upon his six-year-old son almost swallowed by a massive anaconda. He hit the snake with an oar so that it coughed up the boy—still alive.

River's Tiny Killers Far more deadly in water than crocs or giant snakes are small parasitic animals such as flukes, worms, and leeches. They spread diseases such as river blindness and elephantiasis, which disfigure and kill hundreds of thousands of people yearly across the tropics.

Tongue Trap The alligator snapping turtle catches fish when they seize its tongue—which they mistake for a worm.

Paralyzing Toad North America's most poisonous toad is the Colorado River toad. Its venom can cause slurred speech, paralysis, and even death.

Walking on Water The basilisk lizard can run along the surface of the water on a lake or pond for up to 400 yd (400 m).

Dry Spell The African lungfish can survive for up to four years embedded beneath the dry lake bed!

Anglers Snakes in the mountains of Valais, Switzerland, lie on the shores of mountain streams and seize trout when they leap above the water.

Fasting A boa constrictor can go without food for a whole year!

Snappy Meal In 1963 a 26-ft (8-m) anaconda was shot in Trinidad and opened to reveal a 5-ft (1.5-m) alligator in its stomach.

Sneaky Sleeper A snake can sleep with both eyes open!

Kantima Pinchai is one of the brave performers at the Sriracha Tiger Farm in Thailand. She stunned audiences when she placed her head inside the jaws of this crocodile, which can crush with a force of over 2,000 lb per sq inch!

GIANT PYTHON SKIN
EXHIBIT NO: 14127
RED-BALL PYTHON 15 FT (4.5 M)
IN LENGTH

Pythons are known to wander through Singapore's sewer system. Some have appeared in toilets and have been known to bite!

TOO BIG TO HANDLE
The world's bulkiest snake is the anaconda of South America and the Caribbean. It may grow up to 33 ft (10 m) and weigh up to 660 lb (300 kg). Past tales of giants like an anaconda in the 1940s measuring 130 ft (40 m) and 5 tons are now discounted.

Viper Crossing A highway in Shawnee National Forest, Illinois, is closed to automobiles for several weeks twice each year so that it can be crossed safely by copperheads, rattlesnakes, and water moccasins.

Quake Alert Just before an earthquake struck China in 1975, hundreds of hibernating snakes mysteriously emerged from below the ground.

Frozen Solid Garter snakes endure the cold by dropping their heart rates and allowing their bones to freeze solid.

Mouthful! A 16-ft (5-m) long African rock python was once seen swallowing an entire 130 lb (60 kg) impala—horns and all!

Dudu Mia, Bangladeshi snake-charmer, eats some of the 3,500 baby snakes he captured in Bangladesh on April 29, 2002. He claimed to have eaten most of them after capturing them over two days from two houses.

RECYCLED BABIES

Small pregnant desert rodents such as gerbils and jerboas "recycle" their unborn fetuses by absorbing their babies' tissues back into their own bodies. They do this if conditions turn harsh and their offspring are unlikely to survive. If the babies are already born, they eat them instead.

Fat Store When well fed, the camel's hump can contain over 80 lb (40 kg) of fat, which, when broken down within the body to yield energy, produces 16 gal (60 l) of water.

Walk like a A camel trots and gallops like no other animal. It moves both legs on one side of the body forward at a time, rocking from side to side, in a unique method called "pacing."

Jumpers Australia's red kangaroo, the biggest marsupial, can cover 33 ft (10 m) in one bound and clear a 10-ft (3-m) fence. In severe drought, the males save energy by stopping sperm production.

terless Diet A kangaroo-rat obtains one-tenth of the water it needs from the seeds it eats. The other nine-tenths comes from water actually made in its body, as it digests its food.

A camel's body temperature can rise from its normal 100 to 104°F (38 to 40°C), to more than 109°F (43°C) at midday to reduce water loss as sweat. At the other extreme, it can drop to as low as 93°F (34°C) on a cold night to save energy and keep warm.

Long Month A group of camels trekked 534 mi (860 km) across North Australia for 34 days without drinking any water.

Camel races take place weekly in Kuwait. A good racing camel may sell for between $3,000 and $40,000 (£1,800 and £23,000).

Camels can go without water in the cool season for five months, losing up to 40 percent of their body weight in moisture (humans are near death after losing 12 percent). Then they can drink 32 gal (120 l) of water at 3 gal (12 l) a minute —equivalent to a 2-pt (1-l) juice carton every five seconds for ten minutes!

"camels can trek across blazing hot deserts without drinking any water for over a month"

TOP FIVE SPRINTERS

Many deserts are wide open stretches of land, so speed is vital to escape enemies or catch prey. These distances show the number of feet and meters traveled in one second.

1 Cheetah 29 ft (8.8 m)

2 Ostrich 21 ft (6.4 m)

3 Red kangaroo 14 ft (4.3 m)

4 Champion human sprinter 11 ft (3.3 m)

5 Dromedary (camel) 9 ft (2.7 m)

Bladder Supply The water-holding frog of Australia spends more than nine-tenths of its life underground in a skin-like bag waiting for rain so it can dig to the surface, feed, and breed. While buried, up to half of its body weight is very weak urine in its bladder, which is slowly recycled to provide its water needs.

Heavy Hoarder! The North American kangaroo-rat gathers seeds up to 1,000 times its own body weight in its burrow. That's the same as a person filling a 60-ton truck with food!

Praying for Rain The couch's spadefoot toad, which lives in North America's Sonora Desert, stays underground for 11 months each year, coming up to the surface only during the rainy season in July.

Deep Diggers Ants in the Atacama Desert, Chile, dig deep underground passages 10 ft (3 m) below the surface to reach underground streams.

Beware! The gila monster and the Mexican beaded lizard are the world's only two poisonous lizards.

Venomous Small North African desert scorpions such as the yellow, fat-tailed, buthus and the death-stalker don't need size and strength to subdue prey—they use powerful poison from their arched tail-tip sting. Healthy adult humans usually survive despite many hours of agonizing pain, but old, young, sick, or weak people may die, usually after about seven hours.

Legless The glass lizard has no legs, and at times no tail! The tail breaks off and wriggles as a decoy if attacked.

In Australia a thirsty moloch or thorny devil, a spiky lizard, dips its tail in a puddle and the tiny grooves on its scales allow the water to seep by capillary action, all the way along its body to its mouth.

SHAPELY BLOOD CELLS

The microscopic red blood cells of camels are oval—all other mammals have rounded, saucer-shaped ones.

On average, one person is killed each day in Tunisia from a scorpion sting! The North African country consists mainly of the Sahara Desert and is home to millions of the reptiles.

TOP FIVE
DEADLIEST SPIDERS

1 **Sydney funnelweb,** Australia

2 **Black widow, Africa**

3 **Redback, Australia**

4 **Banana spider, North** America

5 **Brown recluse (fiddleback** or violin spider), North America

Poor Guests Many different kinds of woodwasps sting and paralyze caterpillars, lay their eggs inside them, and bury them in soil. The wasp grubs hatch and eat their caterpillar "hosts" alive from the inside out.

On the March The army ants of South America and driver ants of Africa have devoured babies left in cots. They march in columns more than one million strong. Small animals that cannot get out the way are stung to death and torn apart for food by thousands of tiny pairs of pincers.

Gas Sniffers Turkey buzzards are used to detect gas leaks in pipelines in southern California!

Shown here lifesize, the world's smallest chameleon, the pygmy leaf, weighs just 0.1 oz (3 g).

Leaf Sweeper After a big feed, more than one-third of the weight of a proboscis monkey is the leaves that are jammed into its stomach.

Heavy Meals A large African elephant eats more than 350 lb (160 kg) of food each day—the weight of two large humans.

Visitors to the Stockholm Zoo in Sweden are allowed to cuddle spiders (under supervision)! This Mexican orange-kneed bird spider makes itself comfortable on a visitor's face.

The magnificent spider from Australia fishes for food by spinning a fine, silk line 1.5 in (4 cm) long. It uses a sticky globule at the end as bait and its foreleg as the casting rod.

Eight-leg Giants

The largest spider is the Goliath bird-eating tarantula of South America. With leg spans of almost 12 in (30 cm) it would cover your dinner plate. Slightly smaller but heavier is the Salmon Pink bird-eater, also of South America, weighing over 3 oz (80 g). A Salmon Pink ate two frogs and two young snakes in four days, then slept for two weeks.

Tarantulas hunt at night, feasting on animals such as frogs, birds, and lizards. They crush prey with their large fangs.

This amazing colored snake, the eyelash pit viper, has long fangs with which to lunge at prey, mouth open, piercing fur and feathers to inject a deadly venom.

Quick Charge! Despite weighing more than 5 tons, an African elephant can run faster than a human champion sprinter, at speeds of over 25 mph (40 km/h).

Heavy Head A big moose's antlers can weigh more than 55 lb (25 kg). That's like having an eight-year-old child strapped to your head!

Population Explosion If a common housefly mated and laid 500 eggs and they all hatched and reproduced, the fly population would increase by about 30,000,000,000,000 each year!

Top Tree-dweller The largest animal that lives its life in trees is the male orang-utan of Southeast Asia, which can weigh more than 175 lb (80 kg) —as much as a large human.

Long Life The same black garden ants have been kept in ant-nest tanks for about 20 years. Relative to size, a human that lived for the same time would survive for 10 billion years!

Hard Lesson to Learn A scientist saw a mother chimp teach her youngster to break open nuts by hitting them with a stone. When the youngster got bored and looked away, she gave him a slap and made him watch again!

The sticky tongue of this Picasso Panther chameleon can extend up to one and a half times its body length to catch a cricket—then return back into its mouth in a tenth of a second!

TWO SAD ENDS

One of the biggest elephants in captivity was Jumbo. He was captured in Sudan in the 1860s, moved from Paris Zoo to London Zoo in 1865, then to American showman Phineas T. Barnum in 1882. Standing at nearly 12 ft (3.7 m) high, he weighed about 6 tons. Jumbo was killed in a collision with a train in Canada, in 1885—nearly 150 people were needed to drag his body up the embankment. He was skinned and stuffed for the Barnum Museum, but 90 years later was destroyed by fire. His skeleton is still in New York's American Museum of Natural History.

Short Flight The common fly has the shortest life span of all insects. On average, its life expectancy can be anything from 17 to 29 days.

Ripley's® PAINTED VAMPIRE BAT EXHIBIT NO: 18812 PAINTED BY ENRIQUE ANGELES RAMOS OF MEXICO CITY

Babied Bats The mother vampire bat, with a body the size of a baby kitten gives birth to one offspring at a time. She is pregnant for seven months with her single young and she feeds the baby on milk for nine months—much longer than other similar-sized mammals—nearly as long as a human!

Easy Drinking Blood is so nutritious and easy to digest for the vampire bat that it has one of the smallest stomachs and shortest guts of any mammal—less than 8 in (20 cm).

Tank Beetle The rhinoceros beetle has the strength to push an object up to 850 times its own weight.

Fast Jump The flea can accelerate extremely fast, approximately 50 times faster than a space shuttle!

TINY BUT DEADLY

Some arrow-poison (poison-dart) frogs from the Amazon region have enough venom in their skin to kill more than 1,000 people. Licking one can be fatal! Yet the frogs are smaller than your thumb.

During mating, a female praying mantis bites off her partner's head. This sets off reflex muscular actions in his body that makes him release more sperm.

It's a Leopard's Life

Known as the Leopard Man of Skye, Tom Leppard from Scotland has had the whole of his body tattooed in the markings of a big cat. For almost 15 years Leopard Man has lived in a hut made from sticks and stones, on a part of the island that is only reachable by boat and a two-hour hike.

Leopard Man bathes himself in the river and travels by canoe to pick up supplies and his pension once a week. He declares that he has everything he needs and is never lonely.

Leopard Man has had more than 99 percent of his body tattooed—only the skin between his toes and the insides of his ears remain untouched!

Leopards can grow to a weight of 200 lb (90 kg). They are thought to be twice as strong as a human and can drag a carcass weighing 600 lb (270 kg)—the weight of four average-size human beings—20 ft (6 m) up into a tree to feed!

Entombed in Ice

FREEZING FACTS

- Temperature on a pleasant summer's day 77°F (25°C)
- Water freezes at 32°F (0°C)
- Sea water freezes at 28°F (−2°C)
- Typical home deep-freezer is set at −4°F (−20°C)
- Ice-fish blood freezes at −27°F (−3°C)
- Arctic fox shivers at −40°F (−40°C)
- Emperor penguins endure −76°F (−60°C)
- Coldest recorded temperature measured on the Earth's surface on July 21, 1983 in Antarctica −128°F (−89°C)

A 23-ton block of ice containing the remains of a 20,380-year-old male wooly mammoth was discovered in the summer of 1997 by nine-year-old Simion Jarkov near Khatanga, on the Taimyr Peninsula.

French explorer Bernard Buigues arrived on the scene and dug down, with a plan to excavate the entire mammoth. This involved digging the mammoth out, still contained in the block of ice and transporting it by air to a frozen cave. Here, plans were made to thaw out the ice slowly with hairdryers. After just three days, he found the mammoth's skull! But as he dug deeper he discovered the mammoth bones were without flesh. Buigues' idea to clone the wooly mammoth failed.

FREE-FALL

In 1997 an Austrian mountain-rescue climber saw an alpine ibex stumble, bounce, and fall down a huge cliff, pick itself up at the base and walk away. The climber later checked the height of the cliff with a laser tape-measure. It was almost 3,200 ft (1,000 m) high.

Bat keeps it Cool A big brown bat "hibernated" in a laboratory fridge at just above freezing for 344 days—more than 11 months.

King Cat The Siberian tiger is the biggest tiger and the largest of all cats, with a head to body length exceeding 8.5 ft (2.6 m) and a weight of 660-plus lb (300-plus kg). It is also the most northerly and the rarest kind of tiger, living in snowy north-east Asia. There are probably fewer than 200 left.

Bernard Buigues examining the wooly mammoth tusks in northern Siberia, hopeful that the permafrost below contained the fully preserved body of a wooly mammoth.

TOP FIVE
COLD-SURVIVORS

Some species can cope with extreme weather conditions.

1 **Arctic fox** can survive for days at −22°F (−30°C) if well-fed

2 **Musk ox of North America** has longest hair of any mammal at up to 3 ft (1 m)

3 **Yak of the Himalayas, central Asia** survives on ice-fields at 20,000 ft (6,000 m)

4 **Ptarmigan** can survive sub-zero temperatures for six weeks

5 **Snow bunting** nests nearer to the North Pole than any other bird

Pale Prospects Albino or white types are known for most animals, from frogs and snakes to bison, tigers, gorillas, and whales—even albino polar bears! The lack of color is caused by a genetic change or mutation. In the wild, apart from ice and snowy places, albino animals stand out so clearly that they rarely survive long. For example, albino tigers are easily visible to prey as they stalk through undergrowth. It's thought that about one tiger in 10,000 is born nearly or completely white.

Highest Predator The snow leopard is found higher than any other big hunting animal, more than 16,400 ft (5,000 m) up in the Himalayas.

Heavy Sleepers Rodents such as marmots and birch mice in Siberia hibernate in burrows for up to eight months of the year.

Hairy Insulation The musk ox, which lives in the freezing, dry lands of the Arctic, has such a long, thick, and wooly undercoat that when the creature lies down to rest, its body heat does not melt the snow beneath it.

Cold Storage Wood frogs, spring peepers, and several other amphibians thaw out alive and completely unharmed after being almost totally frozen for more than three months of each year.

"tigers can eat 110 lb of meat at a time"

- A big, hungry tiger can eat almost 110 lb (50 kg) of meat in one meal—equivalent to an average person consuming 50-plus half-pounder burgers.

Sleeping with Scorpions

In 2002 Kanchana Ketkeaw from Thailand made herself at home in a glass box where she remained alone for 32 days with just 3,400 scorpions for company! She was allowed to leave the box for 15 minutes every eight hours.

During this marathon stay Kanchana was stung nine times! Some scorpions died during her ordeal, others gave birth, and some extras were added to keep the numbers constant. Each day she fed them on raw egg and ground pork. Kanchana performs with scorpions every day at a local tourist attraction, part of her act involves placing the animals in her mouth. She has been stung hundreds of times—so often, doctors say, that she is probably now immune to scorpion poison.

Unperturbed by their dangerous stings, Kanchana Ketkeaw lives happily among scorpions.

"It was like being in a room at home, only with thousands of little friends"

SIZE COUNTS
Some species of scorpion can grow up to 8.5 in (21 cm) long—as big as a man's hand! These scorpions tend to be less poisonous than the smaller variety that grow up to 4 in (12 cm) in length. A sting from one of these smaller scorpions can cause paralysis.

Termite! The queen white ant (or termite) lays 80,000 eggs a day and is the mother of the entire colony.

Stepping Out If moving our legs at the same rate as an ant, our movement speed would be 800 mph (500 km/h)!

Longest Insect The giant stick insect from Indonesia can grow to an amazing length—up to 13 in (33 cm).

New Bugs Nearly 1,000 insect species are discovered every year.

Lethal Bee The honeybee kills more people around the world each year than do all the poisonous snakes in the world put together.

Steep Crawlers Some insects are able to climb walls and even windows. This is because they have feet with tiny hooks or sticky pads.

Sweet Tooth The aborigines of Australia dig up the nests of honey ants and eat the insects.

CRUNCHY SNACKS!

In Phnom Penh's central market in Cambodia, stalls sell grilled insects and spiders! Hairy tarantulas, which are as big as your hand, are a very popular snack served during the day. Fried worms in Bangkok, Thailand, are threaded onto skewers. In China, small scorpions are considered a delicacy. They are cooked using garlic, herbs, and other spices to enhance the flavor.

Tiny bedbugs feed on human blood. Once well-fed, they can survive for six months before they need to feed again.

High-rise Nest The paper nest of the Brazilian wasp looks and swings like a Japanese lantern, but is actually like a miniature skyscraper. It is made up of at least 20 or more storys.

Air Miles A monarch butterfly can fly 620 mi (995 km) without even stopping to eat!

Nosy Insect An ant has five noses, each of which has a different task to perform.

Sleeping Beauty Snails can sleep for long periods of time—up to three years!

An unusual delicacy—a plate of worms! These creatures are fried and sold by street vendors in Thailand to those who have developed a taste for such a dish!

The high jump champion of the insect world is the froghopper. It can easily jump higher than an Olympic high jump champion! It is only 0.1 in (3 mm) in length but can jump to a height of 27 in (70 cm). If human beings were able to jump as high, they could clear a 650 ft (200 m) building!

TOP FIVE
SOARING BIRDS

1 Alpine choughs 28,000 ft (8,500 m), Himalayas

2 Whooper swans 27,000 ft (8,200 m), northern Britain

3 Bar-headed geese over 26,000 ft (8,000 m), Himalayas

4 Steppe eagle 26,000 ft (7,900 m), Himalayas

5 Bearded vulture 23,000 ft (7,000 m), Himalayas

HIGHEST STRIKE

In 1962 the crew of a U.S. Electra-188 airliner heard a thud to the rear of the airplane at a height of 21,000 ft (6,400 m) over Nevada. On landing, blood and feather remains on the tailplane were identified as those of a common duck, the mallard.

Birds are Best Birds can fly far higher than bats since their lungs take in up to three times more oxygen than bat lungs. At heights approaching 32,000 ft (10,000 m), there's only two-fifths of the oxygen that is in the air at sea level. Also, the temperature of the air is below −40°F (−40°C).

Love Struck Swan A male swan in Hamburg, Germany, fell in love with a swan-shaped pedal boat. Every time someone went near the boat, the swan went wild with jealousy!

Bugs on High Butterflies called queen of Spain fritillaries and small tortoiseshells have been seen actively flying (rather than storm-blown) at 20,000 ft (6,000 m).

Deadly Dive The fastest of all animals is the peregrine falcon. When seeking prey, it reaches speeds of more than 150 mph (240 km/h) in its "power-dive" called a stoop, as it swoops down in mid-air to catch a bird.

Top Flight Meals Mexican free-tailed bats have recently been tracked by radar higher than 10,000 ft (3,000 m) above Texas. Millions leave caves at dusk to eat migrating moths, mainly at heights of 2,000 to 3,200 ft (600 to 1,000 m).

Eating on the Fly The great skua harasses other birds that are flying back from feeding trips over the ocean and makes them disgorge partly-digested food, which the skua catches and eats in mid air.

HIGH FLYERS

- *Concorde* was able to cruise at 59,000 ft (18,000 m)

- Most modern jet passenger planes cruise at 30,000 to 33,000 ft (9,000 to 10,000 m)

- Highest birds fly 28,000-plus ft (8,500-plus m)

- Cirrus clouds (the highest common type) form at 26,000 ft (8,000 m)

Moth cocoons can be unbelievably massive— they can sometimes cover an entire tree.

SPACE ZOO

In 1998 a space shuttle took up "Neurolab," a package of various animals that were tested and studied to gauge their reactions to conditions in space. There were 1,500 crickets, 230 swordtail fish, 130 water snails, 150 rats, and 18 pregnant mice. The swordtail fish, crickets, and water snails were dissected on their return to Earth, to study how their gravity-detecting balance sensors had reacted to weightless conditions. This work is aimed at helping people with certain kinds of deafness that affect the ear's inner hearing and balance sensors.

Shuttle Survivors Canisters of tiny roundworms (nematodes) were the only living survivors of the *Columbia* shuttle disaster on February 1, 2003. As the craft burned up on re-entry, a shuttle mid-deck locker housing the worms' canister was thrown free and fell to Earth in eastern Texas.

Wonky Webs Spiders were taken up to the Skylab space station in the 1970s, where they spun very crooked, untidy webs. Eight garden orb-web spiders provided by a school in Melbourne, Florida, were on the ill-fated *Columbia* shuttle trip in February 2003.

Growth Tests In 1990, 16 laboratory rats were given a growth hormone during a shuttle trip, to see which parts of their bodies grew, and how fast, in weightless conditions. It was part of tests for a new GM form of growth hormone.

Bio-satellites Animal astronauts in the 1970s to 1990s, aboard the seven Russian Cosmos biological satellites, included over 100 rats and fruit flies used for genetic studies, each carrying eight rhesus monkeys. The only problems affecting the fruit flies were "difficulty in mating in zero G."

Ham, the first astro-chimp, tested life-support conditions aboard a U.S. Mercury space mission in 1961, and came back safely.

Space Victims In the late 1950s an estimated 13 dogs and four monkeys died before space scientists were able to bring animals back alive from space.

Panic of First Space Trip

A Russian dog named Laika, captured as a stray in Moscow, took off in *Sputnik 2* in November 1957. Officials said she survived for several days and was then painlessly put to sleep. In 2002, however, new evidence showed that she died after just a few hours, of overheating, panic, and stress. Her *Sputnik* "coffin" continued on 2,570 orbits and burned up during re-entry as a "shooting star" as it fell back to Earth in April 1958.

Laika, the first animal in space, orbited the Earth at an altitude of nearly 2,000 mi (3,200 km).

The Mother Touch!

Two African fertility idols, which according to local folklore could produce pregnancy in women who touch the statues, were acquired by Ripley's in 1993 and became their most popular museum exhibits ever.

When on display in Ripley's Florida office, there were 13 pregnancies in 13 months, mostly among office staff. Soon the statues became headline news and they have since toured the world twice. Over a thousand women claim to have conceived against great odds after touching them.

The statues, which stand at 5 ft (1.5 m) and weigh more than 70 lb (32 kg), have been displayed in every Ripley museum, sometimes twice, to enable as many women as possible to touch them. In the first month of the statues being displayed in the Florida museum there was a frenzy of activity as women traveled to touch them.

Ripley's ®
FERTILITY STATUES
EXHIBIT NO: 8786 AND 8747
ACQUIRED BY ROBERT RIPLEY FROM THE
IVORY COAST OF SOUTH AFRICA IN 1993

There is no rule to say where the statue must be touched in order to increase the chances of conception, but a lot of women touch the woman's baby.

Double Vision

Twins occur about once in every 75 births (every 400 for identical twins), triplets once every 7,500 births, and quadruplets once in every 620,000 births. Only three cases of nonuplets (nine babies at once) are recorded—in Australia (1971), Philadelphia, U.S.A. (1972), and Bangladesh (1977). None of the offspring survived for more than a few days. Earlier reports of decaplets (ten babies) from Spain (1924), China (1936), and Brazil (1946) are not fully substantiated.

In 2003 in England, Nicky Owen (right) gave birth to non-identical twins, having produced identical twins seven years earlier—and being an identical twin herself. Experts calculate the odds of this are 11 million to one.

One of the tallest women ever recorded was Ella Ewing of Missouri, shown here with her parents. She measured an immense 8 ft 4 in (2.5 m) tall. The tallest recorded man was Robert Wadlow (1918–40) of Alton, Illinois. He reached almost 9 ft (2.7 m) in height and was still growing when he died.

Race for Life After birth, the body increases in weight about 20 times from new baby to full-grown adult. Before birth, from fertilized egg to full-term fetus, the body increases in weight six billion times!

Tiny Survivors Premature girls born in Illinois and in England have weighed less than 10 oz (285 g) at birth, almost one-twelfth the normal birth weight—and survived.

What a Whopper! Baby Fedele, born in Italy in 1955, weighed a whopping 22 lb (10.2 kg), three times the average birth weight.

Early Entry Normal pregnancy lasts 266 days from the time of egg fertilization to birth. In Ontario, Canada, James Gill was born after just over half this time, 128 days premature. At 2 lb 6 oz (1077 g) he was less than one-fifth the normal birth weight (about 7 lb/3.4 kg).

Twin Views In Africa, the Yoruba people respect twins, and their mother is given gifts by passers-by. However, the Tumbuka people expel the mother of twins—and father, too—to live on raw food in the forest for two months.

The Greatest In 1989 Augusta Bunge of Wisconsin, became a great-great-great-great-grandmother with the birth of baby Christopher—a span of seven generations.

Move Over Boys After 110 years of giving birth to only boys, daughter Skylar was born in 1992 to the Westerholm family of North Dakota.

Blink, Blink, Blink! Three babies are born worldwide every second.

Womb of its Own In 2003 a healthy baby was born after developing on its mother's liver, which has a rich blood supply.

At only six weeks old, Margrette Klever had hair down to her shoulders!

Little Man Gul Mohammed of India, measured in 1990, stood only 22 in (57 cm) high.

MAGNIFIQUE
Even with today's medical advances, it's not expected that a woman will bear children into old age. In Paris in the 1740s, however, it was reported that at the grand age of 90, La Belle Paule Fieschi had a son.

Probably the most unusual birth ever was in 1954 when Mrs. Boyd Braxton, at 28 years old, gave birth to triplets in different weeks! She is seen here with her six oldest children—aged 2, 3, 4 (twins), 5, and 6 years old—shortly before she was due to give birth to the third of the triplets, the first two having been born 18 days previously! This birth was the result of Mrs. Braxton having a double uterus, which meant that the first two of the triplets could be born at a separate time to the third!

Little Woman Madge Bester of South Africa stood only 26 in (65 cm) high.

Genes that Last Twin brothers John Phipps and Eli Shadrack, born in 1803 in Virginia, lived to over 107 years of age. A pair of identical female twins from St. Louis, Missouri, lived to age 104.

Towering The preserved skeleton of Englishwoman Jane Bunford (1895–1922) measured just over 7 ft (2.2 m). Zeng Jinlian (1964–82) of China would have stood taller, just over 8 ft (2.5 m), but she could not straighten her back due to severe spinal curvature.

Good Old Man In Glendale, California, in 1965, Ruth Kistler had a daughter at the age of 57. In Italy in 1994, 63-year-old Rosanna Dalla Corta had a baby boy following fertility treatment. In 2003, in Chattisgarh, India, Satyabhama Mahapatra gave birth to a baby boy at the age of 65 years!

When Salvador Quini— nicknamed "The Boy Hercules"— from Salta, Argentina, was two years old, he could lift weights that were heavier than himself!

Lizard Likeness!

Erik Sprague, an entertainer from New York State, has spent more than $21,500 (£12,500) in transforming his body to look like a lizard!

In 1997, Erik Sprague had a surgical procedure to split his tongue into the fork-shape that it is today.

As part of his stage act, Erik eats live grubs.

Since the age of three, Erik has loved lizards and always wanted to look like one. His body modifications began with a simple ear-piercing at the age of 18, which became the first in a series of body piercings and tattoos. Lobe stretching, tongue-splitting, teeth-filing, Teflon® implants in his brow, and more body piercings were all part of the transfiguration process for lizard-mad Erik. Erik began touring with an entertainment show in 1999. His act includes eating fire, lying on a bed of nails, swallowing swords, and shooting darts from his nose. It was while traveling with the show that he met his partner Meghan, with whom he now lives in Austin, Texas. Erik's next ambition is to have a tail implant!

IN A BIND

As recently as the early 20th century, foot-binding was practiced in China mainly by upper-class women, especially of the Han dynasty. In one common method the toes were curled over and down under the ball of the foot, and strapped by bandages around the ankle, to create an exaggerated arch to the whole sole to bring the toes and ball close to the heel. The result, known as "lily" or "lotus" feet, was deemed attractive and symbolic of wealth and breeding. The deformity, however, made normal walking almost impossible, so wealthy women with bound feet were usually carried from place to place in a chair or reclining on a bed.

Staple Diet To lose weight, some people have tried stomach stapling to reduce gastric capacity and achieve a feeling of fullness with less food.

Circular plates fitted into the lower lip, to force its extension forward from teeth and gums are considered a decorative body adornment in parts of Africa. The plates are normally worn for ceremonial purposes and can be removed, although they leave the lower lip somewhat floppy. Some lip plates, which are made from wood or clay and often decorated in local patterns with plant sap pigments, are more than 12 in (30 cm) across.

Ripley's®
LIP PLATES
EXHIBIT NO: 22592
WAX HEAD OF AFRICAN "UBANGI"
WOMAN IN CHAD, AFRICA, WEARING
CEREMONIAL LIP PLATE

Power Points Sharpened teeth can be signs of hunting prowess, seniority, or status within a group in several parts of Asia and Africa. The teeth are usually chipped into points using stone or hardwood "chisels."

Super Slimmer Determined dieter, Dolly Wagner of London, England, lost 287 lb (130 kg) over 20 months from 1971 to 1973.

Desperate Measures People have considered almost every procedure to help them lose weight, from removing body fat by liposuction to having their jaws wired together, which limits food intake.

Space Race Wilfred Hardy from England has about 96 percent body coverage, including tattoos on his tongue, gums, and even the insides of his cheeks.

"25 rings and 18 in long"

Risking Their Necks

For centuries, women (and occasionally men) in several parts of Africa and Asia have practiced neck extension. The Paduang and Kareni people of Myanmar (Burma) have achieved total neck lengths of 18 in (40 cm). At an early age, five rings are placed around a Paduang girl's neck. A ring is then added annually until the total number of rings reaches 25! These brass rings, which appear to stretch the neck, are worn for life and only removed if a woman commits adultery. Over such a long period of time, the muscles in the neck weaken and can no longer support the woman's head without the brass rings, which means that she can suffocate as the neck collapses if the rings are removed.

Despite appearance, the brass rings do not actually stretch the neck. Instead they push the shoulders down by weight and pressure.

Tinted Lady "Krystyne Kolorful," a Canadian stage artist, has 95 percent coverage of colorful tattoos.

Instant Diet One liposuction procedure is performed almost every hour in the U.S.A. It is probably the most common procedure in cosmetic surgery and involves fatty or lipid tissue being "dissolved" and removed by suction or scraping, as an "instant" form of weight loss.

A Plate of Parasites Some radical dieters have tried swallowing gut parasites such as tapeworms and roundworms, to reduce their appetite for food.

Unemployed Calcuttan, Murari Aditya, has not cut his fingernails since 1962! The length of all of his nails together is 10 ft 5 in (3.2 m)!

File This Fingernails grow almost four times faster than toenails.

Twenty-year Artwork Rusty Field from England has about 85 percent of his body covered with 2,500 tattoo designs completed over 20 years.

Who's Counting? Bernard Moeller from America has more than 14,000 tattoos.

Ancient Tattoos The world's oldest preserved human, "Otzi" from the European Alps, is dated to about 5,300 years ago. He has various tattoos including stripes on one ankle, a cross behind the knee and parallel lines across his lower back.

Splash! Approximately two-thirds of an average person's body weight is made up of water.

Isobel Varley of Britain is reputed to be the world's most tattooed woman, as well as sporting 49 body piercings.

Turkish architect, Mohammed Rashid charges $5 to anyone who wants to take a photo of his 5-ft 2-in (1.6-m) long moustache!

Indian Sardar Pishora Singh has been growing his 4-in (9-cm) eyebrow hair since 1995!

This Indian holy man, attending the Ambubachi festival in Guwahati, India, has hair that is over 15 ft (4.06 m) long!

HAIR RAISING

- When your hair stands on end, this is a defensive biological reaction which is meant to make you look taller!

- On average, a man's beard would grow to a length of 30 ft (9 m)—if he never trimmed or shaved it in his lifetime!

- Transplanted hair takes about three months to start growing again

- A single strand of hair can help forensic scientists find out a person's age, gender, and race

Al Elderkin of Wrights Pen, England, did not wash, undress, or remove his hat for 40 years! His hair grew through the brim and crown of his tattered hat.

Maud Williams of Oakland, California, had red hair 6 ft 6 in (2 m) long in 1938.

Hair We Go! The body sheds and regrows about 100 scalp hairs and five eyelashes daily.

Hair Miles If all the hair grown all over the body in one year was added together it would measure more than 12 mi (20 km) in length.

Long Stories Many people have had unusual scalp hair growth, with lengths in excess of 16 ft (5 m). Beard hairs can grow just as long. Norwegian Hans Langseth's beard was 17 ft (5 m) when he died in 1927.

Thick and Thin Fair or blonde people have about 130,000 scalp hairs. This number reduces to 110,000 for brown hair, nearer to 100,000 for black hair, and 90,000 for red or ginger hair.

Astrologer Shibsankar Bharati has been growing his beard for over 20 years achieving a total length of 6.5 ft (2 m).

Grace Gilbert traveled with the Ringling Brothers and Barnum and Bailey circus at the turn of the 20th century.

Pictured in 1907, when Grace Gilbert was 32 years old and 5 ft 9 in (1 m 8 cm) tall, her beard was 10 in (25 cm) long!

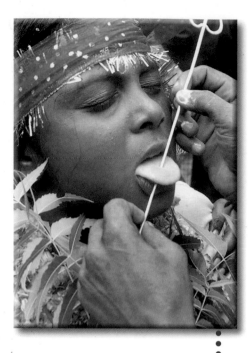

As proof of devotion to the local Hindu religion, Tamil devotees have sharp spears pushed through their cheeks, tongues, or other parts of their body.

Alex Lambrecht of Belgium has more than 140 piercings, which he performed himself! When all the rings, studs, and other adornments are installed, they weigh more than 1 lb (0.5 kg).

Expensive Adjustments

American Cindy Jackson underwent 27 cosmetic procedures in ten years, costing almost $100,000 (£150,000). Her operations included three facelifts, breast reduction then augmentation, and even knee alteration.

Tall Order The desire to be taller can rival that of being slimmer. In many cases, a height increase of between 2 and 4 in (5 and 10 cm) is possible. The procedure involves operations to implant bones into the shin and thigh, with surgery to muscles, tendons, and ligaments.

Rising Fees The cost of height-increase operations varies from country to country, but is about $75,000 (£100,000) in the U.S.A.

"spent 27 years of his life in his bedroom"

Heavy Sentence

Walter Hudson of New York, weighed over 1,400 lb (635 kg) in 1987. Hudson lived on an average daily diet of two boxes of sausages, 1 lb (0.5 kg) of bacon, 12 eggs, one loaf of bread, four hamburgers, four cheeseburgers, eight portions of fries, three ham steaks, two chickens, four baked potatoes, four sweet potatoes, and four heads of broccoli. He drank an average of 12 pt (6 l) of soda with every meal. Hudson spent 27 years of his life in his bedroom and then became famous when he fell in a doorway. It took eight firefighters three hours to rescue him. With the help of American comedian Dick Gregory, Hudson lost 600 lb (272 kg) and began a mail-order business selling clothes for extra-large women. Hudson weighed 1,025 lb (465 kg) when he died in 1991.

Ripley's —

WALTER HUDSON
EXHIBIT NO: 1447
WAX FIGURE SHOWING THE WEIGHT OF THE ONCE HEAVIEST MAN, WALTER HUDSON

John Kamikaze suspended by eight meat hooks, re-enacting a scene from The Water Babies at the Body Craze Event!

Body Craze

The tensile strength of human skin provided a shocking display in a series of performances at Selfridges department store in London.

As the largest and heaviest organ in the human body, skin can be extremely tough and can cope with considerable strain. Performer John Kamikaze and his partner, Helmut, tested this at the Body Craze event held in May 2003 at Selfridges department store in London. Visitors were able to peer through portholes in the shop window and watch them as they performed such feats as swimming through glass shards and suspending themselves from the ceiling by meat hooks pierced through their skin.

For an episode of the Ripley's TV show, Rick Maisel fitted his entire body into a washing machine and was then spun!

Larry Gomez was born with a severe condition that causes hair to grow all over his face and body.

A farmer from Manchuria, China, called Wang had a 13-in (33-cm) horn growing from the back of his head.

THICK-SKINNED!

In the 1920s a member of the Kalinda people of Africa suffered from keloids, which is an overgrowth of scar tissue. As he tried to cut out each thickened skin patch, another scar formed over the wounds. He reportedly ended up with 0.7-in (2-cm) thick skin that looked like a rhino's hide.

Pascal Pinon, born 1887 in Lyon, France, photographed in 1927, aged 40.

Heavy Guy When American Jon Minnoch was rushed to a hospital in 1978, his weight was estimated at 1,389 lb (630 kg). In comparison, giant sumo wrestling champion Emanuel Yarborough weighs 772 lb (350 kg).

Ms Heavyweight One of the heaviest women on record was American Rosalie Bradford who, in 1987, reached a peak weight of about 1,200 lb (544 kg).

Microscopic View The human body consists of at least 50 million million cells. About 3,000 million cells die and are replaced every minute.

Living Lens The eye lens is the only internal part of the body that grows continually throughout life.

Piercing Smile As a symbol of great beauty, the teeth of young women in the Pygmy tribe of Central Africa are shaped into triangles, using a machete.

We're Flaky Dead skin flakes make up 75 percent of household dust.

Life in a Cell The life-spans for different cells in our bodies include 12 hours for a cheek lining cell or bone marrow cell, two days for a stomach lining cell, two weeks for a white blood cell, one month for a skin cell, three months for a red blood cell, 18 months for a liver cell, and almost the body's entire lifetime for a nerve cell.

Tooth Puller Arpad Nick from Hungary pulled a 36-ton Boeing 737 a distance of 33 ft (10 m) using his teeth!

Far Sighted The human eye has the ability to see a lit match from 50 mi (80 km) away on a clear, moonless night, if viewed from a high level such as a mountain peak. Wakes left by ships are visible to astronauts as they orbit the Earth.

Vast Vessels The human body consists of 60,000 mi (96,500 km) of blood vessels, enabling blood to reach every part of the body.

MOVING PARTS

There are some 640 skeletal muscles in the body, with more than 100 in the head, face and neck. It takes:

- 6 to move an eyeball
- 20 to purse the lips for a kiss
- 25 to smile
- 30 to twist a foot inward
- 35 to twist a foot outward
- 45 to frown
- 50 to take a step forward
- 75 to speak

Queen Marguerite de Valois (1552–1615) of Navenne had pockets in the lining of her voluminous skirt so that she could carry the hearts of her 34 successive sweethearts with her at all times! Each was embalmed and sealed in a separate box!

Mouthful of Teeth!

Most humans will have 52 teeth in their lifetime—22 in the milk or baby set and 30 in the adult set. However, cases of three sets have been known, including those of Antonio Jose Herrera of New Mexico. At the age of 10 all his existing teeth were kicked out by a horse, but a new set grew in naturally. In 1896 a French doctor reported a patient who grew a fourth set, known as "Lison's case." Dr Slave lost his normal second teeth at about 80 years of age, then five years later another set appeared, which he retained until his death at 100. At the other end of the age scale, Sean Keaney was born in England in 1990 with 12 teeth.

An Eye for Color A typical person blinks over 300 million times in a lifetime, and can distinguish more than seven million different colors, including over 500 shades of gray.

High Society Air pressure falls the higher you go. So people who live in mountainous regions such as the Andes have adapted over time to survive such conditions. They have shorter arms and legs than average, so that their blood travels shorter distances, and they have over-sized lungs to cope with the lower air pressure.

In the Blink of an Eye On average, you blink 25 times each minute! So in a year, you might blink 13,140,000 times!

Digital Surplus In 1921 an autopsy on a baby boy in London, England recorded that he had 14 fingers and 15 toes.

Bloody Amazing! At any moment, about three-quarters of the body's blood is in the veins, and only one-twentieth is in the capillaries, the tiniest vessels where oxygen and nutrients pass into the tissues.

A child named Babaji is being worshiped by his community because, unbelievably, he was born with a tail.

This Spanish family display their two-, three- and, four-fingered hands!

"you blink about 300,000,000 times in a lifetime"

Two-toed In Africa, among the Kalanga people of the Kalahari Desert and the Wadomo people of Zambezi, there are people with two toes per foot.

Brainy A typical human brain weighs 49 to 53 oz (1,400 to 1,500 g). The brain of eminent 18th-century French scientist Baron Georges Cuvier weighed 64 oz (1,810 g), one of the largest normal brains on record.

Ripley's® SHRUNKEN HEAD EXHIBIT NO: 5065 FROM THE JIVARO INDIANS OF ECUADOR, SOUTH AMERICA

Long Liver The liver can continue to work even after 80 percent of it has been removed, and will return to its former size within a couple of months!

Painless There is no feeling in the human brain, only in the membrane surrounding it, which contains veins, arteries, and nerves. So a person would feel no pain from an injury to the brain alone.

Swallow About 0.5 pt (1 l) of saliva is produced daily, and most of this water is taken back into the body in the intestines. In fact, some 8.5 pt (4 l) of combined salivary and digestive juices are produced daily, but only 3.3 fl oz (100 ml) are lost from the digestive system.

Water Everywhere The human body is two-thirds water, with most (about half) being held in the 640 muscles. Even bones are made up of one-fifth water.

It is possible to make over 1,000 different facial expressions and girners took this to extremes at a Ripley contest in Atlantic City.

A Second Look About one person in 200 has two different-colored eyes.

Three-letter Bits Ten human body parts are only three letters long: leg, arm, ear, lip, gum, rib, jaw, eye, toe, and hip!

Shedding Fast Outer human skin cells are shed and regrown about once every 27 days! Therefore humans may have grown a complete new skin about 1,000 times during their life.

Stop...Sneeze! The heart and all bodily functions momentarily stop when a person sneezes!

LIVE EXHIBIT
In 1822 French Canadian Alexis St. Martin was shot in the side. Dr. William Beaumont treated him, but St. Martin still had a 1-in (2.5 cm) hole in his stomach. For some time after, Beaumont used St. Martin's opening to study the stomach, but St. Martin ran away and, despite the hole, lived until he was 82 years old.

TOP FIVE EXTREME LENGTHS
Straightened out and joined together, these parts of your body would be this long:

1. Nerves including micro-nerves—99,422 mi (160,000 km) (almost halfway to the Moon)
2. Blood vessels—49,711 mi (80,000 km) (twice around the Earth)
3. Tiny tubes of the filter units (nephrons) in the kidneys—over 62 mi (100 km)
4. Sweat gland tubules—31 mi (50 km)
5. Semiferous (sperm-making) tubes in the testes—722 ft (220 m)

Human Pincushion

An abnormality of nerve development means some people feel little or no pain. A few of these people make a living as "Human Pincushions."

Paddy Davidson can spear his cheeks, neck, hands, and feet with nails or skewers. Lauren Oblondo could push a metal pin in through the back of his hand, up inside his forearm and out through his elbow. "Gladys the Impaler" could push a large pin through both her thighs and then balance on it between two chairs. However, such performers usually take great care to keep their equipment sterile, and to know the paths of major arteries and veins, otherwise they could suffer serious wounds and bleeding.

Some people are born with unusually flexible joints, and with practice make them even more supple. The "human owl," Martin Joe Laurello, could twist his neck 180° to look backwards with his body facing forwards.

HEALTHY KISSING

Some Chinese scientists have suggested that kissing can prolong your life. A newspaper report in 1992 stated that kissing is good for your teeth, and burns off up to three calories per kiss—great news for slimmers! Other researchers have suggested the opposite— that, in fact, kissing speeds up your pulse, and so increases, pressure on the heart.

Pakesh Talukdar from India has achieved worldwide fame for such feats as piercing 24 needles into his face and eating bricks.

Finger Press In 1992 Paul Lynch did 124 push-ups supported at his front end by just one finger. Paddy Doyle did 1.5 million push-ups in one year (1988–89), an average of 170 per hour.

Legs to Contend With Queen Mary's Hospital in London is world-famous for treating physical disabilities, and especially fitting prosthetic limbs. In its soccer line-up, every player has only one leg, and the goalkeeper has one arm.

DON'T LOOK DOWN
At Acapulco, Mexico, people high-dive from rock platforms over 82 ft (25 m) high into water less than 13 ft (4 m) deep. But in France Olivier Favre dived from a board 177 ft (54 m) high, and in Switzerland Harry Froboess jumped an amazing 393 ft (120 m) into a lake—from the ill-fated airship *Hindenburg*.

Don't Sneeze "Girners" pull extraordinary faces. J. T. Saylors could cover his nose with his lower lip and chin. Bert Swallowcot went further covering his eyebrows with his lower lip!

No Spare Tire Gary Windebank balanced a pile of 96 car tires weighing over 1322 lb (600 kg).

Running Back In 1994 Timothy Badyana ran a marathon in 3 hours 53 minutes—backwards.

Wrong Footed In 1995 Amresh Kumar Jha stood on one foot (not being allowed to touch anything with the other foot) for over 71 hours.

Month in a Tub In 1992 Rob Colley lived for 42 days in a 150-gal (700-l) barrel on top of a 43-ft (13-m) pole.

Come Again Stephen Woodmore of Kent, England, can speak at a rate of over 637 words a minute!

Twenty-one-year-old "wonder woman" Puangphaka Songskri lies on a bed of nails whilst a colleague breaks cinderblocks on her chest, at the set of a local TV show in Bangkok in September, 2002.

WHO SAYS MOZART ISN'T GROOVY?
Using clues from the shape, construction, and length of the grooves, Dr. Arthur Lintgen is able to name any classical record by just looking at the grooves!

Reverend Kevin Fast of Ontario, Canada, pulled two firetrucks with a combined weight of 16 tons, a distance of 100 ft (30 m). The feat was performed for the Ripley's television show in November 1999 outside the Ripley museum in St. Augustine, Florida.

"Look, No Hands!"
Welsh builder John Evans is able to balance large, heavy objects on his head. He has appeared at numerous events balancing such items as a car on his head for two minutes and 84 milk crates weighing 275 lb (124 kg) for 10 seconds. His other balancing acts included balancing two women who weighed 210 lb (95 kg) each and a succession of 92 people for at least 10 seconds each.

He has also been known to balance bricks, barrels and glasses of beer, and even a piece of wooden furniture weighing 240 lb (109 kg)!

Bone Tired Moyne Mullin of Berkeley, California, could support all her weight on her elbows.

MAKING HER POINT
Vietnamese circus entertainer Hang Thu Thi Ngyuen is so accurate with her aim that she can shoot a bow and arrow at a target as far as 16 ft 5 in (5 m) away, using only her feet, whilst standing on her hands and contorting her body so that it points forward. Since childhood, she has practised for three hours each day.

Tongue Tied American Dean Sheldon held a single scorpion measuring 7 in (18 cm) in his mouth for 18 seconds. He held a total of 20 scorpions in his mouth for 21 seconds in 2000.

Lift out of Order James Garry of Denver, Colorado can lift a 14 lb (6 kg) weight by using only the vacuum created by the palm of his hand.

Alfred Langeven could puff enough air out of his tear-duct opening to play a recorder or even blow up a balloon. Jim Chicon could snort drinks up his nose and squirt them from his eye. People are able do this because the tube-like tear duct connected to the inner lower eyelid drains tears into the nose. Some people are able to use this duct in reverse, for water or air.

Mind on Target

Unlike most illusionists, Britain's Derren Brown definitely doesn't want his act to end with a bang—because he plays Russian roulette!

In 2003, Brown made history by playing Russian roulette live on television! The stunt, staged in Jersey to bypass British gun laws, saw a volunteer load a single bullet into a revolver with six numbered chambers. Brown, who claimed his only clue was listening to the volunteer's tone of voice as he counted from one to six, then fired the gun against his own head until he came to the chamber that he thought contained the bullet. He fired it into the air and saved himself from an untimely end!

Illusionist Derren Brown is able to read and control people's minds, memorize data, and even take away and create pain within people! He does all this with the "power of suggestion," working out details with a combination of observations about a person and through "reading" their reactions to statements or questions.

Ling-Yong Kim of South Korea could solve complex math problems, such as determining indefinite integrals for Einstein's Theory of Relativity at the age of four.

FANCY PHOBIAS

- Agoraphobia—fear of wide-open spaces
- Aibohphobia—fear of palindromes
- Anemophobia—fear of wind
- Arachibutyrophobia—fear of peanut butter sticking to the roof of the mouth
- Genuphobia—fear of knees
- Lachanophobia —fear of vegetables
- Linophobia—fear of string
- Nephophobia—fear of clouds
- Pupaphobia—fear of puppets
- Uranophobia—fear of heaven or a similar spiritual place of respite

Georgie Pocheptsov, born in 1992 in Pennsylvania, started painting at 17 months old! While most children his age were still using finger paints, Georgie was creating works of art showing four-headed giraffes and angels, all in bright, luminescent colors! At only six years old, Georgie started to display his work at the international Art Expo in New York, California, and Atlanta, Georgia.

Immovable Thoughts The brain is one of the few body parts that cannot carry out any movements at all, since it is devoid of muscle tissue.

HUMAN CALCULATOR
In the 18th century German Johann Dase could multiply two numbers—each of eight digits—in less than one minute, and two numbers each of 20 digits, in six minutes. You try: multiply 23,765,529 by 76,904,618 in under 60 seconds!

Keys to a Future Classical composer Frederic Chopin, born in 1810, is one of relatively few child geniuses who went on to achieve worldwide lasting fame. He performed his first international public tour of piano recitals at the age of eight.

Prayers in Hand The Chief Rabbi of Lithuania, Elijah the Gaon, could quote from more than 2,500 religious works he had committed to memory.

Stephanie Hale, from Essex, England, became the youngest national chess competitor in England—at only four years old! She even competed against international chess master Garry Kasparov in an Internet chess game in 1999.

Word Wary Verbophobia is a fear of words. So if you've read this far, you are unlikely to suffer from it, and especially from one of its variants, sesquipedalophobia—a fear of long words!

OUT OF IT
Shamens of the Belaro people in Papua New Guinea, after taking various concoctions of plant and animal juices, are said to enter trances lasting up to 48 hours in which they neither eat, drink, nor respond to stimuli such as loud noises or pinched skin.

An Answer for Everyone Professor Willi Melnikov of Moscow was said to be "relatively fluent" in more than 90 languages.

Something to Say Martha Ann Koop of Tennessee started to talk at the age of six months—about a year earlier than most children.

Seventies Rocker In 1977 Maureen Weston of England went without proper sleep for 18 days during a rocking chair marathon.

Facing His Fear The first person to fly solo across the Atlantic was U.S. aviator Charles Lindberg who completed the journey. He did so despite a mild form of acrophobia, which is a morbid fear of heights.

Pick a Card, Any Card In the 1930s Arthur Lloyd of Massachusetts, was known as the Human Card Index. His special 40-pocket jacket carried 15,000 notecards and he could locate any single card in less than five seconds.

Hypnotizing the Hypnotist Efrarl Rabovich had no interest in hypnotism or the power of the mind until he himself was selected to take part at a local event in Austria in 1921. The hypnotist found him a difficult subject and soon asked for another volunteer. Yet the next day Rabovich was suddenly able to hypnotize people.

Brain Drain For its size, the brain consumes between five and ten times more energy than other organs.

MEGA STORAGE
Weighing 3 lb (1.4 kg) the human brain is the most complex collection of matter known in the universe. The total memory capacity of the brain is estimated at 100 trillion bits of data, which is equal to the information in 500,000 large multi-volume encyclopedias, or in computer terms, about 1,000 gigabytes!

Retiring to the Library Eminent South African general and statesman Jan Christian Smuts (1870–1950) could not read until he was 11 years old, but spent most of his old age, when memory powers normally fade, memorizing more than 5,000 different books.

Quick Study William Sidis of Massachusetts, could type out words in English and French by the age of two, and wrote an article on human anatomy at the age of five.

Empowering the Mind!
Dominic O'Brien has overcome childhood dyslexia and Attention Deficiency Disorder (ADD) to win the World Memory Championships eight times! As a child, he suffered from dyslexia, which led to a difficulty with reading and consistent concentration-lapses throughout his school career. Over 14 years of disciplined training has helped him to correct the "imbalance" that he believes is responsible for these disorders. Along with a colleague, Dominic has used his knowledge of dyslexia and thorough research into the brain and developed the Brainwave Conditioning System, to help others suffering from dyslexia and ADD.

In 2002, in front of a panel of judges, Dominic O'Brien memorized 54 packs of shuffled cards in 12 hours. He then took over four hours to recite all 2,808 cards, with only eight errors!

Hole in the Head!

Cutting or drilling holes into the head, known as trepanation, was practiced on almost every continent in ancient times. It was probably used to let out "evil spirits" from the brain, conditions that we now know as epilepsy, mental illness, or migraines.

Heather Perry from Gloucestershire, England, journeyed to the U.S.A. in order to undergo trepanation, to cure her chronic fatigue and depression.

Ancient trepanation used sharp knives of flint, obsidian (a black, glassy rock) and bronze, and a hand-cranked rotary drill resembling an old-fashioned carpenter's brace-and-bit. Some preserved skulls have four or five holes, often larger than eye sockets. In many cases the bone shows signs of healing, which means the subjects survived. Trepanation is still carried out in some parts of the world today. People use it to create blood flow to the brain for stimulating mental awareness, relieve stress, and as a cure for complaints such as chronic depression.

In 1990, Charles Osborne of Iowa, finally stopped hiccuping after 58 years. Despite the hiccups, he had managed to live a near-normal life and had eight children.

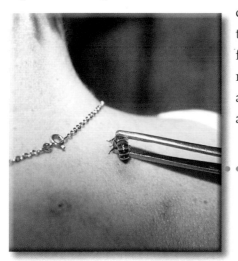

In Moscow, Russia, a clinic treats patients using bee sting therapy. Bee venom has been used for centuries to treat arthritis, skin diseases, and back pain. It is used today as a treatment for multiple sclerosis.

OLD NOSE JOB

In ancient India, petty criminals were often punished by cutting off their noses. To repair the wound doctors developed a method of slicing a triangular flap of skin from the forehead leaving a "stalk" at the bridge of the nose, then folding it over and down with a twist to keep the skin side outwards, and stitching it to a nose-shaped prosthesis of polished wood. A low-fronted turban hid the forehead scar.

A Mouthful False teeth have been found in remains of Romans more than 2,000 years old. Most were made of hardwood or metal but some are ivory, carved from elephants tusks. Even earlier, the Etruscans made removable dentures of gold.

As an antidote for stress at work, a company in the U.K. installed a grass lawn in their office, thinking it would have a calming effect and that it would promote relaxation whilst at work!

Looking Back The ancient Romans used many medical instruments that are strikingly similar to today's tools, such as the rectal speculum—for holding open the "back passage" to look up the large bowel.

Organic Painkiller Some 2,350 years ago Greek physician and "Father of Medicine" Hippocrates advised chewing willow bark to relieve pain. It worked. Much later the active ingredient was isolated and launched as a pain-relieving pill—what we now call aspirin.

Four-day Operation In 1951 Gertrude Levandowski underwent a 96-hour operation in Chicago to remove an ovarian cyst.

Self Help Ira Kahn of Lebanon removed his own appendix while stuck in a traffic jam. However, he was a doctor!

Lost and Found In 1997 Silvio Jimenez underwent an operation to remove tweezers left from previous surgery—47 years earlier.

At Lake Kirkpinar in Turkey, patients are treated with water serpents.

Bled Dry Bleeding the body to release "stale blood" or "foul humors" has been a common treatment through the centuries. Conditions such as jaundice were believed to result from too much blood—so doctors let it out! In the 1300s, 200 leeches were applied to Philus of Padua and he was wrapped in a wet blanket for three days while they gorged on his blood. Unsurprisingly, he died the next day.

In May 2003, Wei Shengchu had 2,003 acupuncture needles placed in his head! Acupuncture is an alternative method of treatment used to heal many health complaints, from stress and headaches to arthritis.

Coldhearted In 1987 a Norwegian fisherman fell overboard and his body became so chilled in the water his heart stopped beating for four hours. He revived when he was taken to a hospital and gradually recovered while linked to a heart-lung machine.

Blood Bath! In Chicago in 1970 Warren Jyrich who suffered from hemophilia or "bleeding disease" received 285 gal (1,080 l) of transfused blood—about 12 bathtubfuls—during a heart operation.

"Smoky," from St. Louis, Missouri, could breathe through a hole in his back and he could exhale smoke from a cigarette through it and could still breathe!

Man-sized Tumors Several operations have been performed to remove tumors weighing more than 220 lb (100 kg), including one ovarian growth of 302 lb (137 kg) and another fluid-filled cyst of 327 lb (148 kg)—this is about the weight of two large adults.

NO THANKS, DOCTOR
In mid-19th century England, a remedy for dysentery was drinking powdered human bones mixed with red wine. An attempted cure for baldness was to sleep with a paste of bull's blood and semen applied to the scalp and covered with a towel. Treatment for earache included poking the ashes of a cremated mouse mixed with honey into the ear. Wine fermented with ground-up lice was given for jaundice, and tea boiled with snails was prescribed for chest infections.

Hard Headed In 1992 in Michigan, Bruce Levon had a head X-ray that revealed a bullet from a shooting that had occured nine years earlier lodged in his skull. Bruce had been unaware of it.

Smile, Please Frederic Green of California was pronounced dead at the age of 82—but in the mortuary the flashbulb of the coroner's photographer woke him up!

Maggots to the Rescue Maggots are fly grubs that thrive on dead and rotting flesh. They are now used routinely in some countries to clean wounds of infected and gangrenous tissue. About 100 "baby" maggots are bandaged onto the wound and removed two or three days later, during which time they have grown in size five times and left the wound picked clean of germs and decay.

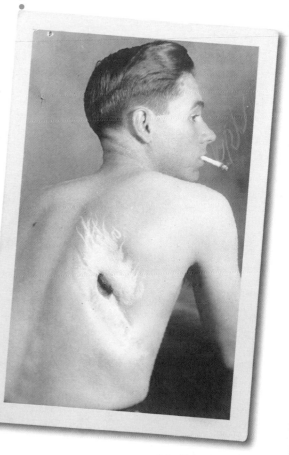

• • • • • • • *In June 2003, thousands of people flocked to the Indian city of Hyderabad in an attempt to be cured of asthma! It was believed that by swallowing a small, whole murrelfish, coated in a special herbal paste, the disease could be cured.*

New Parts Norma Wickwire of the U.S.A. had eight different joints replaced between 1976 and 1989 because of rheumatoid arthritis.

Memory on Hold In 1984 Terry Wallis, aged 20, was involved in a car crash in Arkansas. It was Friday 13 and he went into a coma for 19 years. On Friday June 13, 2003 Terry regaining consciousness and uttered his first words. He is severely paralysed, yet parts of his memory have survived intact for nearly two decades. He could recall events, names, and phone numbers from the time of the accident, but still believed Ronald Reagan was the U.S. president.

Scalp Invader In 1998 a woman returning from the West Indies to England complained of a severe headache. Doctors discovered and removed 91 screw-worms from deep in her scalp. Screw-worms are screw-shaped maggots of a type of blowfly that burrow through wounds into the flesh of animals and people to feed. They hatch from tiny eggs and grow to about 1 in (25 mm) long.

Bedpan Billy Munchausen's Syndrome is characterized by a desire for medical attention and treatment. In England between 1930 and 1979 William McIlroy had over 400 operations in 22 hospitals, using more than 20 assumed names. He finally gave up his visits saying "I'm sick of hospitals."

Plan Melts Away

When Monique Martinot died in 1984, her husband, Dr. Raymond Martinot, cryogenically froze her body in the hope of being able to revive her in the future. In February 2002, Dr. Martinot also died and his wishes to be frozen alongside her were carried out, in the hope that they could both live again one day. However, later that year the French court ruled that they had to be buried.

• • • *Remy Martinot used to keep the corpses of his mother and father in the wine cellar in his home in western France.*

TOP FIVE
BETTING IN THE FUTURE

Some organizations offer long-term cryonic or cryogenic facilities—very low-temperature preservation and storage of bodies. Prices vary but as a general guide:

1 Whole body $100,000–150,000 (£60,000–85,000)

2 Head only $50,000–100,000 (£28,500–57,000)

3 Brain only $20,000–40,000 (£11,500–23,000)

4 Sample of tissue (for DNA, including eggs or sperm) $100–200 (£50–100)

5 Chemical room-temperature preservation of tissue sample (for DNA) $30–100 (£20–50)

Grave Offerings

Every year on November 2, the Day of the Dead, families in Mexico troop to cemetries to visit departed relatives, bearing not only flowers but party fare such as breads, cakes, candy, cigarettes, and alcohol.

Relatives sit around the grave and have a picnic including food such as chocolate hearses and coffins, fancy breads decorated with skulls, and sugar skeletons. It is considered good luck to be the one to find the skeleton hidden inside each loaf baked. Friends give each other gifts of sugar skeletons inscribed with a death motif of their name.

"Happy skeletons" are made in Mexico of papier maché to celebrate the festival of the Day of the Dead, which honors the deceased.

FANTASY TOMBSTONES

- **25-ton granite grand piano**
  Madge Ward, concert pianist, Texas, U.S.A.

- **Giant mobile phone headstone**
  Guy Akrish, Israel

- **Scaled-down Concorde**
  L. Spurlington, model aircraft enthusiast, South Africa

- **Giant light-bulb**
  Sal Giardino, electrician, New Jersey, U.S.A.

Dying by the Minute! About 100 people around the world die every minute.

Time's Up The most "popular" time for dying is the early hours of the morning, from about 2 a.m. to 5 a.m.—which is also the most common time for babies to be born.

Buried But Not Dead!

Following a motorbike crash in 1937, Angel Hayes was pronounced dead. Two hours before his burial he woke from his coma to the shock of his family and friends who had been in mourning for three days. So scared by his near live-burial, mechanic Hayes went on to invent and create a coffin to prevent such a horrible thing from ever happening again. The coffin he created was fitted with alarm bells and flashing lights. In case the occupant would have to wait for a long time before being rescued, supplies such as toilet paper were included. Electrodes were connected to the coffin, which in turn connected to a monitor to alert the outside world of the presence of a living person inside the coffin. To demonstrate just how efficient this invention was, Hayes actually stayed in it underground for two days and two nights!

Hayes' coffin creation was almost home from home—it even had food and drink inside.

Homage on High On All Saints Day in Sacatepequez, Guatemala, residents honor the dead by gathering together in their local graveyard to fly large, decorative kites.

Not Done Yet French soldier Nicola Baillot was captured at the Battle of Waterloo but freed in 1815, aged 24, when a doctor considered him close to death from tuberculosis. In fact, he survived to the grand age of 105.

No Longer Ticking Hannah Beswick of Lancashire, England, was one of many people worried about being mistakenly pronounced dead. Her will contained instructions that her body should be inspected often for signs of life, so her doctor had the body placed inside a grandfather clock to enable regular, timed examinations.

Writing on the Wall The Vietnam Veteran's Memorial in Washington, D.C., carries the names of 38 people who actually survived the war.

Unlucky 13 Author Sholom Aleichem avoided the number 13 at all costs. All his written works went from page 12 to 14. Unluckily, he died on May 13, 1916. However, his family upheld his wishes and changed his epitaph to read May 12.

Unlucky 8 American George E. Spillman of Texas was a "number 8" man—he died at 8 p.m. on August 8, 1988, aged 88.

THE LIVING DEAD!

In 1960 writer Ernest Hemingway read his obituary in many newspapers after his plane had crashed in Africa. He lived for a further year. Other writers have also had premature brushes with the Grim Reaper. Rudyard Kipling stated: "The reports of my death are over exaggerated." Mark Twain made the similar remark: "The report of my death was an exaggeration." Retired funeral home director Charles Tomlinson of Florida went one better and read two of his own published obituaries, in 1995 and 1996.

Ripley's®
GHANESE FANTASY COFFIN
EXHIBIT NO: 21554
BUILT BY PAA JOE FOR A LOBSTER FISHERMAN

A gambler named Louis Vieira and his wife were buried in Pine Grove Cemetery, Connecticut. The ace represents Vieira, the queen his wife, and the dice are just for decoration. The headstone is carved from pink granite so that the hearts on the stone cards look real.

Gruesome Memento Famous English explorer Sir Walter Raleigh was beheaded in 1618 and buried—well, most of him. His wife Elizabeth kept his preserved head in a bag for 30 years!

Uncle's Been Very Quiet . . . A local tradition in parts of Borneo was to squeeze the body of deceased into a jar and keep it in the relatives' house for a year before the "official" burial.

Last of the Great Meals In ancient Rome, Apicius, the gourmet, was so afraid of going hungry that when he became penniless, because of expenditures on his fabulous banquets, he poisoned himself.

"The sitting-room tombstone" Davis Family memorial is located in Kansas, in the middle of nowhere. It was built by John Milbert Davis, a wealthy farmer landowner, as a memorial to his wife, Sara. They were married for 50 years, but he outlived her for another 15. Most of the individual statues are of John and Sara at different stages of their lives, including John with and without a beard, and one without a hand (he lost it in an accident). This picture was taken in 1933. The tomb was not completed until John died in 1947.

Sensitive Soul In 1835 French artist Baron Gros was so upset by criticism of one of his paintings, he drowned himself in 3 ft (1 m) of water.

Buttoned In Africa, a widow of the Tikarland tribe must wear two buttons from her husband's clothing—one in each nostril.

Step Out in Style

A coffin fit for a judge, book in hand.

Funerals may be a sad time when loved ones are laid to rest, but some people have found a way to go out smiling—in custom-made coffins.

A coffin in the shape of a chicken, complete with chicks!

Coffin makers in Ghana handcraft individually styled models! They come in all sorts of shapes and sizes, from animals such as eagles, cows, chickens, or crabs, to objects such as planes, boats, and luxury cars, to shoes, hoes, shovels, and even bottles! Fishermen can be buried in a fish, an athlete in a giant sneaker, a fruitseller in a papaya!

The occupant of this coffin will be flying into the afterlife in this airplane!

GHANA AIRWAYS

• *Mickey had pillows and*
• *blankets and the heat from*
• *a single light bulb to keep him*
• *warm during his entombment.*

Buried Alive

Mickey Bidwell of Binghamton, New York, U.S.A. was buried alive 6 ft (2 m) under frozen earth for 53 days in 1932. The box in which he was buried measured 7 ft (2 m) long, 21 in (53 cm) wide and 24 in (61 cm) high. There was only 4 in (10 cm) clearance between the box lid and his chest. Food was lowered through an opening in the box, and visitors each paid a dime to look through the hole that also provided him with his air supply. He gained about 10 lb (4.5 kg) while underground, and spent time answering fan mail. Between 1930 and 1936, Mickey spent a total of 365 days underground!

A Great Exit Perhaps the most costly and elaborate funeral of all time was Alexander the Great's in 323 BC. His jewel-studded hearse drawn by 64 horses traveled more than 994 mi (1,600 km) on specially-made roads from Babylon to lay him to rest in the city he had created—Alexandria, Egypt.

Year-Long Funeral The cortege of Chinese General Yi Chun traveled from Peking to Kashgar Sinklang, a distance of 2,299 mi (3,700 km). The funeral lasted exactly one year, from June 1, 1912 to his laying at rest on June 1, 1913.

Well Laid Out The elaborate funeral suit of Chinese Princess Tou Wan, who passed away over 2,000 years ago, was made from 2,000 pieces of jade sewn with gold and silk-covered wire.

Up in Smoke American Bill Johnson of California asked for his ashes to be shot into the sky as firework rockets.

Rest in Pieces Hapsburg emperors had their bodies preserved in monastery crypts in Vienna, Austria, their mummified guts in St. Stephan's Cathedral, and their hearts in the Augustiner Church.

• *Mick Fowell from Norfolk, England, has*
• *an unusual coffee table in his front*
• *room—a coffin. Fortunately, it's empty!*

HAVING THE LAST LAUGH

The ancient Greek soothsayer Calchas foresaw many great events, including the Trojan War. He was so amused to find out that he had outlived the hour of his death as predicted by the spirits, that he laughed until he died—literally.

Hanging Around Gene Roddenbury, the creator of *Star Trek*, arranged to send his ashes into space on a Pegasus rocket, which will circle the Earth for years.

Hard Reminder In New Guinea, when an Asmat warrior dies, his son inherits his father's skull and uses it as a pillow at night.

Silent Mourning In Australia, a widow of the Warramunga aboriginal people does not speak for a year after her partner's death and communicates in the form of gestures and expressions.

The Million-Pound Pound

When Simon Whitaker from Oxfordshire, England, placed a £1 coin (about $1.80) for sale on the eBay auction website, he never expected to face a whopping potential £1 million profit!

What began as a joke escalated fast after Whitaker's friend suggested he contact British national newspaper *The Sun* to record the event. Soon afterwards, offers started to flood onto the auction site for £20, £90, £120, £200—up to a phenomenal £19,500! However, just when things couldn't get any more ridiculous, on the eighth day of bidding an offer came in for over £1 million ($1.7 million)! Realizing the potential fees he stood to pay eBay in the unlikely event the sale actually went through, Whitaker cancelled the auction.

Prior to the story of Simon Whitaker's auction appearing in the news, the pound coin had only received sensible offers in the region of 10–15 pence (17–25 cents).

alllife my sale

information | on sale now | what sold? | browse | contact

allmylifeforsale

Welcome to allmylifeforsale. I am in the process of listing everything I own on Ebay. Feel free to look around and sort through some of my junk. Click here to see all of the items that I will be listing on Ebay in the coming weeks.

Keep checking back to see who bought what and what they are doing with my stuff. Did you ever give me anything? Here is your chance to get it back!

John D. Freyer

Click here to see a QTVR of my house

< information >< on sale now >< sold >< contact ><browse>

Assessing Self-Worth

To test the value of his life, student John D. Freyer of Iowa undertook a project in 2001 to sell off all his possessions, and even his friends! His website—allmylifeforsale.com—listed all the items he had for sale, from clothes and toilet rolls to a tape from his answering machine that included a message from his mother. Other items listed were a 1970s-style telephone, a photocopier, and even his childhood teeth! The most popular of the items for sale, however, were experiences such as a hot-tub session or a dinner date with one of his friends. The aim of the project was to determine how much the life of a student is worth.

John Freyer's website was linked to eBay, so that potential bidders could log onto the auction site and start bidding for any of the items listed on his website. On his site, each item was cataloged with a brief description of how he came to acquire it and any stories linked with it.

DEAD COURIERS
American cartoon artist Paul Kinsella has set up a website where the living can send telegrams to the dead. It costs around $5 (£3) per word to post a message, which is then given to a terminally-ill person who memorizes it to take into the afterlife. All recipients must have been dead for at least 30 days.

Txt Wdng :>) A Norwegian couple who met via text messaging got married in an Oslo phone booth in 2003. Long-distance lovers Grete Myrslett and Frode Stroemsoe conducted their romance by phone and picked out their wedding rings before ever meeting in person. The 100 wedding invitations were all sent by text message.

Go to Your Room! In 2002, Chris Phillips from Hampshire, England, worked from his bedroom to set up his own Internet business while still in school. A year later, at 18 years old, he sold 90 percent of the company, which now employs over 100 staff and has seven offices based in the U.S.A. and Canada, for a staggering £2 million ($3.5 million)!

No Joke Scientists in Australia have developed software that allows people to log on to computers by laughing.

"analyzing dogs' voices"

Skysurfers Tim Porter and Chris Gauge took the concept of "surfing the net" to a new level when they attached a laptop to one of their boards and attempted to send an Internet message while in freefall.

Rent-a-Cow Swiss dairy farmer Paul Wyler has posted photos of his cows on the Internet with the idea of renting the animals out to cheese-lovers.

Japanese toymaker Takara developed a gadget to enable owners to understand their dogs. "Bowlingual" analyzes a dog's bark and various other noises using a wireless microphone on the dog's collar.

Zoologist Dr. Susan Savage-Rumbaugh has devised a method of communication for the ape world. Her research has proved that it is possible to teach chimpanzees how to communicate by using symbols as part of sign language.

Pot Luck A coffee pot bought ten years ago for £25 ($43) by computer students at Cambridge University, England, became such cult viewing on the Internet that it recently sold for £3,350 ($5,750)! Tired of trekking through their seven-story building only to find the coffee pot empty, the students had set up one of the first webcams so that they could watch it without leaving their desks. The pot became a huge hit as hundreds of thousands of net surfers logged onto the image from all over the world.

Ringing Revenge In 2003, U.S. columnist Dave Barry got his revenge on telesales firms by publishing the phone number of the American Telesales Association in *The Miami Herald* and urging readers to call them. Thousands took his advice, forcing ATA to stop answering the phone!

Take my Dad Nina Gronland of Trondheim, Norway, was so irritated by her father living with her that she decided to put him up for auction on an Internet site! The advert for 52-year-old cab driver Odd Kristiansen read: "Giving away my dad to a nice woman in Trondheim. Dad is tall, dark, and slim and in his best age. I am tired of him living with me. Furniture comes with him. Serious!"

Saved in Seconds A church in Hokksund, Norway, offers salvation in 12 seconds to anyone who reads a prayer on its website.

BUY A USED TOWN
The Northern California town of Bridgeville became the first town to be sold online when it was bought by a mystery bidder on the Internet auction site eBay for nearly $1.8 million (£1 million) in December 2002. With 82 acres (33 ha), Bridgeville comes complete with a post office, a cemetery, and more than a dozen cabins and houses. It was put up for sale when the previous owners couldn't afford the $200,000 (£116,300) needed to renovate the town. Bidding started at $5,000 (£3,000) and almost 250 bids were made, comfortably exceeding the asking price of $775,000 (£450,000).

Safe Siesta There are more telephones in New York City alone than there are in the whole of Spain!

Inflated Bill A man from Yorkshire, England, received a gas bill for a staggering £2.3 million ($3.9 million) in 2003 after a computer mix-up. When the gas company was told of the man's complaint, they checked the error and revised the bill to the princely sum of £59 ($101).

SEX CHANGE
Internet users in China can buy voice-altering machines that make a man sound like a woman and vice-versa. The devices, which hook up to a telephone, cost $12 (£7) each and have been selling well, mainly to people trying to find out whether their partner is up for an affair.

> ## "Northern California town sold online for $1.8 million"

Champion Surfers The U.S.A. holds the record for surfing the Internet, coming in at just over 24 percent of the world's total usage.

Hot Mail The amount of junk mail that Americans receive in one day could produce sufficient energy to heat 250,000 homes.

Tired of being asked when he was going to settle down and marry, David Weinlick plucked a date out of thin air—June 13, 1998. At 28 years old, with the deadline looming and no bride in sight, he decided to advertise for her on the Internet! His friends and family picked the bride from an adventurous list of candidates following a session of interviews. Elizabeth Runze was the lucky one who got to walk down the aisle in the Minneapolis shopping mall, just hours after meeting David for the first time ever!

Bliss Online From the start of 2004, couples in Russia have been able to wed via the Internet.

Bride's Net Profit A Florida woman surfing the Internet was stunned to find that her boyfriend had posted a marriage proposal to her on it. Natalie Thilem of Fort Lauderdale was looking for jewelry on the eBay website when she found attached to a heart-shaped diamond engagement ring a proposal from Shane Bushman. She said yes!

An Islamic court ruling decreed that it is acceptable for a man to divorce his wife by sending her a text message, reading "I divorce you" three times.

Doctor Flies to the Rescue

When Scottish surgeon Angus Wallace stepped on board his flight from Hong Kong to London in 1995, he was unaware that he was just hours away from having to perform major surgery on a fellow passenger—using only a coat hanger and various other rudimentary tools.

Professor Angus Wallace carried out the operation using a catheter, brandy bottle, tools from a medical kit, and a wire coat hanger, all found on board the airplane.

A healthy passenger doesn't feel any effect from reduced air pressure, but Paula Dixon had previously suffered a collapsed lung as a result of a motorbike crash, and so was susceptible to respiratory problems. Wallace had to relieve a tension pneumothorax—air trapped as a result of a malfunction inside the lung—using only the tools available to him on board the plane. The operation was a complete success and Wallace later received a professional award for the act.

Part-time Moms In 1936, at the age of 17, Louise Madeline Pittman of Atlanta, Georgia, decided to divide her time between two sets of parents because a hospital mix-up when she was born made it impossible to determine her real mother.

Fare Hearing In 1995, doctors in Sweden restored a deaf man's hearing by removing a bus ticket that had been lodged in his ear for 47 years!

Dangerous Weapon Every year around 8,800 people are injured using toothpicks.

Grrrr! Actress Sarah Bernhardt once consulted a doctor about having the tail of a tiger grafted to the base of her spine.

Dimbeswar Basumatary from India has amazed doctors by being able to stare at the Sun for hours on end without so much as blinking! Of course this should never ever be attempted by anyone!

Deadening the Pain An Argentinean man was refused treatment for toothache in 2002 because his medical records showed that he had died in 1980! Rafael Lanizante thought it was a joke until he saw his own death certificate. While the mix-up was investigated, there was at least some good news from Mr. Lanizante—with all the confusion, his toothache had disappeared!

Sick Bets In 1980, a Las Vegas hospital suspended workers for having a pool on when patients would die.

Deep Bite When Kevin Morrison of Rockford, Illinois, was bitten by a 3-ft (1-m) nurse shark in 1998, doctors had to surgically remove the shark from his chest.

Slow Bullet Bruce Levon of Gross Pointe, Michigan, was accidentally shot in the head in 1983—but didn't know it until doctors spotted the slug in an X-ray eight years later!

Have You Had Your Head Examined?

Believe it or not, this bizarre machine was used to determine a person's health and happiness! The wire cage fitted over the head and the machine "read" bumps on the sitter's head. A print-out displayed the development of each of the 32 faculties that believers felt determined the well-being of a person. This pseudo-science, known as phrenology, was used to determine the best presidential candidate in the 1848 election. Zachary Taylor won but died soon after.

Made in about 1908, this machine purported to be able to determine the sitter's well-being.

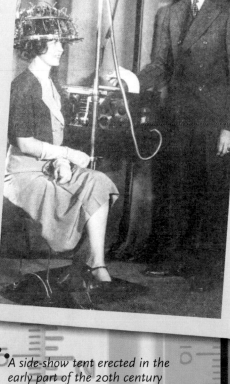

A side-show tent erected in the early part of the 20th century housed phrenologists who made a living by carrying out readings.

BREASTFED BY DAD

In 2002, it was reported that a Sri Lankan man, whose wife died while giving birth to their second child, was able to breastfeed his elder daughter. Mr. B. Wijeratne from Walapanee, near Colombo, discovered his talent after his 18-month-old daughter Nisansala refused to take formula milk. He said: "She was used to her mother's milk and rejected the powdered milk so I tried feeding through a bottle. Unable to see her cry, I offered my breast. That's when I discovered that I could breastfeed her." Doctors say that men with a hyperactive prolactine hormone are able to produce breast milk.

This pacemaker, worn by Scott McIver, is the size of a U.K. 50 pence piece. The first ever pacemaker was too large to fit in the human body!

Talked to Death Edward Dilly (1732–79) of London, England, never stopped talking—even in his sleep. Physicians certified this as his actual cause of death.

It took 600 hours to create this skeleton inside a bottle! The bones were carved from hard maple wood and then dropped through the narrow neck and assembled inside the bottle.

Out-of-Date A Roman metal pot unearthed at an archeological dig in London in 2003 was found to contain 2,000-year-old ointment.

Left Right, Left Right A French woman was born in 1869 with two pelvises and four legs. She married and gave birth to two normal children.

Sleepless in Romania In December 2003, doctors in Budeasa, Romania, were mystified by a woman who claimed not to have slept for eight years. Maria Stelica, 58, developed insomnia when her mother died in 1995 and had stayed awake ever since.

Self Scan Dale Eller, 22, walked into a police station in Columbus, Ohio, in 1990 and requested an X-ray to locate his brain. He showed baffled officers a hole in his skull, which he said he had made with a power drill, and through which he had inserted a 3-in (8-cm) piece of wire in a failed attempt to find his brain. Surgeons later removed part of a wire coat hanger from his head.

Persistent Patient Between 1929 and 1979, British hypochondriac William McIlroy underwent 400 operations and stayed at over 100 different hospitals, using 22 aliases.

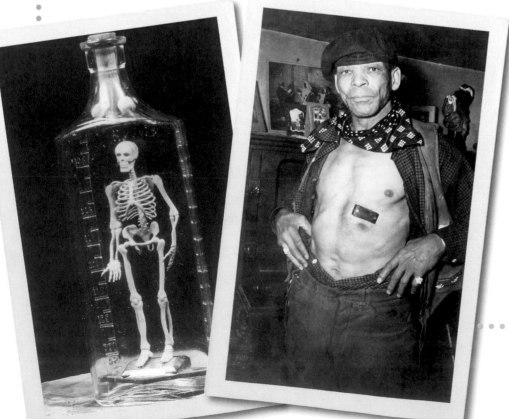

Sioux "Chief" Couzzingo, from Oxford, Ohio, fastened his broken rib to his breastbone using a screwdriver—without anesthetic!

Hiro Takeuchi works for the Hello Tomorrow and New Body Institute in Japan, where he creates artificial human body parts from silicon and vinyl chloride. These parts, which include ears, breasts, legs, and arms, are bought for 30,000 yen ($245 / £137) or more, by people who have lost body parts through disease or accident.

Channel Flipper Bryan Allison, 24, was hospitalized in Buffalo, New York, in 2001 after falling 20 ft (6 m) while throwing a television set from the second-floor balcony of his home. He was watching a videotape replay of a 1989 National Hockey League playoff game and became incensed once again that his team had lost. Angrily, he picked up the TV set and hurled it off the balcony—but forgot to let go!

Hart of the Problem Dianne Neale, a 49-year-old American, suffered epileptic seizures in 1991 whenever she heard the voice of *Entertainment Tonight* host Mary Hart. The TV presenter even apologized on air for the distress she caused her!

John Evans suffered severe injuries after he was struck by a train. He woke up to find his left hand had been attached to his right arm!

CHOCOLATES TO LIVE FOR

German confectioner Adolf Andersen believes he has created the world's first anti-ageing chocolates. He claims the ingredients in Felice pralines—dark chocolate, mango, and soya milk—not only make you happy, but immediately make you feel 15 years younger.

TV Seizure At 6.50 p.m. on December 16, 1997, 685 people in Japan, mostly children, simultaneously suffered epileptic seizures. After an investigation, it transpired that they had all been watching the television cartoon *Pocket Monsters*, and that the seizures had been caused by the program's flashing red and blue lights.

Feeling the Heat The highest manufactured temperature was created by scientists at Princeton University in 1978. They managed to generate a temperature of 70 million degrees Celcius!

Spoken Word Scientists have created a machine that scans the words of a book, no matter what typeface, and feeds the information into a computer, which translates into spoken English for the visually impaired.

Gene Jugglers

While American petowners clamor for designer dogs such as the Labradoodle (a cross between a Labrador and a poodle), scientists across the world are experimenting with nature to create new cross-breeds.

The new breed of featherless chicken, developed in Israel, is designed not to suffer from the heat as much as feathered birds do.

Israeli scientists recently came up with a bright pink featherless chicken, its ugliness offset by the fact that it doesn't need plucking. And in August 2003, a Japanese safari park unveiled the world's only living zenkey—an animal that looks like a donkey in pyjamas, as well it might since it is a cross between a donkey and a zebra.

Developed in Dubai, the "cama"—half camel, half llama—is the first of its kind!

BOFFIN FACTS

- Peanuts are an ingredients used to make explosives
- Our atmosphere is showered every 24 hours by 750,000,000,000,000,000 meteors
- Fragments of breaking glass can move at up to 3,000 mph (4,800 km/h)
- All the gold that has ever been mined in the world to date would only make a block the size of a tennis court and as high as a 400 oz (11,340 g) gold bar
- A hit golf ball spins about 8,000 revolutions a minute

The "zenkey," developed in Japan, has a donkey mother and a zebra father.

Scientists from Britain and the Netherlands have developed a way to levitate frogs magnetically! By placing the frog into a magnetic tube and creating a weak magnetic field in its atoms, an opposing force is then generated. This overcomes the force of gravity—just like two poles pushing apart. It may only be a matter of time before humans can be levitated in this way!

A Drop in the Ocean Scientists calculate there are roughly the same number of molecules in a spoonful of water as there are spoonfuls of water in the Atlantic Ocean.

SCHOOL OF FISH

Scientists at Plymouth University, England, claim that fish can tell the time. They trained fish that were kept in a tank to feed themselves by pressing a lever to release the food. Although food was only available for one hour, the fish quickly figured out when it would arrive. Experts had recently proved that fish had at least a three-month memory.

Medical Scents Scientists in Brazil have come up with a perfume in pill form to be taken three times a day.

Dodging Raindrops Scientists Trevor Wallis and Thomas Peterson of the National Climatic Data Center in Asheville, North Carolina, have discovered that a person walking in the rain gets 40 percent wetter than a person who runs in it.

Shaky Robot In 1992, scientists in San Francisco invented a robot that could mix 150 different drinks and add up the bar tab!

Naval Campaign Karl Kruszelnicki, a scientist at the University of Sydney, Australia, has written a study of belly-button fluff after examining samples from 5,000 people.

Gone But Not Forgotten

The Tasmanian tiger was declared extinct in 1936, but a pup preserved in ethanol for 130 years may hold the key to reviving the species. Australian scientists have successfully replicated DNA from the specimen and plan to bring the species back from extinction!

The Tasmanian tiger has not been seen for over 70 years, but scientists now hope to recreate the animal within the next ten years.

The preserved Tasmanian tiger pup is the key to the revival of the species.

ROBO DANCER

Japanese scientists have developed a dancing robot that is capable of following a human dancer's lead. The Mobile Smart Dance Robot predicts the dancer's next move through hand pressure applied to its back. Equipped with a computer, sensor, batteries, and four wheels, it can move in any direction and has enough memory for the necessary steps to dance a waltz.

Pages with Half-Life The notebooks in which Marie and Pierre Curie recorded details of their experiments on radium nearly 100 years ago are still dangerously radioactive.

Two climbers in the Oetztaler Alps discovered a glacier-mummy—a freeze-dried man. "Otzi," as he was called, had been preserved in ice for about 5,000 years at an altitude of about 10,000 ft (3,000 m). Scientists in Italy defrosted him in the hope of learning more about his lifestyle.

Non-Stick In its liquid form, mercury can be poured out of a jug and yet leave the inside of the jug completely dry.

Sniffer Bees Researchers at the University of Montana have been training honeybees to sniff out landmines. Apparently bees not only have a better sense of smell than dogs, but they also learn faster.

Cold Logic Albert Einstein not only developed the Theory of Relativity—he also designed refrigerators!

Bite-Sized To cater for Japan's rising population of single people, scientists have created a range of dwarf vegetables, including mini cauliflowers and half-size radishes.

Bacteria Revival Scientists in Chicago have revived 2,800-year-old frozen bacteria and algae, that were found lying dormant in an Antarctic lake.

German scientist Ursula Plate of the Medical University of Lübeck has developed a cure for those with a fear of flying! The 3-D glasses simulate a turbulent, but safe, flight from Hamburg to Munich.

Carp Get the Beat Scientists at the Rowland Institute for Science in Massachusetts have taught Koi carp to detect the difference between classical music and the blues!

Laid Back Turkeys In the run-up to Christmas, turkey farmers in Britain play "relaxation" CDs to their birds. Farmers suggest that playing music to their turkeys has a calming effect on them and, as a consequence, keeps their meat tender.

BID FOR FREEDOM

Gaak, a "living robot" programmed to think for itself, made a daring escape from its compound in Rotherham, England, in 2002. It broke out of its paddock, traveled down an access slope, through the front door of the Magna Science Centre, and was eventually discovered at the main entrance to the car park after nearly being run over by a visitor! Professor Noel Sharkey said: "There's no need to worry, as although they can escape they are perfectly harmless and won't be taking over just yet."

Terror of the Roosts Two Scottish inventors have devised a robotic bird of prey designed to scare off pigeons by swooping on their territory. The flying fiberglass peregrine falcon can move its head and call like a real bird. Creator, Bob McIntyre, says, "The bird is very high tech. It can even give you a call on your cell phone to let you know when its battery is running down."

Flylight U.S. government scientists have developed a tiny robotic fly with solar-powered wings that weighs only 0.004 oz (0.1 g)—less than a small size paper clip!

Tattoo on Trust Austrian electrician Niki Passath has created Freddy, the world's first tattooing robot. But you can't choose your design—Freddy's computerized brain, which is programmed with artistic outlines, takes care of that.

Barb's Pills Dr. Adolph Von Baeyer (1835–1917), a chemist in Berlin, Germany, who discovered barbituric acid (which gave us barbiturates) named his find not after an ingredient but in honor of a sweetheart named Barbara!

Numbers Game Benjamin Franklin, the statesman, scientist, and inventor, was born on January 17, 1706, was one of 17 children, started his career in Philadelphia at 17, and died on April 17, 1790.

The almost perfectly preserved skeleton of this meat-eating baby scipionix dinosaur was found intact! Remnants of the liver, large intestine, windpipe, and muscles can even be seen! Scientists understand that it lived approximately 110 million years ago.

No Tip Necessary A hotel in Atlantic City, New Jersey, unveiled Rich, a 5 ft (1.5 m) tall robot whose duties included mingling with guests and delivering room service meals. The management refused to let him gamble in the casino for fears that he could be equipped to cheat with hidden cameras.

The Ignoble Prize You've heard of the Nobel Prize—well this is the Ignoble Prize! Winners must achieve two things: they have to make people laugh, and they have to make them think. Entrants in 2003 for the prizes for physics and medicine categories have submitted reports on "An Analysis of the Forces Required to Drag Sheep over Various Surfaces" and "Navigation-Related Structural change in the Hippocampi of Taxi Drivers."

Faith in the Air

Churchgoers who for years have endured hard, wooden pews may have had their prayers answered by an inflatable church that was developed near London, England.

Apart from the inflatable pews, the 46-ft (14-m) high building contains a blow-up organ, altar, pulpit, candles—even inflatable stained-glass windows! As many as 60 worshipers can fit into the invention.

Visitors try the seats of the inflatable church on display at the National Christian Resources Exhibition in 2003!

It takes less than one hour to inflate the plastic bouncy-church!

Close the Cover Dutch designer Hans Rademaker has created a bookcase that can be converted into a coffin after the owner's death.

Let's Call it a Vodka In 1997, researchers at the University of Idaho developed a cold-climate potato that produces its own antifreeze.

Who Needs a Wife? A German firm has built the first talking washing machine. Speaking in a friendly female voice, "Hermine" gives advice on how to load the machine and get the best results from the wash. She can also understand complex spoken commands.

Backyard Snow A U.S. company sells a machine that will make real snow in your yard overnight!

PROBLEM LICKED
Rick Hartman, a toymaker from Issaquah, Washington, has invented a motorized ice cream holder in order to eliminate tongue stress caused from licking ice cream. "Ice-cream technology has been stagnant for the last 200 years," says Hartman. A motor inside an acrylic cone is connected to an activator button, which, when pressed, makes the cone whirl without the tongue moving.

The invention of the snowshoe was displayed by Charlie Miller, a famous guide from Boston, who walked 223 mi (360 km) on them!

Eat it All Researchers at Campinas State University in Sao Paulo, Brazil, have created an edible cling film, made from amaranto flour.

Fear Spray Mary Elizabeth Feldman of Charleston, South Carolina has invented Ghost Away, a chamomile-based spray to use against ghosts and monsters!

Eau de Anything Christopher Brosius of New York City creates fragrances for people who want to smell like lobsters, dandelions, sugar cookies, or even dirt!

Ear Ring Reginald M. Grooms of Conway, South Carolina, invented an alarm clock that is worn inside the ear.

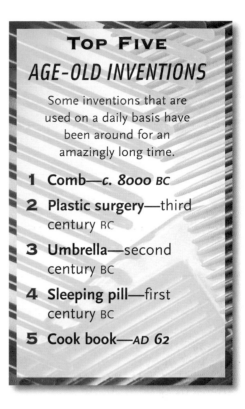

TOP FIVE
AGE-OLD INVENTIONS

Some inventions that are used on a daily basis have been around for an amazingly long time.

1 Comb—*c. 8000* BC

2 Plastic surgery—third century BC

3 Umbrella—second century BC

4 Sleeping pill—first century BC

5 Cook book—AD *62*

Wake-up Shoes Scientists at Boston University, Massachusetts, have developed vibrating insoles to be worn inside shoes. The random vibrations amplify balance-related signals between the feet and the brain, which become dulled with age. It is hoped that the new shoes will prevent elderly people from losing their balance and suffering falls.

This 14.8-ft (4.5-m) long vehicle is shaped like a submarine, but the periscope is made from a video camera and the turret from a washing machine! Invented by Jo L'Tessier, the vehicle is powered by electricity and can reach speeds of up to 12 mph (20 km/h)!

The annual International Birdman Festival in Bognor Regis, England, attracts the most inventive minds, including Sir Richard Branson. Entrants create personal flying machines and test them to the limit by jumping off the end of the pier.

New Ideas Not Welcome In 1875, the director of the U.S. Patent Office suggested that the department be closed down because, in his opinion, there was nothing left to invent. How wrong he was!

No Quack-Ups Argentinean inventors have come up with a strap-on rubber duck, which they claim will combat tiredness in drivers. The Duckmaster fastens around the neck and starts quacking if the user's head slumps forward.

Mood Mouse A company in California has developed a computer mouse that can sense the emotions of the person using it. The Emotion Mouse can measure pulse, temperature, and skin resistance to identify states of sadness, happiness, or anger.

Sudden Inflation Japanese inventor Katsu Katugoru, whose greatest fear is drowning, has created inflatable underwear! Inconveniently, the garment accidentally inflated to 30 times its original size in a crowded subway.

For Him! To evoke memories of the celebrated Oktoberfest, Munich's annual homage to beer, German pub landlord Peter Inselkammer has created a new perfume that smells of rancid beer and cigarette butts! It costs around $160 (£90) a bottle.

Roll On When Joseph Gayetty invented toilet paper in 1857, he had his name printed on each sheet.

Fear Banished Light bulb inventor Thomas Edison was afraid of the dark.

Hot Table Richard E. Mahan of Houston, Texas, invented an electrified tablecloth to stop insects landing near the food!

Make a Note! Laszlo Biro, inventor of the ballpoint pen, lost a fortune by forgetting to patent it in the U.S.A.

PIZZA BUBBLES
Ducio Cresci, a cosmetics manufacturer from Florence, Italy, has devised a new range of bathroom products that smell like pizza. Using tomato extract plus essential oils of basil and oregano, he has created a luxury bubble bath, soap, and body lotion—all with the great aroma of pizza. He says: "The bubble bath smells especially strong when you are bathing in it, but once out of the water it leaves an irresistible trace of scent on your skin." Cresci, a former TV presenter, has not stopped there. His Experimenta range also includes cappuccino soap, baked Tuscan bread body lotion, and oils smelling of chocolate, cake, and chewing gum.

Plenty of Pin Money In 1849, the safety pin was created by New York mechanic Walter Hunt—by accident. He was idly twisting a wire while trying to think of something that would enable him to pay off his $15 (£8) debt.

For Dunkers Dominic Skinner from England invented a coffee cup with a built-in biscuit shelf to store three biscuits—without getting them soggy.

These automatic spectacle cleaners were presented by a hopeful Indian student for the Young Inventor Award in Bangalore.

First Shoe-Trees Rubber shoes were first made in Brazil around 1820 by tapping a rubber tree and letting the liquid latex drop on the bare feet of local workers! After the rubber dried, the shoes were removed and exported to the U.S. for sale.

"Pyon-pyon" or hopping shoes are a recent creation from Japanese Dr. Joshino Nakamatsu, who already has an astonishing 2,300 patents to his name. Made of plastic with a spring to disperse the weight of the wearer, they put a bounce back into your step.

Flying Papers In 1972 Robert Lamar of Houston, Texas, patented a design for a truck that would automatically throw newspapers onto subscribers' lawns.

Ideas in Motion Acting on the theory that physical stimulation of the buttocks helps relieve constipation, in 1966 U.S. inventor Thomas J. Bayard invented a vibrating toilet seat.

CREATIVE FLOW

- The first electric kettles took 12 minutes to boil
- Enough Velcro® is produced each year to stretch twice around the world
- The first hearing aid weighed 16 lb (7 kg) and had to be placed on a table
- In their first year on sale, only 51 safety razors were sold in the U.S.
- Early video recorders were the size of a piano
- Shoes were not made for both right and left feet until 1785

Needle Point In 1914, Natalie Stolp of Philadelphia devised an implement designed to discourage men from rubbing a leg against a lady's thigh on a crowded train or carriage. A spring attached to the lady's underskirt responded to pressure by releasing a short, sharp point into the offender's flesh.

The donut was invented by a sea captain to fit the handle of a steering wheel. During a storm in 1850 Captain Hanson Gregory, skipper of the good ship Donat, squeezed a "solid sinker" weight down over a wheel handle in order to keep both hands free to steer the ship, and so the donut was born!

Cleaning the toilet seat has never been easier than with Swiss inventor Juerg Lumpert's "disinfection element." The clean-crazy creation uses an ultraviolet wavelength of light, which hovers above the seat, negating the need for disinfectant.

"cleaning the toilet using hovering lightwaves"

No Wet Dogs Celes Antoine of Forestville, Maryland, invented a self-supported umbrella for dogs!

Pecking Order In 1902, Andrew Jackson Jr. of Tennessee patented an eye protector shaped like a pair of miniature glasses for chickens to prevent them being hen-pecked.

Hats Off! In 1920, Alan Dawson of Jacksonville, Florida, invented a hat with a built-in comb.

Close the Cover In 1986 American Ralph R. Pire of Lindenhurst, New York, devised a mechanical arm apparatus attached to the shoulder that allowed the wearer to pat himself on the back whenever he felt in need of a psychological lift.

This novel, naval invention simulates the rolling and pitching of a ship in a storm and was used to test levels of sea sickness among sailors.

Tin Boat Hovercraft inventor, Christopher Cockerell, constructed his prototype model from an empty tin of cat food, a coffee tin, and a vacuum cleaner.

For Stepping Out An Australian inventor has developed pantyhose that have three legs—in case one of the other two gets a run.

A Head of Beer Randy Flann of Milwaukee, Wisconsin, has invented headgear that comes in the shape of a football, a baseball, or a basketball, and also a keg that contains beer!

EAR-WAX MIRROR
Justin Letlow from Bend, Oregon has invented an ear mirror to help people clean their ears and avoid "earwax embarrassment." It features two small, adjustable mirrors connected by a flexible plastic handle. Users hold one mirror close to their ear and the other in front of their eyes. Explaining the need for his invention, Mr. Letlow says, "I can't think how many times I've been watching a game on TV, and they zoom in on the coach, and there's this big old piece of earwax."

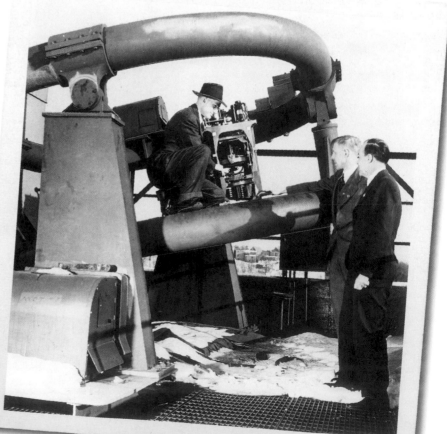

It's possible to travel at 12 mph (20 km/h) with the Segway™ Human Transporter, invented by Dean Kamen. It is a two-wheel vehicle with powerful motors, tilt sensors, and gyroscopes to detect your center of gravity.

Floating Furniture In 1989 William A. Calderwood, of Arizona, devised a range of helium-filled furniture, tethered to the floor that, when not in use, could float up to the ceiling!

The New Black A group of scientists have developed a new paint color—superblack. It's blacker in hue than all other blacks and absorbs 99.7 percent of light, so almost no light is reflected from its surface.

Kissing Shield For those who enjoy kissing but dread the thought of catching a disease, Deloris Gray Wood of Missouri has invented the kissing shield. A thin, latex membrane stretched over an attractive heart-shaped frame, the shield is worn over the mouth and is described by its inventor as being ideal for vote-hungry politicians who have to kiss a lot of babies.

"Qrio," a humanoid robot, shows off its amazingly human flexibility and ability to dance! It weighs just 15 lb (7 kg), is 23 in (58 cm) tall and was presented at the Robodex exhibition in 2003!

Santa Detector American inventor Thomas cane has come up with a device to ensure that children no longer miss the arrival of Santa Claus. A wired stocking is hung over the fireplace and as soon as Santa emerges from the chimney, lights on the stocking start flashing to wake the children of the house.

Animal Lover In 1999, American inventor Stephen B. Hoy devised an edible greeting card for pets.

Safety First To reduce pedestrian casualties in 1960, David Gutman from Philadelphia invented a special bumper to be fixed to the front of cars. The bumper not only cushioned any impact but also had a huge pair of claws that grabbed the pedestrian around the waist to prevent him falling to the ground.

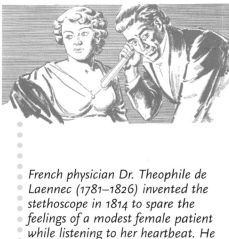

French physician Dr. Theophile de Laennec (1781–1826) invented the stethoscope in 1814 to spare the feelings of a modest female patient while listening to her heartbeat. He rolled a sheet of paper into a cone.

Special Delivery

In September 2003 Charles McKinley shipped himself from New Jersey to Dallas in an airline cargo crate because he thought it was the cheapest way to fly.

The 25-year-old shipping clerk made the unscheduled trip because he was homesick and a friend told him he could save money by flying as cargo, although in fact he could have flown first class for the same cost if he had realized how much he would have to pay in fines! Before climbing into the crate, McKinley filled out forms saying it contained a computer and clothing. The box was loaded onto a pressurized cargo plane and flew from Newark, New Jersey, to Niagara Falls, New York, then to Fort Wayne, Indiana, before continuing to Dallas. The courier who delivered the crate to McKinley's parents' home first became suspicious when he thought he saw a pair of eyes peering out. He feared it contained a dead body until, in front of his startled parents, McKinley broke out of the box on their doorstep. After the courier alerted the police, District Attorney Bill Hill said of McKinley: "He violated the law of stupidity if nothing else."

Stowaway Charles McKinley went without food or water for the 15-hour journey home to Dallas, Texas. The crate in which he stowed away was just 5 ft 8 in (1.7 m) tall.

WEIRD CARGO

- Eileen Cresswell, a 63-year-old grandmother, was arrested for masterminding an international drug smuggling plot

- A student smuggled a tortoise into England—inside his sock!

- A Swedish tourist tried to smuggle eight baby snakes, including four venemous king cobras, into Australia

- A U.S. man was arrested after trying to smuggle four pigeons into Canada under his shirt

The Solar Challenge attracts hundreds of solar-powered cars from across the world to compete in the 2,300-mi (3,700-km) race.

Foul Cargo In 2003 customs officers at Amsterdam's Schiphol airport in the Netherlands opened a smelly suitcase—and found it full of rotting baboon noses!

Jumbo Fuel Bill A full jumbo jet tank contains enough fuel to drive the average car around the world four times.

Watery Graveyard Over 1,500 shipwrecks lie in the waters surrounding New York Harbor.

TICKET FLURRY

Walter H. Burtin of Washington, D.C., was arrested and charged with committing 34 traffic offences in ten minutes—he passed 15 red lights and nine stop signs, disregarded four official signs, twice drove on the wrong side of the street, drove through a safety zone, failed to slow down at an intersection, drove without a permit, and was caught speeding.

Israeli newlyweds buck the traditional modes of transportation to travel to their wedding reception on a plow!

Short Hop The shortest scheduled flight in the world is British Airways' twice-daily flight between the islands of Westray and Papa Westray off the north coast of Scotland. It takes just two minutes to reach its destination!

Baboon at the Switch At Uitenhage Station, South Africa, a baboon once stood in for a crippled signalman. The intelligent ape infallibly operated six levers as it was directed.

Over the Limit In 1903 England became the first country to impose a speed restriction on the road. Vehicles were limited to 20 mph (32 km/h).

No Frills Flight In May 2003 the world's maiden naked flight carried 87 nude passengers from Miami, Florida to Cancun, Mexico. Arranged by a travel agency specializing in naturism, all the passengers except for the captain and the crew stripped off their clothes when the plane reached its cruising altitude.

A staggering 500,000 stamps have been painstakingly stuck to this VW Beetle, exhibited at an international stamp fair in Germany.

Horse Power Today, a rocket can fly to the Moon quicker than an 1800s stagecoach could travel from one end of England to the other.

Don't Look Up On August 27, 1933, Lieutenant Tito Falconi of the Italian Air Force flew a plane from St. Louis, Missouri, to Joilet, Illinois—a distance of 250 mi (402 km)—in 3hr 6 min 30 sec—flying the entire journey upside down.

Burning Up the Road A 3-mi (5-km) long road in Orchard, Texas, was built of sulphuric slag, and when it rained the hot exhaust pipes of automobiles set it on fire.

A streetcar invented by I. Mathewson of Gilroy, California, in 1876 had its gasoline motor disguised as the head of a horse so that it would not frighten real horses!

Cracking Cheeses During a vital wartime engagement between the fleets of Uruguay and Argentina in 1841, the Uruguayan flagship *Santa Maria* ran out of cannon balls. So the ship's American commander, John Coe, ordered the guns to be loaded instead with hard Dutch cheeses, and the Argentinean navy was routed!

Costly Number Sichuan Airlines of China paid $190,000 (£106,000) for the phone number 8888-8888 in the hope that it would make its customers happy. The number eight is considered lucky because it sounds like the Chinese word for "getting rich."

Olive Squeeze American Airlines saved an estimated $40,000 (£22,000) in 1987 by removing one olive from each salad served with first-class meals.

Light Lunch Charles Lindbergh took only four sandwiches with him for sustenance on his famous transatlantic flight.

"Best Lowrider Car" "Best Hopping" and "Best Car Dancing" are just some of the competitions the Lowrider Experience exhibitors can enter. They can also show off their luxury interiors.

This 115-ft (35-m) long sofa was constructed for European Car Free Day in Italy, in 2001, during which members of the public protested against too many cars on the road. The sofa seated more than 100 people.

Anti-Clamp Crusader

In 2003 a man wearing a Superman-style costume roamed the streets of London, England, illegally freeing wheel-clamped cars—with an angle grinder.

Under the guise of Angle Grinder Man, he illegally released at least 12 cars in the capital. He even set up his own Angle Grinder Man website with a call-out number for clamped motorists. "I'm performing a public service," said the anonymous crusader. "And I like wearing the costume."

RIVER OF NO RETURN
In September 2003 an 81-year-old Canadian woman failed her driving test for the sixth time by reversing into a river. She was trying to back out of a parking space in Thunder Bay, Ontario, but went 25 yd (23 m) too far and plunged over an embankment.

Monster Jam A 1980 traffic jam stretched 109 mi (175 km) northwards from Lyon in France.

Drinks Caddy Bill Francis of Lakewood, Colorado, turned a 1964 Cadillac car into a full-sized bar in his recreation room.

Holy Rollers Romanian priests bless cars in the belief that it will make the vehicles safer on the roads. The ceremony involves splashing holy water on the engine and seats of the car.

TRAVEL-LOG

- One in 300 of all road accidents in Canada involves a moose
- There are approximately 800,000 people flying in airplanes around the world at any given moment
- The wingspan of a Boeing 747 is longer than the length of the Wright Brothers' maiden flight
- In Ethiopia there is just one car for every 1,468 people
- Car airbags inflate at 200 mph (322 km/h)

Angle Grinder Man—the auto hero who illegally freed wheel-clamped cars using an angle grinder.

Tandem sport takes on a new meaning when parachutists take to the skies while riding a bicycle!

No Ewe Turn As part of a 1996 safety initiative, authorities in the Dutch town of Culemburg released six sheep into their busy streets to control the speed of rush-hour traffic!

Women's Touch In 1955 Chrysler developed a car called the Dodge La Femme that was to be sold exclusively to women. The car came with a matching purse, umbrella, and raincoat!

Risky Front Seat In 2003 a woman was arrested for dangerous driving after she drove 2 mi (3 km) to a police station in Dubrovnik, Croatia, with her drunken husband on the car bonnet!

Last Laugh A Romanian man was so upset at failing his driving test that he set his car on fire. He said: "When I came home I thought I saw the car laughing at me. So I put gas on it and lit it up."

Bean Power In Brazil in times of crop surplus, coffee beans were used to power steam locomotives.

Winding Roads If all the roads in the United States were joined together, they would encircle the globe 150 times.

Undertaken A Dutch hearse driver was fired in 2003 for losing a coffin on the way to a funeral.

Going in Style Betty Young was buried at Phillips Memorial Cemetery in Foster, Rhode Island, inside her 1989 Cadillac Coupe de Ville!

Hello Dolly Arlene Lambert of Toronto, Ontario, drives a car that is covered with hundreds of plastic baby dolls.

Ripley's®
GIANT RUBBER TIRE
EXHIBIT NO: 15280
MEASURES 12 FT 10 IN (4 M) IN
DIAMETER, IS 137 IN (54 IN) WIDE
AND WEIGHS 12,000 LB (5,440 KG)

This is the world's largest tire and costs $30,000 (£16,500) to produce. There is enough rubber in one of these tires to make 5,276 average-sized car tires! It takes three days to make one tire and can support 250,000 lb (113,400 kg). They are used on front-end loader Caterpillars, which are used in open pit mining.

AMERICA OTR LOADER-DOZER

Firestone HALF TREAD

S/185-57 L-5 /L-5S

Head for Heights

To 41-year-old Frenchman Alain Robert, tall buildings are personal challenges. He climbs their outside surfaces to dizzying heights, sticking to glass, brick, concrete, and steel like a human fly—without any safety ropes to keep him from hurtling to his death.

EARLY BOOKING

Dutch architect Hans-Jurgen Rombaut has designed the Moon's first hotel, complete with a low-gravity games area where guests would be able to fly and abseil wearing special suits. As there is no wind on the Moon, the building is of a fragile design but it has a half-metre thick hull to protect visitors from extreme temperatures and cosmic rays. Guests will stay in teardrop-shaped habitation capsules that hang from two huge pillars to create the impression of constant travel. Rombaut hopes the hotel will be open for business by 2050.

He started climbing at the age of 11 and has scaled more than 60 buildings, using only specially adapted climbing shoes. His claims to fame are conquering the 984-ft (300-m) high Eiffel Tower in Paris, New York's Empire State Building at 1,250 ft (381 m) and the 1,482-ft (452-m) Petronas Twin Towers in Kuala Lumpur, Malaysia.

Alain Robert often dresses as Spiderman for his death-defying climbs.

Nothing Wasted In 2002 Taiwanese researchers unveiled a new house brick made with sludge from sewage works. They said it was a good way of using up waste and insisted that the bricks didn't smell.

God's Glass House Built in 1980 at the behest of TV evangelist Robert Schuller, the $20 million (£11 million) Crystal Cathedral near Los Angeles is made from over 10,000 panes of glass. In fact the only non-glass components were white steel trusses and wooden fittings.

Brief... The old tower of Grevenmacher in Luxembourg, a part of the town wall erected in 882, was the only structure not demolished by an air raid against the town in 1944. Yet 34 years earlier the tower had been declared unsafe.

Backyard Beacon Denver and Clover Randles of Ohio spent 18 years building a 45-ft (14-m) high lighthouse in their yard, even though they live 400 mi (645 km) from the ocean!

BOTTLED UP

In 1956 Tressa "Grandma" Prisbrey found that her collection of pencils, which eventually numbered 17,000, had outgrown her house trailer in Santa Susana, California. So she began constructing a building to display them, using a material that was cheap and plentiful—discarded bottles. Over the next 25 years she created the Bottle Village, the ultimate recycling venture. As well as collecting bottles, she would visit the local dump to find old tiles and car headlights. When she finished it, the village consisted of 22 buildings, made out of approximately one million bottles set in cement.

Fruit Topping A building in Dunmore Park, Scotland, is topped with a 53-ft (16-m) high stone pineapple.

Waterproof postcards are embossed with waterproof stamps when customers post them at the aquatic post box off the coast of Hideaway Island, Vanuatu. A 9-ft (3-m) dive is needed to reach the postbox first.

Dog Tired A hotel in Vancouver provides a resident dog that guests can book for a stress-relieving stroll.

Full Deck The Pack o' Cards public house in Combe Martin, Devon, England, has 52 windows (the number of playing cards in a pack), four main floors (the number of suits) and 13 doors on the ground floor (the number of cards per suit).

Home to Roost The roof of a house in Santiago, Chile, collapsed in September 2003 under the weight of accumulated pigeon droppings. Ana Maria Bustos said she ended up with a year's worth of pigeon guano on her living-room floor.

Stable Environment Farm animals have been banned from blocks of council flats in the Russian city of Kiev after a survey revealed that residents were keeping over 3,000 pigs, 500 cows and 1,000 goats. The city authorities said that cows were being kept on balconies and even in bedrooms and bathrooms. Unrepentant flat owners pleaded that the animals helped keep the flats warm in winter.

Towering Ambition

In the Watts district of Los Angeles stands a curious monument to the ingenuity and determination of Simon Rodia, an Italian immigrant labourer. Over a period of 33 years, Rodia, working alone, built around his house the Watts Towers. The tallest tower is nearly 100 ft (30 m) high and contains the longest slender column of reinforced concrete in the world. Rodia finally laid down his tools in 1954 at the age of 79, deeded the property to his neighbor for nothing, and disappeared!

Watts Towers comprise nine structures made of steel and mortar.

One of Rodia's towers is embedded with pieces of ceramic tile, pottery shards, sea shells, and broken glass.

Cracking Up Raymond Isidore of Chartres, France, spent a total of 23,000 hours to make his home and all its furnishings out of a million broken dishes.

TOP FIVE
ODD BUILDS

1 Star Floating Palace, cinema built 1907—U.S.A.

2 Fortress pumping station, built 1856—England

3 Pompidou Centre, inside-out art gallery—France

4 Ingalls Hockey Rink, shape of a whale—U.S.A.

5 Fake castle, with false facades—England

Colored lightbulbs are impacted inside 1,000,000 cu ft (30,000 cu m) of ice at the Ice Lantern Festival Exhibition in China. The ice is sculpted into animals and even buildings, such as this mosque.

Not to be Forgotten Built at Margate, New Jersey, in 1881 by James V. Lafferty as a real-estate promotion, Lucy the elephant is a 65-ft (20-m) high building of wood and tin. In her time she has served as a tavern and a hotel, and is currently a tourist attraction.

Botched Blast A Romanian wrecking crew failed to demolish a block of flats in the town of Flaminzi in 2001 but their "controlled" explosion left 24 neighboring houses uninhabitable after blowing out every house window within 200 yd (183 m).

High-rise Zoo After neighbors reported hearing roars coming from their Manhattan apartment tower in 2003, police found a 400-lb (180 kg) male tiger being kept as a pet in a tiny fifth-floor apartment! His housemate was a 5-ft (1.5-m) long alligator. Owner Antoine Yates said he was trying to create a Garden of Eden.

PAPERED OVER
Old buildings in Virginia are being protected from damage by using toilet paper. Experts say a poultice of toilet paper and water soaks up the salt that destroys bricks. Conservators at Williamsburg historic park used 700 rolls of toilet paper to test the idea on a smokehouse.

Pet Pitch A Japanese real estate agent tried to sell off the last few apartments at a Kawasaki complex in 2002 by offering free puppies and kittens to potential buyers.

Sweating it Out The Panchaiti Shrine in Jalalpur, India, was financed by a loom owner who each day contributed coins equal to the weight of the perspiration from the foreheads of his weavers. In 25 years the hard-working weavers donated 4,000 rupees (about $90 / £50).

第十七届哈尔滨国际冰雕比赛开幕式

Cold Comfort

Quebec's newest tourist attraction is a luxurious ice hotel situated on the shores of Lake St. Joseph. Constructed from 4,500 tons of snow and 250 tons of ice, the hotel is rebuilt each year and is open from January until it begins to melt in late March.

The beds are solid blocks of ice with a wooden platform for a foam mattress and there are two art galleries of ice carvings in the form of reliefs projecting from the walls like a frieze. The Grand Hall features a spectacular ice chandelier and in the bar all the furniture and glasses are made of ice. "We don't serve our drinks 'on the rocks'," say the hotel, "we serve them 'in the rocks'!" The N'Ice disco has room for 400 dancers and there is even an ice chapel where "white weddings" take on a whole new meaning!

Rooms at the Ice Hotel, Quebec, average around 27°F (−3°C). Guests keep warm while they sleep by wearing polar fleeces and deer skins.

Sweden also has an ice hotel, which uses 30,000 tons of snow and 10,000 tons of ice.

OFFICE PUT TO SLEEP
An office block in Liverpool, England, was demolished in 2001 because it made people literally sick. The Inland Revenue headquarters at St. John's House was diagnosed as having Sick Building Syndrome after workers complained of a succession of illnesses, including sore throats, runny noses, coughs, and various stress-related symptoms.

Croc Idyllic In the heart of Australia lies a hotel in the shape of a 250-m (820-ft) long crocodile. The Gagudju Crocodile Holiday Inn near Ayers Rock has rooms running along the length of the body to the tail. The swimming pool is situated in the creature's alimentary canal.

Catered Canines In 2000 the Regency Hotel in Manhattan prepared special breakfasts for dogs! The morning feast was served at tables by waiters wearing white gloves and tuxedoes.

Castle of Convenience The Sultan of Brunei's Palace has 1,788 rooms, 257 toilets, and an underground garage for his 153 cars. It would take a visitor over 24 hours, spending 30 seconds in each room, to view the entire palace.

Getting Over It The great bridge of Ceret, France, was built with fines collected from married couples each time they argued. For each quarrel a fine of one centime was collected.

The 1,188-ft (362-m) long "Tibetan Bridge" in Italy is made from just three ropes that connect the island of Procida, near Naples, with Vivara Rock.

Behind Bar Snacks In Beijing, China, there is a restaurant called Chain Cool that has a prison décor. Patrons eat in cells behind iron bars from a menu offering such dishes as "Cruelty" and "Rehabilitation."

Asleep in the Deep
Situated 30 ft (9 m) down in Bora Lagoon in the Florida Keys, Jules' Undersea Lodge is the world's first underwater hotel. A converted underwater research station, it was opened in 1986 and stands on legs 5 ft (1.5 m) off the bottom of the lagoon. To enter, guests, who have included former Canadian Prime Minister Pierre Trudeau and Steve Tyler of rock band Aerosmith, must scuba dive 21 ft (6.5 m) below the surface of the sea. The hotel boasts a restaurant and two rooms, both with private baths, and can cater for six guests at a time.

Amenities at the Jules' Undersea Lodge, Florida, include a fridge, microwave oven, books, and video recorder, plus a giant porthole to enable guests to observe passing fish.

Butter Sculptor

The *Last Supper* carved entirely from butter was sculpted by 74-year-old Norma Lyon of Des Moines, Iowa, in 1999, working in her cooler at 42°F (5°C).

For over 40 years Norma has sculpted a life-sized cow for the Iowa State Fair using 600 lb (272 kg) of butter. Using a wood, wire, metal, and steel mesh frame she softens buckets of five-year-old butter outside the cooler before moving into the cold and applying layers until a cow emerges, measuring 5.5 ft (0.2 m) high and 8 ft (2.5 m) long. After leaving the cow to set for 20 to 30 minutes she finely sculpts the head and the body, working down the legs to the hooves—24 hours of butter sculpture! Norma's work includes a Harley-Davidson motorcycle, and a life-size sculpture of John Wayne.

ARTY FACTS

- Van Gogh only sold one painting in his entire lifetime— *Red Vineyard at Arles*

- Jean Dakessian, an artist in California, painted 50 oil pumps to look like insects and animals

- Salvador Dali once held a party at which every guest came dressed as a bad dream

- Paul Gauguin worked on the building of the Panama Canal

Norma Lyon's biggest project yet, The Last Supper sculpted from a staggering 1,800 lb (815 kg) of butter in 1999.

Brush Stroke

Arriving for work in October 2001, Emmanuel Asare, a cleaner at a fashionable art gallery in London, Eyestorm, found that the room had been left in a complete mess following an exhibition party. Empty beer bottles, paint-covered newspapers, and candy wrappings were strewn all over the place. So he diligently set to work sweeping up the bits and pieces and dumping them in garbage bags. Next day he reported for duty, only to be told by gallery bosses: "That was no rubbish you cleared—that was a £5,000 ($8,000) work of art by the great Damien Hirst!"

Day Job Dutch master Vincent van Gogh (1853–90) painted one picture each day for the last 70 days of his life.

Night Shift French artist Anne-Louis Girodet (1767–1824) found that he worked better at night. So that he could see in the dark, he would light up to 40 candles around the brim of his hat, later calculating his fee according to the number of candles burned while he painted the picture.

DIFFERENT HANDLES

When French artist Louis François Roubillac (1705–62) started work on his sculpture of composer George Friedrich Handel he decided he didn't like Handel's ears. So he modelled the ears of a London lady instead.

Made from Scratch Californian artist Tim Hawkinson likes to model sculptures from parts of his body. His favorite work of art is a 2-in (5-cm) tall piece called *Bird* that was made entirely from his fingernails!

Foot Prints Upside-down Kansas City artist, Jimmie McPherson, was able to draw pictures with both his feet at the same time.

Food Drawer Michelangelo (1475–1564) created a still-life drawing of wine, fruit, bread, and spaghetti as a shopping list left for his cook who was unable to read.

Smile in the Mirror Leonardo da Vinci's famous painting *The Mona Lisa* was originally bought by King Francis I of France to hang in his bathroom.

Winner's Cup American sculptor Tom Friedman pinned a Styrofoam cup with coffee stains to a piece of wood, added a ladybug, and called it *Untitled*. In 2001 it sold at auction for $30,000 (£18,000).

In 2003, students from London's Camberwell College of Arts spent 630 hours creating the world's biggest popcorn sculpture—a 13 ft (4 m) statue of King Kong, weighing 1,720 lb (800 kg)— that's as much as four gorillas!

Waste Disposal Drivers using the Eastshore Freeway at Emeryville, California, in 1987 were amazed to see over 100 driftwood sculptures spread out along a mile of roadside. The eye-catching sculptures, which included a train, were created from waste material carried in by the tide.

Bumper Crop Jon Bedford, an artist from Santa Fe, New Mexico, has created amazing sculptures out of chrome car bumpers! He transforms the scrap metal into birds and animals, including a life-size rhinoceros!

BAGS OF TALENT
Using ordinary brown paper grocery bags, Anton Schiavone, an artist from Bangor, Pennsylvania, created magnificent life-size replicas of the masters, including Leonardo da Vinci's *The Last Supper* and Michelangelo's *La Pieta*.

The brown paper bag replica of Michelangelo's La Pieta by Anton Schiavone.

Desk Work Yugoslav performance artist Marina Abramovic spent 12 days on three raised desks at a New York City gallery in November 2002. Existing solely on water, she lived in full public view for the entire time. She said the idea of the performance was to heighten her senses and transmit energy to her audience.

Eye Liner Visual artist Jochem Hendricks of Frankfurt, Germany, creates works of art by drawing with his eyes instead of his hands. He uses an eyescanner that converts data to actual lines.

Motor Mountain Located in Jouy-en-Josas, France, the 65-ft (20-m) high sculpture *Long-Term Parking* by Arman comprises 60 cars embedded in 1,600 tons of concrete.

Angry because his art was unknown in Rome, Italian painter Salvator Rosa (1615–73) disguised himself as "Dr Formica" and prescribed "the art of Salvator Rosa" as a cure for mental depression. Rosa's ruse worked and he soon became one of the city's most famous artists.

Capsized In 1961 the Museum of Modern Art in New York proudly displayed *Le Bateau*, a painting by celebrated French artist Henri Matisse. It took seven weeks before someone spotted that it had been hung upside-down.

Soft Approach In 1999 Indian sculptor Anant Narayan Khairnar finished a 7-ft (2-m) tall statue of Mahatma Gandhi—made entirely from cotton! It took him 11 months to complete the sculpture.

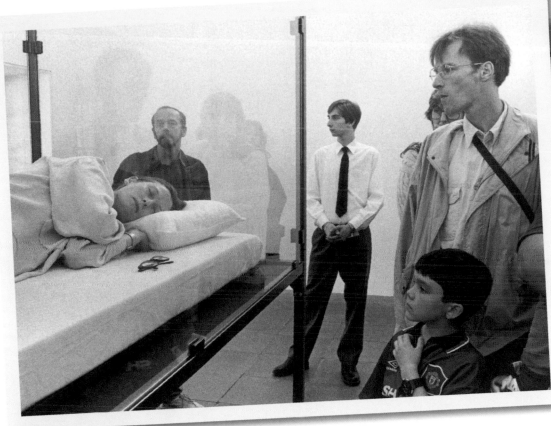

In 1995 London's Serpentine Gallery showed The Maybe, an exhibit by Tilda Swinton, which consisted solely of her sleeping on a mattress on a shelf in the center of a room for eight hours a day.

Barred When French artist Cézanne applied to enter the École des Beaux-Arts, he was turned down!

True Grit French painter Sarah Biffin was born without limbs. She was able to paint by clasping the paintbrush or pencil tightly between her teeth.

Snappy Gift American artist Charles Willson Peale, not only painted George Washington but presented him with a set of dentures made from elks' teeth!

Moving Exhibits The Andy Warhol Museum located in Pittsburg, exhibits unusual art and sculpture as well as playing host to Tibetan monk dance routines.

Sole Survivor The murals in the court of the Algerian Palace of Hadj-Ahmed Constantine were painted in the 19th-century by a shoemaker. Hadj-Ahmed thought all Frenchmen were artists so he ordered a captive French shoemaker to decorate the palace wall or suffer death.

Sinking Funds *Drains*, a sculpture of a sink stopper by U.S. artist Robert Gober, sold for over $55,000 (£32,000) in 1995. Gober said the work represented "a window onto another world."

Ape Fan Congo, a chimpanzee at the London Zoo in the 1950s, was such a talented artist that the great Pablo Picasso bought one of his paintings.

Lick of Paint Huang Erh-nan, a Chinese artist of the 1920s, did not paint with a brush. Instead he used his tongue.

WATERED COLORS

An accident in 1983 left Belgian scuba diver Jamy Verheylewegen crippled for 18 months. During this time, he produced more than 400 paintings underwater, using oil paints on synthetic fiber. His boards were mounted on an easel that was weighed down with lead.

He Gave His All

Thinking he was dying from tuberculosis, Japanese sculptor Hananuma Masakichi wanted to leave a gift to the woman he loved. So, working with adjustable mirrors, he used around 2,000 pieces of wood to carve a full-size image of himself. He plucked out his own nails, teeth, and hair to finish the work. He later recovered and, having lost these vital parts, also lost his girlfriend!

Ripley's ®

MASAKICHI WOOD MODEL
EXHIBIT NO: 12983
CARVED IN THE 1890s AS A SELF-
PORTRAIT FOR THE GIRLFRIEND MASAKICHI
THOUGHT HE WOULD LEAVE BEHIND

Toast of Japan

Japanese artist Tadahiko Ogawa
has used slices of toasted bread
to recreate such famous works of art
as Da Vinci's *Mona Lisa* and
Michelangelo's *Creation*.

Ogawa draws his pictures, traces them on to aluminum
foil, and then cuts the foil into toaster-size pieces. He
wraps the foil around the bread and cuts the foil away
from the areas he wants to brown (toast). Each piece of
bread is individually toasted to the desired color—
lightly toasted to burned! The toast is then put together
as a mosaic to create the final work. Ogawa has
completed about 50 old masters including Da Vinci's
The Last Supper and Botticelli's *Birth of Venus*.

Mona Lisa *made from
63 pieces of toast—
lightly toasted to burned!*

Ripley's ®

CREATION
EXHIBIT NO: 13843
OGAWA'S "CREATION" IS MADE
ENTIRELY FROM PIECES OF TOAST

Portrait of Barry Humphries as Dame Edna Everage made of toast, on the side of a building in Melbourne, Australia, in 2002.

This artwork by Haris and Aimal Jahed is drawn on 13 floors of a skyscraper in Hamburg, Germany, and measures 141 ft (43 m) high.

Knot Alone In 1989 New York City performance artists Linda Montano and Tehching Hsieh created a work of art by spending a year tied together at the waist by an 8-ft (2-m) rope.

Father Figure Francesco da Ponte (1470–1541), celebrated Italian painter, was the father of one famous artist, grandfather to four famous artists, and great-grandfather to six famous artists!

Final Snub Sir Godfrey Kneller (1646–1723), famed English painter, was such a snob that he refused to be buried in Westminster Abbey—because it was the last resting place of too many mediocre artists.

Art of the Streets Artists Steven Lowy and Pascal Giraudon of New York sell prints of manhole covers, using steamrollers to imprint the designs on paper!

People at Haines Point, Washington, D.C., are dwarfed by an aluminum sculpture of a partly-buried giant. Named The Awakening, *the sculpture was created by J. Seward Johnson, Jr. in 1980.*

TOP FIVE
MOST EXPENSIVE PAINTINGS

1 **$82.5m (£50m)** *Portrait of Doctor Gachet,* Vincent van Gogh (1990)

2 **$78.1m (£46m)** *Au Moulin de la Galette,* Auguste Renoir (1990)

3 **$76.73m (£45m)** *The Massacre of the Innocents,* Peter Paul Rubens (2002)

4 **$71.5m (£42m)** *Portrait de l'artiste Sans Barbe,* Vincent van Gogh (1998)

5 **$60.5m (£35m)** *Still Life with Curtain, Pitcher, and Bowl of Fruit,* Paul Cézanne (1999)

Cents of History Art Grant of San Francisco, California, created a two-dimensional sculpture of a stagecoach using one million pennies.

PAINTINGS THAT REALLY LIVE! An exhibition at Soho's New Museum of Contemporary Art in New York City in 1988 offered visitors the unique experience of shaking hands with "paintings," featuring artists actually standing inside large frames on the walls for up to 7 hours!

Speed Worker Denny Dent, a U.S. artist pays tribute to musical artists by painting a portrait of them faster than the time it takes to play one of their songs!

"Cadillac Ranch" livens up historic Route 66 in Texas. A collection of artists known as "Ant Farm" created the flamboyant sculpture as a tribute to America's favorite mode of transportation.

Art House A painting by Albert Bierstadt, a 19th-century landscape artist, measured over 150 sq ft (14 sq m) and was so large that a house had to be built around it!

Don't Get Up British artist Tracey Emin created a work of art that consisted of her old unmade bed—complete with dirty sheets, an empty vodka bottle, and old tissues. It was sold for $225,000!

Dotty Driver Artist Tyree Guyton has decorated his car in Detroit, Michigan, with thousands of polka dots.

Artist Peter Rocha has also made jellybean portraits, including one of former president, Ronald Reagan.

Ripley's——® **JELLYBEAN ROULETTE WHEEL**
EXHIBIT NO: 13154
THIS ROULETTE WHEEL IS MADE FROM 14,000 JELLYBEANS, IN 25 DIFFERENT COLORS, WEIGHING 80 LB (36 KG)

Public Autopsy!

Nearly 50 people paid about $20 dollars each for ringside seats to watch the public dissection of a 72-year-old deceased German businessman in England in 2002. This ambitious artistic performance by Professor Gunther von Hagens was Britain's first public autopsy in over a century.

German pathologist, Gunther von Hagens has developed a technique of plastination—impregnating human organs and entire corpses with liquid plastic to stop the body from decomposing. His 2002 show "Body Worlds," featured 25 skinned human corpses. He has also worked with horses, including one exhibit that showed a mounted rider whose outstretched arm holds his own brain.

Von Hagens styled himself on the doctor in Rembrandt's painting, The Anatomy Lesson of Dr. Nicolaes Tulp, *by wearing a black fedora (hat) and a surgical gown. The autopsy of this 72-year-old man was broadcast on British television.*

The Basketball Player *created by Gunther von Hagens, using a real body.*

In 1991 British artist Marc Quinn produced Self, *a sculptural self-portrait of his head made from nine pints of his own blood donated over a period of five months.*

Lookalikes Patience Lovell Wright (1725–86) created life-size wax models of famous English royalty and politicians. She was the first recorded sculptor in the American colonies.

• *"Asian Field," an exhibit by English artist Antony Gormley, in Beijing in 2003, is made from 192,000 clay figures—each one no bigger than your hand!*

BLIND ARTIST PAINTS WITH FEELING

British artist Gary Sargeant lost his sight—but still manages to paint. He visits the scene of the picture and with the help of his wife measures dimensions, either with his blind stick that is marked in finger-length notches and walking out distances between objects, or feeling textures by touch. By measuring and using masking tape, he builds up the canvas and then starts work. As the paint builds up he "reads" it, and from his many years of experience painting as a sighted person interprets what the picture should look like.

Final Move Though French Cubist Marcel Duchamp embraced sculpture in favor of painting, he later embraced chess in favor of sculpture!

Slow Starter When Pablo Picasso was born, he was left for dead by a midwife who believed him to be stillborn. However, a nearby relative quickly spotted the baby was alive and came to the rescue by reviving him!

Massive Collection The Hermitage and Winter Palace in St. Petersburg, Russia, is home to almost three million works of art. The palace itself has an amazing 1,786 doors, 1,945 windows and over 1,000 rooms!

Long Hall The Louvre Museum in Paris, home to Leonardo da Vinci's *Mona Lisa*, has an exterior that is 2.5 mi (4 km) in length!

A Head for Writing

Tapan Dey can write with a pen clipped to his hair or with one protruding from his mouth, a nostril or even an ear!

Indian street performer Dey from Basirhat, West Bengal, must be the world's most unconventional writer. Even when he uses his hands, he still insists on doing things differently—and writes with all four limbs at the same time by inserting pens between his fingers and toes! The 27-year-old can also write amazingly well in four different languages—Hindi, Assamese, English, and Bangla. Dey, who wants to redefine the art of calligraphy, says: "I was inspired when I saw a young boy in Calcutta writing with both hands. I thought I could do better."

Tapan Dey puts pen to paper using a pen that is pinned on to his hair!

From Russia With . . . Suspicion Karl Marx once wrote to his friend, Friedrich Engels, expressing his distrust of the entire Russian population!

BOOK BAN

- *Little Red Riding Hood,* folktale—U.S.A., alcoholism

- *Huckleberry Finn,* Mark Twain—U.S.A., racism

- *The Adventures of Sherlock Holmes,* Sir Arthur Conan Doyle—U.S.S.R., occultism

- *Frankenstein,* Mary Shelley —South Africa, indecency

- *The Merchant of Venice,* William Shakespeare— U.S.A., offensive to Jews

Start to Finish English writer Mary Shelley (1797–1851) wrote *Frankenstein* when she was just 19. By contrast, Alice Pollock of Haslemere, England, had her first book, *Portrait of My Victorian Youth,* published when she was 102.

True North English novelist Charles Dickens (1812–70) thought his writing would improve if he slept facing north! He always carried a compass with him to check his direction.

Sights Unseen Even though he was totally blind and journeyed without a companion, British writer James Holman (1786–1857) wrote a number of excellent travel books graphically describing his adventures in many lands.

The strangest library in all history! Saheb Ibn Abad (938–995), the Grand Vizier of Persia, always traveled with 117,000 books— even when he went to war. His mobile library was carried on 400 camels, which were trained to walk in alphabetical order so any book could be located immediately.

Ripley's

Grain of Truth

The 65 words, 254 letters of the Lord's Prayer inscribed on one single grain of rice! Rice writers were employed at the Ripley's odditoriums in the 1930s to produce grains to sell as souvenirs. This piece is thought to have been done by E.L. ("The Amazing") Blystone of Ardara, Pennsylvania—he used no form of magnification to work and his personal record was an amazing 1615 letters on a single grain!

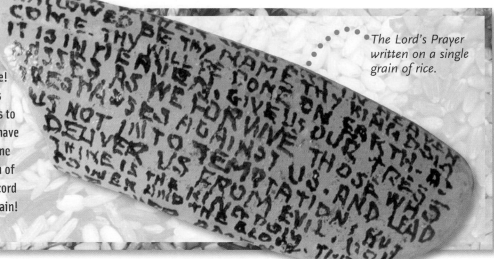

The Lord's Prayer written on a single grain of rice.

Multi-tasking French painter Claude Monet (1840–1926) often worked on as many as six paintings at the same time!

Fueled by Coffee The French writer Voltaire (1694–1778) drank an average of 70 cups of coffee a day!

BOUND WITH HUMAN SKIN

After John Horwood was hanged in 1821, when he was found guilty of murder, his body was given to Bristol Royal Infirmary in England for dissection. The anatomist, Richard Smith, published his findings in a book and paid a local tanner to turn the murderer's flayed skin into leather with which to bind the tome together. The book went on public display for the first time in 2003.

Slow Reader In 1650 the Bishop of Winchester, England, borrowed a book from Somerset County Records Office. It was eventually returned to Somerset County Library in 1985, having built up a fine of £3,000 ($5,000). Its title? *The Book of Fines.*

A banana mailed to a Connecticut hospital with two postage stamps in 1988 arrived safely! The address for Rachela Colonna and the message—"I love you" in Italian—were written on the peel and the stamps were covered with clear tape.

A woman who bought a hardback version of the then unknown *Harry Potter and the Sorcerer's Stone* for £10.99 ($18) in 1997 sold it for £13,000 ($21,600) at auction in 2002. Amazingly successful, Harry Potter (Daniel Radcliffe) is seen here in *Harry Potter and the Chamber of Secrets* (U.S. 2002) with Ron Weasley (Rupert Grint).

Potter Mania A 93-word "teaser card" written by J.K. Rowling and holding clues to the plot of *Harry Potter and the Order of the Phoenix* was sold to a private U.S. collector six months before publication of the novel—for $46,600 (£28,680)!

Think Ink Denied the use of pen or pencil, René Auguste de Renneville (1650–1723), a prisoner in the Bastille for 11 years, wrote 6,000 lines of romantic poetry and a ten-volume history book using split chicken bones dipped in a mixture of soot and wine.

Flexible Letters The 26 letters of the English alphabet can be made into 403,290,000,000,000,000,000,000,000 different combinations.

ALPHA BITS

- The Cambodian alphabet has 74 letters, while the Rotokas in Papua New Guinea has just 11 letters—a, b, e, g, i, k, o, p, r, t, and u.

- The only 15-letter word that can be spelled without repeating a letter is "uncopyrightable."

- If you were to spell out numbers, you would have to go to "one thousand" before you found the letter "a."

- There is no single word to say "yes" or "no" in Japanese.

- The only ten-letter word you can spell using just the top row of letters of a keyboard is "typewriter."

Dorothy Nusbaum of Washington, D.C. was ambidexterous and could write two different sentences simultaneously. She could also write backward with her left hand!

Tintype Laurent de la Baumille, 18th-century poet and playwright, while held as a prisoner in the Bastille in 1752, wrote a tragedy by scratching the words onto two tin plates with a needle! Although the plates were confiscated, he had memorized the words and the play was later performed in French theaters.

Italian poet Alighieri Dante (1265–1321) had a phobia about candlesticks. So he trained a cat to hold a lighted candle in its paws while he wrote.

Frontier Library The front door of the Haskell Free Library and Opera House at Derby Line, Vermont, is in the U.S.A. But the back door is in Quebec province, Canada. During World War II, Canadian visitors to the front door had to show their passports.

Favorite Tale Countess Yekaterina Skavronskaya (1761–1829) of Russia enjoyed the same story 24,090 times! She was lulled to sleep by the same fairy tale told by the same servant every night for 66 years—until the day she died.

Book behind Bars The last prisoner in the Bastille was a book! By order of King Louis XVI, the *Dictionnaire Encyclopédique* was sentenced to life imprisonment for the crimes of liberalism and disloyalty to the state.

POET'S CRUMBS

In 1857, Alfred, Lord Tennyson, Queen Victoria's Poet Laureate, earned less than her official rat-catcher!

Career in Shreds After laboring for 13 years writing a book about Swedish economic solutions, business consultant Ulf af Trolle finally took his 250-page manuscript to be copied. Yet it took just seconds for his life's work to be reduced to 50,000 strips of paper when a worker confused the copier with the shredder!

WORD WISE

- *Gone With The Wind* was Margaret Mitchell's only book

- The Bible is the most shop-lifted book in the U.S.A

- The first book on plastic surgery was written in 1597

soft **sheep**

clouds

Flock of Poems

English writer Valerie Laws spray-painted words from a poem onto a flock of sheep in 2002 to see whether the animals would then arrange themselves to form a new poem as they wandered about the field. Northern Arts awarded her a grant of $3,400 (£2,000) for the project, which, she said, would be an exercise in both "random" literature and quantum mechanics.

One of the poems created by Valerie Laws' experiment read: "Warm, Drift, Graze, Gentle, White below the sky. Soft, Sheep, Mirrors, Snow, Clouds.

Uphill The Maori name for a particular hill on New Zealand's North Island runs to a staggering 85 letters—taumatawhakatangihangakoauauotam ateaturipukakapikimaungahoronukup okaiwhenuakitanatahu. Translated into English, this name means "The place where Tamatea, the man with the big knees, who slid, climbed, and swallowed mountains, known as landeater, played his flute to his loved one."

Times of Plenty One issue of the *New York Times* contains more information than the average person in the 16th century would have read throughout their entire life.

Undaunted Author John Creasy, a British author, received a total of 774 rejection slips before finally getting his 564 books published.

Miniature copies of the Koran (top), Hindu holy book the Bhagavad-Gita (middle) and the Holy Bible (bottom).

HOLY BIBLE

Bevelie It or Not!

Apratneply it dsoen't mtaetr waht oderr the ltetres in a word are, the olny ipmoratnt tihng is taht the fisrt and lsat ltetre be in the rhgit palce. The rset can be a toatl mses and you can stlil raed it whituot a porbelm. Tihs is bacesue the hamun mnid deos not raed evrey ltetre by itlesf, but the wrod as a wolhe.

TEMPTING TITLES

- *A Pictorial Book of Tongue Coating*
- *Amputation Stumps: Their Care and After-treatment*
- *Holiday Retreats for Cats and Dogs in England*
- *All About Mud*
- *Canadian National Egg Laying Contests*

Do it Yourself George Bernard Shaw created a new way for spelling fish: "Ghoti" to highlight inconsistencies in pronunciation of certain letters. "Gh as in "enough", "o" as in "women," and "ti" as in "nation."

Arab Influence Many words we use daily are derived from Arabic words such as "algebra," "average," and "tabby." Algebra means a reunion of broken parts; average means damaged goods; tabby means a cloth with stripes.

Heavy Going The Arabic *Legislations Encyclopedia* is so massive it weighs a staggering 925 lb (420 kg) and has an index that takes up six volumes!

A Key Change The first typed manuscript was submitted to a publisher by author Mark Twain.

Thriller Bee Show

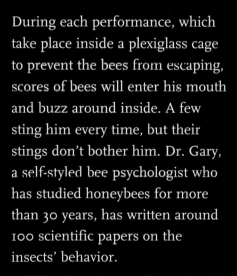

Dr. Norman Gary, professor of entomology at the University of California, tours the world with his Thriller Bee Show, playing Dixieland jazz on the clarinet while as many as 100,000 bees swarm all over him and often even enter his mouth!

Apart from a passion for bees, 60-year-old Dr. Norman Gary plays the clarinet (in bee flat!) in a band called The Beez Kneez.

During each performance, which take place inside a plexiglass cage to prevent the bees from escaping, scores of bees will enter his mouth and buzz around inside. A few sting him every time, but their stings don't bother him. Dr. Gary, a self-styled bee psychologist who has studied honeybees for more than 30 years, has written around 100 scientific papers on the insects' behavior.

TOP FIVE
MOST PLAYED SONGS

20th century favorites
on U.S. radio and TV

1 **"You've Lost That Lovin' Feelin,"** The Righteous Brothers

2 **"Never My Love,"** The Association

3 **"Yesterday,"** The Beatles

4 **"Stand By Me,"** Ben E. King

5 **"Can't Take My Eyes Off You,"** Andy Williams

Blowing Bubbles

The world's most unusual music venue is situated 30 ft (9 m) beneath the surface of the sea off the coast of Florida. In July 2003 nearly 400 people dived below the waves to hear the 19th annual Lower Keys Underwater Music Festival.

Music, including The Beatles' "Yellow Submarine" and extracts from "The Little Mermaid," was piped down through speakers suspended from boats on the surface. Some musical festival participants declare that they have seen fish and other marine creatures also enjoying the concert!

TOP FIVE
MUSICAL DEATHS

Five famous musicians who experienced untimely deaths in strange circumstances.

1 "Mama Cass" Elliot of The Mamas and Papas choked to death on a sandwich, 1974

2 Brian Jones of The Rolling Stones drowned in his swimming pool, 1969

3 Terry Kath of Chicago died playing Russian roulette in 1978. His last words were: "Don't worry, it's not loaded"

4 Keith Relf, singer with The Yardbirds, was electrocuted while tuning his guitar, 1976

5 Graham Bond, blues musician, mysteriously fell to his death under a subway train at London's Finsbury Park Station, 1974

QUIRKY NOTES

- Beethoven poured jugs of iced water over his head to help creativity
- A violin contains some 70 separate pieces of wood
- Replica kettle drums were once used as currency in Indonesia
- There are over 50,000 official Elvis impersonators worldwide
- Seven percent of Americans think Elvis is still alive
- The 1952 symphony, "Victory at Sea," written by Richard Rodgers, lasted 13 hours

Instruments at the Lower Keys Underwater Music Festival include trumpets, harps, guitars, and even trumbones.

Festival participant Bill Becker flies the American flag as Mel Herlehy strums an underwater guitar.

Biker Beat An "orchestra" of 100 bikers revved up their motorcycles at different intensities at an exhibition in Stockholm in 2000 to perform "Vrooom," a five-minute piece by Swedish composer Staffan Mossenmark. They were conducted by Petter Sundkvist, who waved racetrack flags instead of a baton.

No Sing-along In 2002 Cambodian Prime Minister Hun Sen announced that he was banning all karaoke clubs from the country. He said that any clubs still open would be destroyed by military tanks.

White House Blues President William Howard Taft (1857–1930) was so tone deaf that he couldn't recognize the national anthem. He had to be told when to stand up.

Divers and snorkelers "play" instruments underwater while other divers and snorkelers "listen."

Musical Pigs Farmer Raymond Collier of Hampshire, England, plays classical music to his pigs to boost productivity. He insists that the pigs sleep better after listening to a symphony—unlike his neighbors who have complained about being kept awake at night.

Flight of Fancy In 2003 Bono, lead singer of Irish rock band U2, paid £1,000 ($1,670) to have his favorite hat—a trilby—flown first-class to Italy. He had forgotten to pack it for a charity gig with Luciano Pavarotti.

Death Watch Elvis Presley used to enjoy visiting his local morgue to observe the corpses. He also had a fixation with guns and would use his TV set for target practise.

Early Works Elvis Presley was 21 when he had his first hit. By that age Mozart had written over 250 compositions.

Real Emotion In 1971 while Calgary's KFSM radio station was playing Carole King's "I Feel the Earth Move," the studio collapsed.

Distant Star Pyotr Ilyich Tchaikovsky (1840–93) was awarded a generous annual allowance by wealthy widow Nadezhda von Meck—provided that they never meet. She was convinced that she would be disappointed if ever she met her idol in person.

Rossini Riddle Italian composer Gioacchino Rossini (1792–1868) wrote 53 grand operas before his 11th birthday. How come? He was born on February 29 and his birthdays came only once every four years!

Playing it Cool

The Exhibition of Ice Art takes place at the Nocka Strand in Stockholm. The exhibits, which include musical instruments as well as famous Swedes, are made with water from Sweden's Tome River.

Visitors to the Exhibition of Ice Art protect themselves with warm coats and shoes before they view instruments that are made from 120 tons of clear water ice.

New Wrinkle You're never too old to rock! Twin sisters Kin Narita and Gin Kanie had a hit single in Japan at the age of 99.

Hundreds of 12-ft (4-m) long alphorns are played at the Alpine Horn Festival in Switzerland. Players use a wooden cup-shaped mouthpiece to adjust the sound that emits from the instrument.

Hot Reaction Elizabeth Billington, England's greatest singer of her day, had such a powerful voice that when she sang in Naples in 1794, the Italians accused her of causing the eruption of Mount Vesuvius. She was subsequently driven out of town by the irate residents.

TRAGIC COINCIDENCE
American rock star Duane Allman was killed in a motorbike accident in Macon, Georgia, in 1971. By a macabre coincidence, fellow Allman Brothers member Berry Oakley was killed in another motorbike crash just three blocks away a year later.

Don Tranger from Meadville, Pennsylvania, was able to play three trumpets simultaneously, in 1937.

In the 1930s Chas Cheer was known as the man with the xylophone head. Tunes could be played on his skull as he formed the notes by opening and closing his mouth.

View from Afar "When Irish Eyes Are Smiling" was written by a German, George Graff, who had never set foot in Ireland in his life.

Memorable Chord French musician Yves Klein composed a "Monotone Symphony," which consists of a single chord held for 20 minutes.

Bagpipe Blunder In the 1960s a Scottish record company released a bagpipe record on which the music was back to front. The error arose after the master tape had been processed from a tape that was accidentally played in reverse. Hundreds of copies were sold before the mistake was spotted.

- Ten thousand young Chinese musicians gathered on July 2, 2002 to play six types of percussion instruments in celebration of the fifth anniversary of Hong Kong's handover from Britain to China.

Prophetic Words Lena Gilbert Ford, the lyricist of the song "Keep the Home Fires Burning," died in a fire at her home.

Simon Says Just one man knows whom Carly Simon was singing about in her 1972 hit "You're So Vain." Dick Ebersol, president of NBC Sports, bid $50,000 (£30,000) at a 2003 charity auction for the right to hear the information from Simon herself. The only condition was that he had to swear not to tell anyone else.

Beating the Weather Celebrated drummer Gene Krupa could predict the weather according to the sound of his drums. A dull sound indicated rain while a vibrant tone meant fair weather. In 1944 he claimed never to have made a wrong forecast in 15 years.

Moody Madonna As a teenager Madonna was sacked from a New York Dunkin' Donuts shop for squirting jam at a customer.

Fatal Reversal Known for playing the world's smallest harmonica, Mexican musical maestro Ramon Barrero made an untimely inhalation during a performance at Iguala in 1994 and choked to death on his instrument.

The musical bicycle was invented before radio. Samuel Goss of Chicago fitted piano wires and hammers onto the frame of a bicycle in such a way that different tunes could be played according to the speed of the machine.

CLASSIC STRATEGY

In 2003, Stoke-on-Trent Council in Staffordshire, England, announced that Beethoven's Symphony No. 9 in D Minor would be continuously played in a multi-story parking garage in an attempt to drive away homeless vagrants. It was hoped that the symphony's frequent changes of pitch and time would be so irritating that it would deter the homeless from sleeping there.

Fatal Debut While performing at the New York Metropolitan Opera in 1995, 63-year-old tenor Richard Versalle suffered a fatal heart attack and fell 10 ft (3 m) from a ladder after singing the line "Too bad you can only live so long" from the opening scene of *The Makropulos Case*, a Czech opera about an elixir that ensures eternal youth. Since it was the show's New York premiere, the audience thought it was all part of the plot.

Space Rocks American astronaut Charles Conrad so loved the music of Jerry Lee Lewis that he took a cassette into space on board *Apollo XI*.

Bach to Bach Johann Sebastian Bach came from a family of 62 professional musicians.

The King's Toys Elvis Presley owned 18 television sets, 100 pairs of pants, 21 capes, 8 cars, 7 motorcycles, 3 tractors, 7 golf buggies, 3 mobile homes, and 6 horses!

Determined Diva Romanian folk singer Joan Melu played a two-hour performance, including an interval, at the Capitol Theatre, Melbourne, in 1980, despite the fact that no one turned up to watch her. She even gave an encore!

Short but Sweet An instrumental album recorded by the artist Gadfly lasts for a mere 32 seconds.

Born to be Famous

Not all musicians were born to greatness: Shirley Bassey used to pack chamber pots; Joe Cocker was a gas fitter; Bette Midler worked as a pineapple chunker; Sting had a job as a bus conductor; Cyndi Lauper started out cleaning dog kennels.

Ozzy Osbourne once worked as a slaughterhouse worker.

Rubini, the 19th-century king of the Italian tenors and hero of the La Scala Opera House in Milan, once sang a high note with such force that he broke his own collar-bone!

Ripley's®

LOUIS ARMSTRONG PORTRAIT
EXHIBIT NO: 22073
CREATED FROM NEARLY 30,000 CRYSTAL RHINESTONES BY KEN BURKITT OF CANADA

Monsieur Mangetout

Michel Lotito munches his way through an appetizing plate of car parts.

When Michel Lotito, a Frenchman from Grenoble, sits down to dinner, the menu might start with a pair of aluminum skis, followed by a supermarket trolley (with a side plate of razor blades) and finish off with a television set, washed down with a few glasses.

Lotito, who goes under the stage name of Monsieur Mangetout (Mr. Eat-All), has made a career out of devouring metal, crockery, and glass without suffering any ill-effects.

Since the age of nine, he has been crunching through coins, cutlery, plates, bicycles (he says the chain is the tastiest part), and even a coffin—empty of course. His finest hour came in Caracas, Venezuela, in 1978 when he began eating a Cessna 150 light aircraft. Taking a few snacks each day, it took him two years to finish it. Lotito attributes his ability to eat and pass these items naturally to the fact that he was born on June 15, 1950—halfway through the middle day of the middle month of the middle year of the 20th century. Puzzled medical experts, however, have a more logical explanation: they found that the lining of his stomach and intestines is twice the thickness of the average human.

Bukur, a gypsy of Felsendorf, Transylvania, was so overjoyed at the birth of twins that he placed the newborn infants in a huge pot and danced for a full hour with the pot and babies balanced on his head.

SKIN DEEP

At the 2003 New York International Fringe Festival, Russian dancer Ksenia Vidyaykina did not stop at stripping off her clothes—she then appeared to strip off her skin, too! In a performance called "Trapped," she removed a chiffon toga and then proceeded to peel fake rubber skin from her thighs, complete with dripping red stage blood. She said that the idea was to show the beauty and bravery of stripping off her various layers.

Two young sisters from Mongolia, Anu and Mandukhai, show off their stage contortionist tricks in two lockers at Hamburg station in Germany.

Monty Melee A French stage version of *The Full Monty* closed early following a fist-fight between two actors mid-way through a performance. Pierre Cosso, who was taken to hospital with a broken nose, came to blows with Christian Mulot in a row over the levels of noise backstage during his solo spot.

Foot Perfect The Zamalzain, leader of a Basque dance troupe, must leap high in the air and land on a wine glass so lightly that he neither shatters nor spills a single drop of wine.

Chihuahua Cha-Cha Clansko in the Czech Republic stages an annual dance championship with a difference. It is for dogs, which can compete either in solo competitions or with their owners in the couples contest!

The Other RSC Originating in California in 1981, the three-man Reduced Shakespeare Company perform all of the Bard's 37 plays and 154 sonnets—in just 90 minutes.

A Car All at Sea A London Palladium production of the musical *Chitty Chitty Bang Bang*, held in the presence of the Prince of Wales, was abandoned before the interval when the main character— the car—collided on stage with a ship.

FROZEN DANISH
A production of *Hamlet* was staged in a 26-ft (8-m) high ice theater in 2003. The theater in Jukkasjaervi, northern Sweden, is modelled on London's Globe Theatre and so has no roof. Temperatures dipped as low as −24°F (−31°C) during rehearsals.

Pay That Sticks Dancing gypsies in Tirana, Albania, perform with such vitality that onlookers traditionally pay them by placing coins on their foreheads. The dancers sweat so much that the coins stick to their skin.

Shaolin Monk Warriors perform lying on a bed of nails at the Valle Giulia Festival in Rome, Italy. They are able to withstand high levels of discomfort and pain by practising the art of meditation.

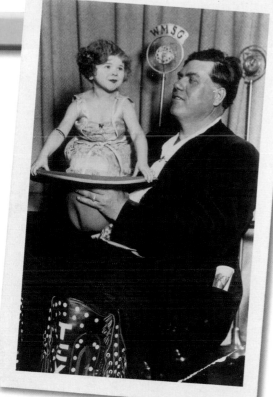

Jim Tarven was a giant, standing at 7 ft 11 in (2.4 m) tall. He weighed in at 390 lb (176 kg). In contrast, the other half of the double act was Mary Schmidt (in the hat) who was only 3 ft 5 in (1 m) tall and weighed only 84 lb (38 kg). This picture was taken in 1930 when they were part of the Sells-Floto-To-Mix Circus.

Top Marx A production of the *Communist Manifesto* became the surprise hit of the Buenos Aires theater circuit in 2003. The adaptation of the 1848 masterpiece (featuring Karl Marx) drew large audiences when performed by theater company Lucharte at a local bread factory.

Quick Closure Lord Lytton's play, *The Lady Of Lyons*, opened and closed at London's Shaftesbury Theatre on December 26, 1888. After waiting patiently for an hour, the audience was sent home because nobody could raise the safety curtain.

One Good Turn . . . Madame Favart, star of the Opera Comique, Paris, was the first performer to entertain soldiers during wartime. In 1746, at the height of the conflict between France and Austria, she took her entire troupe to the front to amuse French troops. Indeed she proved so popular that the enemy Austrians also asked her to put on a show for their army. So she ended up entertaining both sides!

Theater Buffs Naked ushers were hired by a theater in Berlin to show guests to their seats at the 2003 premiere of *Art Breaks Free* by Christoph Schlingensief.

A giant skeleton representing Death stands in a lake with bony fingers holding open the Book of Life. The stage suspended over the water was the scene for Verdi's opera Un Ball in Maschera at the Bregenz Festival in July 2000. The actors appear dwarfed by this vast set.

Looking Back A secret society of African acrobats, known as the bird men of Guinea, only accept new members if they can swivel their heads a full 180 degrees!

Roaring Success French actor Charles Dullin (1885–1949) had the most dangerous audience imaginable—when he recited poetry in a cage of lions.

No Strings Attached
A 1930s Vaudeville contortionist called Brawerman (or "King Brawn") was able to pass his entire body through an unstrung tennis racket.

LIE STILL

Legendary French actress Sarah Bernhardt (1844–1923) used to learn her lines while lying in a coffin. The silk-lined coffin traveled everywhere with her on tour. She also slept in it and used it as a setting for entertaining a series of lovers, among them Napoleon III, novelist Victor Hugo, and the Prince of Wales—the future King Edward VII of England.

Back Seat Sell-out At the Edinburgh Fringe Festival in 1981, the Bogdan Club performed the play *2001* in the back of a Hillman Avenger car. The maximum audience for each performance was four, but safety officials complained because the theater on wheels had neither exit lights nor space between the aisles.

Your Eyes Only Charles Monselet (1825–88), France's leading theater critic for 42 years, never saw a play in his entire lifetime! Instead he always waited in a nearby bar during a premiere where friends later reported their impressions of the play.

Up in Stages An outdoor theater was created annually near Puchheim, Austria, by laying planks across horizontal branches of a tall linden tree. Four stages were set up to create a four-story theater, capable of accommodating 140 actors.

Animal Antics Audiences in ancient Greece were stunned by performers who would pinch part of a goat's neck, cutting off the artery leading to its brain, causing the animal to fall asleep! The goat would then wake when the pressure was released.

The ballerinas of ancient Knossos on the island of Crete used to finish their dance by jumping over a charging wild bull—always leaping between the animal's horns!

Ripley's——

Fading Star In a 1787 performance of *Hamlet*, the lead man was so overcome with stage fright on the second night that the play went on without him! Many spectators said they preferred the play without the central character!

THE SMALLEST THEATRE IN THE WORLD

Gordon's

Marcel Steiner performs Macbeth in his own theater—built on a 650cc motorcycle! On another occasion, he performed The Tempest in the parking lot of the Royal Shakespeare Company at Stratford, England, while the RSC was doing a grander version of the same play inside!

Making-up Monsters

Movie make-up techniques have changed—
dramatically. For the cult movie *An American
Werewolf in London* (U.S. 1981), the pre-digital
make-up and body prosthetics were considered
ground-breaking in the movie industry at the time.

HUMAN VOICE

Director Peter Jackson said:
"The character of Gollum is a
completely digital creature, but I
was determined that I wanted an
actor to actually create the
character." One thing that
belonged entirely to Andy Serkis,
however, was his distinctive voice.

Traditional make-up was also
applied by Rick Baker in films such
as the remake of *Planet of the Apes*
(U.S. 2001) and *Thriller* by Michael
Jackson. But traditional movie
make-up could soon be a thing of
the past. Hollywood has gone
digital. The system employed on
Lord of the Rings: The Two Towers
(U.S./NZ 2002) is called motion capture photography. Actor Andy Serkis
would go into a studio wearing a suit with reflective dots all over it, each
dot corresponding to a joint in his body, and act out the scene. Twenty-five
cameras then fed the information into a computer, which captured his
movements and translated them to form the digital version
of Gollum. It was this animated Gollum that was seen on screen.

*Thanks to advances in digital technology,
fantastic visual effects can be achieved
without make-up. In the movie* Lord of
the Rings: The Two Towers, *the character
of Gollum was digitally produced to have
300 muscles that actually moved plus 250
different facial expressions. It was part
acting, part animation.*

*The transition from man to beast
in* An American Werewolf in
London *took Oscar-winning
make-up artist Rick Baker
ten hours a day to complete.*

Tom Hanks is related to Abraham Lincoln. He is a direct descendant of Nancy Hanks, Lincoln's mother.

ACTORS' FIRST JOBS

- Warren Beatty—rat-catcher
- Sylvester Stallone—lion-cage cleaner
- Errol Flynn—sheep-castrator
- Sean Connery—polisher for coffin-maker
- Keanu Reeves—manager of a pasta shop in Toronto
- Burt Lancaster—lingerie salesman
- Michelle Pfeiffer—checkout girl at a grocery store
- Alan Ladd—hot-dog seller
- Kirk Douglas—window-cleaner
- Jayne Mansfield—saucepan seller

Siamese Twin At birth, American actor Andy Garcia, had a twin about the size of a small ball joined to his left shoulder. The twin was surgically removed but died soon afterward.

Agent Who? At the age of ten, Leonardo DiCaprio was advised by his agent to change his name to a more American-friendly Lenny Williams.

Ill Wind Vivien Leigh hated kissing Clark Gable on *Gone With The Wind* (U.S. 1939) because she said he had terrible breath.

Pampered Pooch It's a dog's life. When Ava Gardner died in 1990, she left her pet corgi Morgan a monthly income plus his own limo and maid.

Sticky Drain The blood used for the shower scene in Alfred Hitchcock's 1960 horror movie *Psycho* (U.S. 1960) was really chocolate syrup. The scene took seven days to shoot.

Like No Udder In early Clarabelle Cow cartoons, the cow's udder was always discreetly draped by an apron for fear of upsetting those with high morals.

Silver Lining Mel Gibson won his leading role in the movie *Mad Max* (Aus 1979) because the producers were looking for someone who looked weary, beaten, and scarred. The night before his screen test, Gibson had been attacked by three drunks.

Judy's Roots Judy Garland was a descendant of former U.S. President Ulysses S. Grant.

Extra "Extras"

Some movie-makers go to extreme lengths to achieve a realistic scene. In Richard Attenborough's movie *Gandhi*, (U.K. 1982) more extras appeared on screen than in any previous historical epic. Other movie-makers have been known to draft in regiments, even whole armies, to take part in a scene, as in the Nazi-made epic, *Kolberg* (Ger 1947).

On the set of Gandhi (U.K. 1982), the director employed 300,000 extras to play mourners in the opening funeral scene.

Kate's Honey Kate Winslet, star of *Titanic* (U.S. 1997), first appeared on screen dancing with the Honey Monster in a TV commercial for Sugar Puffs breakfast cereal.

Movie Mania In India every day more than 15 million Indians go to the movies.

Chaplinesque Charlie Chaplin once came third in a Charlie Chaplin lookalike contest.

No Hopers While at school, the now successful actors Gene Hackman, Dustin Hoffman, and Robin Williams were voted "Least Likely to Succeed" by their classmates.

Eyes Wide Shut Screen tough guy Edward G. Robinson hated playing hoodlum roles. In fact, the sound of gunfire made him squint so badly that his eyelids had to be taped open.

Spiderman In 1993 a newly discovered species of spider was named *Calponia harrisonfordi* in honor of Hollywood star Harrison Ford's movie role fear of arachnids.

Bela Lugosi (1882–1956) was the vampire who couldn't stand the sight of blood. Famed for his blood-thirsty portrayal of Count Dracula in movies, Lugosi often fainted at the sight of real blood.

LIMELIGHT

A North Wales lighthouse with room for a 12-strong audience staged a movie premiere in 2003. South Stack lighthouse on Anglesey Island showed a 15-minute film by Elaine Townson called *The Birds and a Suitcase* (U.K. 2002). Not the easiest venue to reach, the audience had to climb down more than 400 steps to get to the remote cinema.

King-sized Waste For the remake of *King Kong* (U.S. 1976), producers ordered the construction of a 40-ft (12-m) high, 13,000-lb (5,896-kg), electronically controlled robot with a 20-ft (6-m) arm span covered with two tons of horse hair to simulate fur. Yet the expensive creation appeared for only ten seconds of the movie, the majority of which featured an actor in a gorilla suit playing on miniature sets!

Movie Marathon Thai film buffs watched 36 films in two-and-a-half days in 2003, beating an American record set two years earlier. The 17-person group watched films for 64 hr 58 minutes as part of the Bangkok International Film Festival. They took a 15-minute break after every third film.

Unbuttoned Alfred Hitchcock didn't have a belly button. It disappeared when he was stitched up following surgery.

"20 donuts a day for five weeks"

Renée Zellweger had to go from a size 6 to a size 14 for her starring role in Bridget Jones: The Edge of Reason (U.S. 2004).

Sole Sister Reese Witherspoon had 63 pairs of shoes specially made for her movie *Legally Blonde 2* (U.S. 2003).

Swedish Ban The family film *E.T.* (U.S. 1982) was banned in Sweden for youngsters under eleven because of fears that it showed parents being hostile to their children.

Good Old Mom When Cary Grant played the son of Jessie Royce Landis in *North by Northwest* (U.S. 1959), he was 55 and she was 54!

Renée Zellweger, seen here in Bridget Jones's Diary (U.S. 2001), ate 20 donuts a day for five weeks to pile on 14 lb (6.5 kg) for the sequel, Bridget Jones: The Edge of Reason (U.S. 2004). Her diet also included a burger with large fries, savoury scones with gravy, and a high-fat milkshake—all for breakfast!

More than 1,600 pairs of latex ears and feet were used during the filming of The Lord of the Rings: The Two Towers, *(U.S./NZ 2002) each cooked in a special oven.*

TOP FIVE
HOLLYWOOD ACTRESSES

(based on earnings in 2002)

1 **Julia Roberts** $20.3m (£12m) per film

2 **Cameron Diaz** $20m (£11m) per film

3 **Drew Barrymore** $15.6m (£7m) per film

4 **Jodie Foster** $15.6m (£7m) per film

5 **Reese Witherspoon** $15.6m (£7m) per film

Scary Cartoon Mickey Mouse was banned in Romania in 1935 because the authorities thought a 10-ft (3-m) high rodent on screen was likely to scare the nation's children.

Mouse Mail Mickey Mouse received 800,000 fan letters a year.

Presidential Rejection A movie script written by President Franklin D. Roosevelt about *Old Ironsides*, one of the United States' most famous warships, was rejected by Hollywood.

Dad's Watching Actress Evelyn Venable, voice of the Blue Fairy in *Pinocchio*, (U.S. 1940) was forbidden to kiss on screen—upon the orders of her father.

Horse Play Mack Sennett, producer of *The Keystone Cops*, began his career playing the hind legs of a stage horse!

Straight Man Buster Keaton's contract with MGM in the 1920s prevented him from smiling on screen.

Language, Please! Clara Bow (1905–65) had it written into her contract with Paramount that none of the crew would use profane language in her presence. In return she was offered a $500,000 (£300,000) bonus if she remained free of scandal. She failed to collect.

Duck Out Donald Duck was once banned in Finland because he doesn't wear pants!

Flawed Stars

Things may appear perfect in the movie world but they are not always what they seem: Demi Moore was born cross-eyed; Clark Gable is listed on his birth certificate as a girl; the Oscars were made of wood during World War II —to conserve metal; and Johnny Depp has a phobia about clowns.

Clint Eastwood is allergic to horses.

Gnome Man's Land

Twice a week, Ron Broomfield dresses as a garden gnome, complete with the obligatory cap, pipe, and fishing rod, and joins a few hundred of the brightly colored little chaps in his garden!

Unsurprisingly there is no place in this menagerie for a wife. "I'm not married any more," confesses Ron, "but, to be frank, there's no room for a woman. Gnomes have become my life." Ron's hobby has so far cost him more than $33,000 (£20,000), but it's all in a good cause as he uses the gnomes to help raise money for charity.

• Sixty-nine-year-old Ron Broomfield shares his home in Alford, Lincolnshire, England, with nearly 1,000 garden gnomes.

• People collect all sorts of little men. The fourth annual Michelin collectors' convention was held in July 2003 in Clermont Ferrand, France.

Eyes on the Past

A collection of nearly 2,000 glass eyes was auctioned in 1998 by Sotheby's. The collection contained different colored eyes—from light blue and green, to hazel and brown. Sold separately to adults and children worldwide, the collection dates from mid-19th century England. It is believed that in the 9th century BC Egyptians created artificial eyes by pouring wax or plaster into the orbits of the dead after removing their eyes. A precious stone was inserted into the middle to represent the iris.

Sotheby's auction expert, Catherine Southon, poses with the glass eyes before they were sold at auction.

Bride Wore Green Susan Lane of Toluca Lake, California, creates wedding dresses and bouquets out of recycled trash—including plastic bags, egg cartons, and cotton balls!

Tallest Cake The world's tallest bridal cake was prepared for the wedding of Dutch crown-prince Willem-Alexander to Princess Maxima in February 2002. The top of the cake towered 59 ft (18 m) above the town square in Ommen, the Netherlands.

Harvest Time Otto Wegner of Strasbourg, France, took 15 years to build a clock made entirely of straw—it even had a straw mechanism—and it worked!

Hard to Match A 9-ft (3-m) high model of Cologne Cathedral was built with 2,500,000 matches by Hans Swoboda of Chicago.

Beach Mansion A sandcastle built by M.S. Di Persio of Bradley Beach, New Jersey, measured 8 ft 2in (2.5 m) high and comprised 33 floors, 1,637 windows, 84 doors, and 752 steps!

Thousands of collectors attended a G.I. Joe Collectors' Convention in Washington in 1999, to mark the 35th anniversary of G.I. Joe!

Jacqueline Voisenet has an amazing collection of 647 chamber pots, gathered over a period of 12 years.

GAME ON

- Enough rope has been included in Clue and Cluedo games to encircle the world

- The yo-yo was based on a Filipino fighting weapon

- There are 1,929,770,126,028,800 possible different color combinations on a Rubik's Cube!

- If all the dresses bought for Barbies since her creation in 1959 were laid end to end, they would stretch from London, England, to Sydney, Australia, four times

- Every day more money is printed for Monopoly games than for the U.S. Treasury

Medical Melange

In the Mütter museum you can find such diverse exhibits as a plaster cast of Siamese twins Chang and Eng (plus their attached livers), the cancerous tumor that was surreptitiously removed from the upper jaw of President Grover Cleveland, and a piece of the thorax of John Wilkes Booth, Abraham Lincoln's assassin! Other exhibits include bladder stones removed from U.S. Chief Justice John Marshall, and a giant colon, which is displayed in a glass case. Chevalier Jackson's collection contains objects that had been swallowed and removed as well as 3,000 items retrieved from human bodies, such as a small metal battleship, ammunition, a pair of opera glasses, and dentures. Arguably the oddest attraction, however, is the body of the "Soap Woman." She died of Yellow Fever in the 19th century and was buried in soil containing chemicals that turned her body to soap!

The Mütter Museum in Philadelphia is home to some of the world's strangest displays, such as skulls, a cancerous tumor, and even bladder stones!

Navel Power Graham Barker of Perth, Australia, has been collecting his own navel fluff since 1984. He keeps the 0.5 oz (15.4 g) ball of fluff in his bathroom to show visitors.

Worth One's Salt John Rose of Lebanon, Indiana, has an incredible collection of over 2,000 salt and pepper shakers.

Fencing Master Jesse S. James of Maywood, California, used to be hooked on barbed wire and collected over 200 different types!

Mettle Morris Karelfsky of Tamarac, Florida, has made more than 500 chairs—some only one-sixteenth of an inch thick—out of tin cans.

Matchless James A. Davis of Caryville, Tennessee, constructed a violin made from 5,327 matches. He kept it in a special case built from 18,593 matches.

À la carte Jacques Rouetof of Paris, France, has a collection of over 15,000 menus, including one from the Elysée Palace in 1905, honoring the King and Queen of Spain, listing 29 courses!

READY FOR TURBULENCE

Dutchman Nick Vermeulen is the man to know if you're a queasy traveler. Nick is the proud owner of a growing collection of over 2,000 airline sickbags!

Maybe Tomorrow "Procrastinate Now" is the motto of the Philadelphia-based Procrastinators Club of America. According to the rules, anyone who fills out the membership application form and sends it in promptly can forget about joining!

Filipino shoemakers spent 77 days in 2002 making a pair of shoes 18 ft (5.5 m) long and 7 ft (2 m) wide. The shoes, each of which could hold 30 adults, were a French size 753. They were made from 720 sq ft (67 sq m) of leather, 495 lb (225 kg) of adhesive and 3,300 ft (1,000 m) of thread.

MACABRE MUSEUM

The Tragedy in U.S. History Museum in St. Augustine, Florida, which closed in 1998, contained many macabre exhibits. Among them was the car in which actress Jayne Mansfield was decapitated in 1967, and the ambulance in which President Kennedy's assassin, Lee Harvey Oswald, was taken to the hospital after being shot by Jack Ruby.

Jim Jamboree When the Jim Smith Society held its 14th annual convention at Kings Island, Ohio, in 1983, it boasted some 1,200 members—all named Jim Smith. Remarkably, five of them were women!

Upright Citizens In the 1970s in Austria there was a private club for men who wished to be buried standing up.

Dirty Bits The Museum of Dirt, in Boston, Massachusetts, houses bottled fluff and stuff from around the world, including genuine dirt from such diverse places as Antarctica and the Clampett's mansion from the television show *The Beverly Hillbillies*.

Top Dunker Felix Rotter from Germany is the proud owner of a collection of more than 6,000 teabag labels from around the world.

Lifting the Lid Barney Smith of Alamo Heights, Texas, founded a museum containing over 600 decorated toilet seats.

Famous Locks John Reznikoff from Stamford, Connecticut, has collected the hair of more than 100 dead celebrities, including John F. Kennedy, Elvis Presley, Abraham Lincoln, and Marilyn Monroe.

Banana Bonanza The Washington Banana Museum at Auburn, Washington, boasts more than 4,000 banana-related artifacts.

This incredible miniature basket is just 0.28 in (0.7 cm) high!

Overtime Sweden's Lotta Solja has a collection of over 275 parking meters.

UNMISSABLE!

- International Brick Collectors' Association Convention
- International Mars Society Convention
- Rathkamp Matchcover Society Convention
- Belgian Society of Bagpipe Players Convention
- National Button Society Convention

Artless Most museums celebrate the best in art: the Museum of Bad Art in Boston, Massachusetts, however, is a shrine to the worst! The collection ranges from "the work of talented artists that have gone awry, to work of exuberant, although crude, execution by artists barely in control of the brush."

Seventy-one-year-old Henri Chesnais took three years to build a replica of Mont Saint-Michel in his back garden, using 300 tons of stone! He has been creating miniature replicas of different buildings since he retired in 1992.

Bunny Mania!

Born under the sign of the rabbit, Akira Tanimura has amassed a collection of over 10,000 rabbit-related items, cuddly toys, and ornaments.

Akira, a Professor at Osaka University, was born in both the Year and the Month of the Rabbit—April 1927. His symbolic birthday may have encouraged his lifelong fascination with rabbits!

Akira Tanimura lives with his 10,000-piece rabbit toy collection at his home in Hyogo, Western Japan.

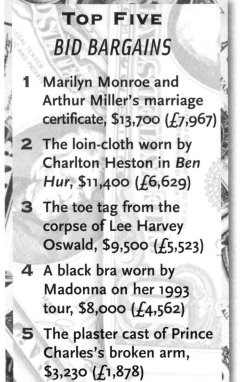

Nail Biter The Glore Psychiatric Museum, in St. Joseph, Missouri, is dedicated to mental illness. The oddest exhibit is a display of 63 buttons, 453 nails, 9 bolts, 115 hairpins, 42 screws, and 942 various pieces of metal—all of which were found inside a patient at St. Joseph 70 years ago.

Ancient Trappings The Museum of the Mousetrap at Newport, Wales, features around 150 mouse and rat traps. There is a 5,000-year-old device from Ancient Egypt and even a French trap in the shape of a guillotine!

Splinter Group There are more than 700 members of the National Toothpick Holder Collectors' Society in the U.S. Some collections are worth more than $250,000 (£145,339).

Neckwear At Leeds Castle Museum in Kent, England, there is a collection of dog collars spanning four centuries.

The Waltons Deep in Schuyler, Virginia, lies the Walton's Mountain Museum, dedicated to the popular TV series of the 1970s. There are precise replicas of John Boy's bedroom, the family parlor and the general store.

MEMBERS ONLY!

- Sausage Appreciation Society
- Wallpaper History Society
- Richard III Appreciation Society
- Bus Enthusiasts Society
- Flotation Tank Association

A surprisingly common phobia is a fear of buttons! Yvan-Pierre Delerue obviously doesn't suffer from it as he has amassed a million-strong collection. In 1996 he inherited part of the collection of buttons from his grandmother and has been continuing to collect them since, making his collection the largest in Europe.

Buried Treasures The National Museum of Funeral History in Houston, Texas, is home to one of the biggest collections of coffins in the world. There is an exact replica of Abraham Lincoln's coffin plus the actual hearse that conveyed Princess Grace of Monaco at her 1982 funeral, not to mention a "Funerals of the Famous" gallery recalling the send-offs of celebrities from Charles Lindbergh to Elvis Presley.

Double Drumsticks Over 6,000 stuffed animals were auctioned in 2003 when Walter Potter's Museum of Curiosities came up for sale in England. Among the items offered were a four-legged duck and a two-headed lamb.

Toothpick Tower Joe King of Stockton, California, built a 24-ft (7-m) high model of the Eiffel Tower from 110,000 toothpicks and 5 gal (19 l) of glue.

Ripley's®
GEORGE WASHINGTON CAKE
EXHIBIT NO: 14257
MADE FROM SUGAR, FLOUR, SHORTENING, AND BUTTERCREAM

A Piece of Cake!
Pastry chef, Roland Winbeckler, of Kent, Washington State, took a break one day from making wedding cakes in his shop and instead made a life-sized replica of George Washington, standing 6 ft 2 in (1.88 m) tall! Made from completely edible ingredients, the cake was priced at $4,300 (£2,499). Among Winbeckler's other life-sized replica cakes are ones made to look like Marilyn Monroe, Cher, lions, and tigers.

The George Washington cake displayed at the Ripley's museum in Hollywood weighed over 30 lb (13 kg).

Ivan Medevesk displayed his collection of 507 stuffed frogs in Zagreb, Croatia, in 1997. The "Fantasy in the Froggyland" collection, which he bought in 1964, was created by Hungarian Ferenc Mere in the early 20th century.

Cutting Edge Paul Richter of Leipzig, Germany, has collected over 17,000 razor blades.

King of the Road Elvis Presley's driver's license sold at auction for $7,400 (£4,400).

Keen Stroke Arnold Schwarzenegger bought President Kennedy's golf clubs for $772,500 (£460,000) in 1996.

The Final Word In Atwoodville, Connecticut, it is illegal to play a game of Scrabble while waiting for a politician to speak.

Wide-eyed English nurse Florence Nightingale kept a small owl in her pocket—even during the Crimean War.

Dreadlock Deal A 4-in (10-cm) strand of Bob Marley's hair once sold for $4,500 (£2,600).

Monument to Spice The Mt. Horeb Mustard Museum in Wisconsin is home to more than 3,400 types of mustard. The collection even includes a chocolate-fudge flavor mustard!

Bank Bacon The Piggy Bank Museum in Amsterdam, the Netherlands, exhibits around 12,000 piggy banks, including ones in the shape of the Taj Mahal and Winston Churchill.

Token Relic A Roman coin, thought to have been minted around AD 315, was displayed in a museum in Tyneside, England, for several days in 1975, until a nine-year-old girl pointed out that it was in fact a token given away with a soft drink. The "R" on the coin, which the curators thought stood for "Roma," instead represented "Robinsons," a soft drink manufacturer!

Ripley's®
RIBBON QUILT
EXHIBIT NO: 13274
MADE ENTIRELY FROM PRIZE RIBBONS
WON AT STATE FAIRS

Gladys McCrae of St. David, Arizona, made this flag quilt in 1980 using prize ribbons she had won over the years for her homemade jams and preserves, which she entered into state fairs. First prize ribbons are blue, second prize red, and third white. Just a few years after making the first quilt, Gladys had enough prize ribbons to make another one!

Tomato Pasting

The Spanish town of Buñol becomes a sea of red mush once a year as 200,000 lb (90,720 kg) of ripe tomatoes are hurled during a two-hour brawl known as La Tomatina.

A festival-goer wallows in the tomato pulp running though the streets, which is created during the world's biggest tomato fight.

At dawn, windows and doors in the streets are covered in preparation for the onslaught. Large trucks drive up the cobblestone streets and from the back of them, mushy tomatoes are thrown at the waiting crowds. The attack is usually over in about two hours when everyone heads down to the river to participate in communal baths. The festival dates back to 1944 when the town fair was marred by hooligans throwing tomatoes at the procession. At least 20,000 participants from all over the world now turn up for the fruity fun.

FESTIVE FACTS

- **Mashed Potato Wrestling**—July, South Dakota
- **Cherry Pit Spit**—July, Vermont
- **Zucchini Festival**—August, Vermont
- **Most traveled corn dog,** October—Texas

Women of the Balanta tribe in Binar, Portuguese Guinea, take part in an annual festival where they dance while balancing huge baskets on their heads that contain their husband or sweetheart!

SHRINE TO CHOCOLATE

Among the exhibits at the 1893 Chicago World's Colombian Exposition was a 38-ft (11.5-m) high temple, weighing 30,000 lb (13,608 kg) made entirely of chocolate. The exhibition also featured a statue of a knight on horseback—made out of prunes!

Granny Take a Leap The first Grandmothers' Festival was held in 1992 at Bodo, Norway. Several game grannies took part in a number of activities, the star being 79-year-old Elida Anderson who became the world's oldest bungee-jumper.

Garlic Overkill Gilroy, California, calls itself the garlic capital of the world. Each year it hosts a Garlic Festival, during which it features such delicacies as garlic ice cream and garlic chocolate. It even offers garlic-flavored dog biscuits.

Human Roast The speciality of Chamouni, who billed himself as the "Russian Salamander," was to climb into an oven with a raw leg of mutton—and emerge only after the meat had been thoroughly roasted.

Swinging Couple Aerialists Miguel and Rosa Vazquez were married on a high trapeze platform in December 1983 at a performance of the Ringling Bros. and Barnum & Bailey Circus at Venice, Florida—before carrying on with the show.

Hair Feat Eat your heart out, Marge Simpson! At a 1986 fair in Washington State, Jane Barako from Seattle, using only hair spray, had her hair styled to a height of 3 ft (1 m).

Long Man In the 1920s, Clarence Willard of Painsville, Ohio, performed a 12-minute Vaudeville act in which he added 6 in (15 cm) to his height by stretching the muscles of his knees, hips and throat!

Gentle Giant At Toledo Zoo, Ohio, in 1931 an elephant weighing 13,000 lb (5,897 kg) sat on a board supported by four ordinary, 14-oz (397-g) glass bottles without breaking them.

Moose Gems An annual Moose Dropping Festival that takes place at Talkeetna, Alaska, features jewelry made from moose droppings!

Diving enthusiasts Mr. and Mrs. Huemer exchange rings during their 1997 underwater wedding in Grosau Lake, Austria.

A devoutly religious man in Kathmandu, Nepal, contorts his body during worship at the Pashupatinath Temple.

Saint of Serpents

The statue of St. Domenico in Cocullo is surrounded with snakes at the beginning of the annual St. Domenico's procession in Cocullo, Italy, on May 1, 2003. Legend has it that snakes were offered to the Angizia goddess as a gesture of goodwill, and that St. Domenico protects people from snake bites and rabid animals.

The statue of St. Domenico is brought out into the churchyard annually, where snake-catchers surround it with reptiles.

Chimp Charm Lucy, a chimp with an Amsterdam circus, was so desperate for a mate in 2001 that she kept jumping from her podium to kiss men in the audience. The circus director remarked: "She prefers fat men. And because she's an adult she has a lot of force in her arms. It's not easy to pull her off men she likes."

Bottled Up Argentine contortionist Hugo Zamaratte can fold his 5 ft 9 in (1.8 m) body into a bottle just 26 in (66 cm) high and 18 in (46 cm) wide.

Loose Lips One of the chief attractions at the 1933 Believe It or Not! Odditorium at the World's Fair in Chicago was Mrs. Margaret Hayes of New York who, as a gurning champion, had perfected the art of swallowing her nose!

Big Mouth Sam Simpson of Avalon, California, could hold three billiard balls or a baseball in his mouth—and whistle at the same time.

Nambla, a clown wearing extreme make-up, including a lit candle placed on his head, enters into the spirit at the Burning Man Festival in the Nevada Desert. Up to 30,000 people travel to this annual arts festival held in the barren desert, where a temporary civilization is created. Participants go to great lengths to create and take art into the desert, set it up and then burn it on the final day of the festival.

Man of Stone Harry J. Overdurff of Dubois, Pennsylvania, was a man who turned to stone. Baffling scientists, his flesh solidified to be as hard as a rock. Unable to move any part of his body except his lips, he could support 800 lb (363 kg) balanced on his body between his head and knees.

Leg Lock In 2001 during rehearsals a contortionist got one of his legs stuck round his neck for two hours. Kazakhstan-born Birkine was carrying out his daily routine with the Netherlands National Circus when his leg locked as he twisted it behind him. He had to remain on his pedestal until an osteopath arrived. He later lamented: "I think I didn't warm up properly."

Bubble Wrap Richard Faverty of Chicago, Illinois, can blow bubbles large enough to completely enclose his body.

Short Cut During the 1970s, Professor Len Tomlin of England had a traveling flea circus featuring Bonzo, a flea that mowed a tiny lawn with a miniature lawnmower.

Elephant Charged Mary, a circus elephant, charged with killing three men at Erwin, Tennessee, in 1916, was lynched on a steel cable before a crowd of 5,000.

Termites Take Off Every March the 700 members of the American Association of Aardvark Aficionados celebrate National Aardvark Week!

Tongue Tied Habu Koller could lift weights of 105 lb (48 kg) with his tongue!

REVERSE BEEF

New York prankster Brian G. Hughes (1849–1924) told the press that he was financing an expedition to South America to bring back a little-known creature called a reetsa. When news appeared that one had been captured, thousands of New Yorkers lined the city docks waiting to catch their first glimpse of the elusive beast. The gangplank was positioned—and then an ordinary steer was led down backward off the ship. "Reetsa" is "a steer" spelt backward!

Bare Faced Prank Las Vegas promoter Michael Burdick created an uproar in 2003 when he announced that he was selling $10,000 (£5,800) safaris to men wishing to hunt down naked women in the desert with paintball guns. Women's groups protested until Burdick revealed it was all a hoax.

Sea Monster Thousands of New Yorkers were fooled by a sea serpent constructed by German archaeologist Albert Koch. He unveiled the 114-ft (35-m) long skeleton of what he claimed was an extinct marine reptile at Broadway's Apollo Saloon in 1845. Soon visitors paying 25 cents a head flocked to view the monster, which Koch said he had dug up on an expedition to Alabama. An anatomist, however, exposed the serpent as a fraud, revealing that it was actually a composite of several specimens of an extinct whale called a zeuglodon. A typical zeugolodon measured only 40 ft (12 m) long. Koch had simply joined a few bits and pieces together.

In 1842, as part of an elaborate hoax, the New York Herald astounded the world with an astonishing headline— "Mermaids are Real!" Nearly a century later, in 1939, Robert Ripley displayed a "mermaid" at his New York City Odditorium. There are very few of these hoax mermaids now in existence. Made from the front half of a monkey and the back half of a fish, for several decades they tricked audiences into thinking they were the real thing!

Home of the Whopper On April 1, 1998 Burger King published a full-page advertisement in *USA Today* announcing the introduction of the "Left-Handed Whopper" to its menus, designed to accommodate the 32 million left-handed people in America.

Wasp Sting In 1949 Phil Shone, a radio disc jockey in New Zealand, warned listeners that a mile-wide wasp swarm was heading straight for Auckland. He urged people to combat the threat by wearing their socks over their trousers when leaving for work and by placing honey-smeared traps outside their homes. Hundreds of gullible listeners took his advice.

April Fool On April 1, 1996, the *New York Times* stated that fast food chain Taco Bell was purchasing the Liberty Bell, to be known henceforth as the Taco Liberty Bell. Thousands rang the National Historic Park to protest!

Extreme Flyer

On July 31, 2003, Austrian extreme sports fanatic Felix Baumgartner became the first person to fly unaided across the English Channel.

Felix Baumgartner wore only an aerodynamic jumpsuit, a parachute, a carbon-fiber wing, and an oxygen tank as he flew through the air. He had prepared for his flight with three years of rigorous training, which involved strapping himself onto the top of a speeding Porsche.

Thirty-four-year-old Baumgartner, who had previously made history by parachuting from the world's tallest building, Malaysia's Petronas Towers, and from the statue of Christ in Rio de Janeiro, completed the epic crossing to France with a 5.9 ft (1.8 m) carbon fiber wing strapped to his back. Jumping from a plane 30,000 ft (9,000 m) above Dover on the English coast at a temperature of −40°C (−40°F), he relied on his oxygen supply as he began hurtling toward the ground at speeds of up to 225 mph (362 km/h). After gliding for 22 mi (35 km), he opened his parachute and landed on the French coast near Calais. The journey took 14 minutes. Baumgartner said: "It was pretty cold up there, but you don't feel like you are going down more than 27,000 ft [8,230 m]. You feel like you are flying for ever. All I thought was, I hope I make it to the other side."

On July 17, 1999, divers from Bad Neustadt, Bavaria, divided into two teams, and played cards 10 ft (3 m) underwater in a pool!

Dog Bitten in Half
In 2002 Japan's Takeru Kobayashi broke his own record during the 87th annual Nathan's Famous Fourth of July Hot Dog Eating Contest in New York. In the 12 minutes allowed he beat his previous record of 50 by half a hot dog and bun. The runner-up could only manage 26.

In 2003, Kobayashi lost a similar hot dog eating contest to a Kodiak bear on the TV show "Man vs Beast."

Giant Jigsaw Residents of Saint-Lo, France, painstakingly assembled a gigantic jigsaw puzzle in 2002. It measured 50 ft (15 m) by 82.5 ft (25 m) and was made up of 150,000 pieces.

In a Pickle Canadian Pat Donahue in 1978 ate 91 pickled onions in just over one minute.

FLYING BLIND
Mike Newman of England, became the fastest blind driver of a car in the world when his Jaguar XJR averaged 144.7 mph (232.8 km/h) over two runs at an abandoned airfield in 2003. The 42-year-old bank official, who has been blind since he was eight, was guided via a radio link with his stepfather who was traveling in a vehicle four car lengths behind.

Steep Faith Italian mountain guide Tita Piaz once climbed the notorious Winkler Tower—9,000 ft (2,743 m) of sheer rock—with his five-year-old son strapped to his back! Ironically Piaz, who had climbed the Dolomite tower 300 times without mishap, died in 1948 following a fall from a bicycle.

Slug Fest In 1982 Ken Edwards of Cheshire, England, ate 12 live slugs followed by two Brillo pads for dessert—in less than two minutes.

Santa Assembly Over 1,200 Santas Clauses gathered in a German theme park in November 2002. Four hundred and sixty-five Santas had congregated in Switzerland two years previously.

Light at the End In 1906 William "Burro" Schmidt started digging a tunnel through California's El Paso Mountains. He dug 1,872 ft (571 m) through 2,600 tons of rock, completing the task 32 years later.

Out of Earshot Seventy-seven-year-old Bulgarian Kolio Botev claimed a record in 2002 after living for 60 years with a bullet lodged behind his right ear. Since accidentally shooting himself in 1942, he declined all medical offers to remove the bullet for fear that the operation would kill him.

Panting Finish When Jacob Emery of Pembroke, New Hampshire, was given just 12 hours notice to appear at Exeter as a representative in the state legislature, he found he had no pants worthy of the occasion. His resourceful wife devised a plan: she managed to catch a sheep, shear it, card the wool, spin and weave it, in time to produce a pair of pants fit for Emery to wear —all in one night!

Week in Oatmeal In 1988 pub landlord Philip Heard of Hanam, Bristol, England, sat in a bathtub filled with cold porridge for a total time of 122 hr 30 min.

Doorman A carpenter walked from one end of Britain to the other in 2003 — carrying a 40 lb (18 kg) pine door on his back. Brian Walker took five weeks to complete the 871-mi (1,401-km) trek from Land's End in Cornwall to the Scottish outpost of John o'Groats. He said he was inspired by his father having once carried a door home from a builder's yard 4 mi (6.5 km) away.

Heavy Footed In 1989 Michael Stobart of Loughborough, England, walked 6 mi (10 km) in 24 hours with Dorothy Bowers standing on his feet!

Backwards Record In 1990 Welshman Steve Briers recited the entire lyrics of the Queen album "A Night at the Opera"—backwards. It took him just under 10 minutes.

Maaruf Bitar of Lebanon practices his favorite hobby—underwater cycling off the coast of the Mediterranean city of Sidon.

In 1929 William Bulson of Paterson, New Jersey, pulled a 3,800 lb (1,724 kg) automobile with his teeth while walking on his hands!

Mark McGowan used his nose to push a peanut 7 mi (11 km) along London's roads. He used a protective covering on his nose to avoid scraping the surface of the skin. He had to replace the peanut several times when it wore out, fell down drains, or was stepped on by people passing by!

Englishman Garry "Stretch" Turner is a member of the extreme show "Modern Primitives—The World of Freaks—Rituals." He performed at the Pepsi Music Club, Vienna, on March 17, 2002, clipping pegs to his face to stretch his skin. In September 2002 he clipped 153 clothes pegs to his face at a bookstore in England.

Looking Back It took Peter Rosendahl of Las Vegas, Nevada, 9 hr, 25 min to ride a distance of 46 mi (75 km). It wasn't the distance covered that took him so long, it was the fact that he was riding a unicycle the whole way, backwards!

Italian Job Italians Daniele Sangion and Giorgio Valente pushed a Fiat Uno weighing 1,852 lb (840 kg) a total distance of 33 mi (52 km) along a 5,216-ft (1,590-m) track near Venice, Italy, on October 18, 1998.

Speedy Sculpting It took just one hour for American John Cassidy to make 367 different balloon sculptures on May 10, 1999 in Philadelphia.

In 2003, four Chinese women lived with 2001 snakes in Happy Valley Park—for 153 days! The women even shared beds with the reptiles as part of an endurance challenge.

Heroic Feats A seal in the River Tees, England, swam to the aid of a drowning dog. The brave creature pushed the dog toward some mudflats, saving its life!

GREAT FEATS

- In 1891 Parisian baker Silvain Dornon walked on stilts from Paris to Moscow in 58 days

- Canadian Robin Susteras won a car in a 1992 competition by standing for 96 hours with one hand touching the car

- Canadian strongman Louis Cyr lifted 18 fat men—weighing a total of 4,337 lb (9,561 kg)—on a plank placed across his back

Dressed as Mahatma Gandhi, 31-year-old Akchinthala Sheshu Babu stands motionless in New Delhi on April 6, 2002 for over 40 hours, taking no time out for drinking or visiting the toilet!

Pieces of Pi It took Englishman Creighton Carvello 9 hr, 10 min to recite by heart the value of pi to 20,013 places!

Bogged Down

The World Bog Snorkeling Championships take place in Wales. Since the competition began in 1986, eager competitors have flocked to the event from all over the British Isles, as well as the rest of Europe, Australia, and America, to raise money for charity.

The objective is to swim the length of the course as quickly as possible without using conventional swimming strokes. The person to complete the course in the quickest time wins, although none of the competitors smell very good afterwards!

Entrants must swim 60 yd (55 m) with their snorkels through a murky, weed-infested bog.

Bathtime Each July, during the Vancouver Sea Festival, competitors take to the Straits of Georgia in their bathtubs to race across the 43 mi (55 km) course in the Nanaimo to Vancouver bathtub race!

Cutting Up In early May in Japan, teams compete to wreck their competitors' kites. The team members tie broken glass and razor blades to their kites and launch them for a kite shredding competition. The team with the kite that stays in the air the longest wins.

For competitors in the World Bog Snorkeling Championships snorkels, masks, and flippers are essential pieces of equipment. Wet suits are not compulsory, but advisable for swimming through the slime and muddy water!

WACKY RACES

- Lawnmower races take place each year in Sussex, England

- Lobsters race down a saltwater filled track at Aiken, South Carolina

- Once a year, grandfathers and grandsons get together in teams in Fort Worth, Texas, to race curled-up armadillos by rolling them over a flat course

- At the World's Greatest Lizard Race in Lovington, New Mexico, contestants are disqualified if they eat their rivals!

Hot Buns and Iced Cakes

Men and women from 15 countries sweat it out to see who can last the longest at the World Sauna-Sitting Championships in Finland. Every 30 seconds, 1 pt (0.5 l) of water is poured on to the stone oven to raise the temperature. Natalia Trifanova was crowned Sauna Queen. "I'm pink but happy," she said afterward.

Leo Pusa (right) won the contest in 110°C (230°F) of heat, on August 5, 2000, in a time of 12 minutes, 5 seconds! In 2003 Timo Kaukonen won with a time of 16 minutes, 15 seconds.

In 1933 in an ice sitting contest Gus Simmons (left) sat on an ice block for an incredible 27 hours, 10 minutes, but was disqualified because he was running a temperature of 102°F (39°C).

Fishing with Feelings

The World Flounder-Tramping Championships were first staged in 1976 to settle a wager as to who could catch the biggest flounder in Scotland's Urr estuary. The flounder, a flat-fish, lies on the bottom of the shallow estuary and buries itself in the mud when the tide goes out. Some 200 competitors wade into chest-high water with bare feet, searching for the tell-tale wriggle beneath their toes. The fish can be captured either with a three-pronged spear or by hand. The flounder must be alive at the weigh-in.

Dead Heat

Goodwater, Alabama, hosts an annual Casket Race, whereby a live "body" carrying a cup of water is carried by a pallbearer over a winding course. The winner is the pall bearer who spills the least water!

Pudding Bash

For 150 years a pub in Lancashire, England, has staged the World Black Pudding Knocking Championships. Competitors travel from as far as Canada Australia, and the U.S.A. Each competitor gets three throws of a black pudding—a regional sausage made from pigs' blood and fat—to dislodge a series of Yorkshire puddings from a platform 20 ft (6 m) up a wall of the bar.

Fast Flock

In 1993 Margaret Davis of County Durham, England, won the first Scottish Sheep Counting Championships by accurately counting 283 animals as they ran by!

As part of the celebrations to mark the 500th anniversary of a town in Belarus, willing participants paid 100 Belarus rubles ($1) for the opportunity to catch as many fish as possible in three minutes with their bare hands!

RUNAWAY CHEESE!

Gloucestershire, England, is home to an annual cheese-rolling contest. As the starter counts to three, 7 lb (3.2 kg) circular Double Gloucester cheeses are set in motion down a steep hill. At a further count of four, the runners start to chase their cheese! Anyone who manages to catch theirs before it reaches the bottom of the hill, gets to keep it. The prize is worth the effort, but the risk of injury is high!

The World Toe Wrestling Championships are held each year in Derbyshire, England. Opponents sit on the floor facing each other and "wrestle" using only one of their big toes while the other foot is raised off the floor. The first to pin down their opponent wins!

Pun Fun! The O'Henry Pun-Off World Championships, held annually in May in Austin, Texas, sees eager competitors gather to partake in witty word play.

Mower Madness Anyone aged between 16 and 80 who owns a lawnmower that can be modified in order to reach crazy speeds, can head to Glenview, Illinois, to take part in the annual Lawn Mower Drag.

Snow Place to Go Trenary, Michigan, is home each February to the Outhouse Classic—an event in which authentic wood or cardboard outhouses are mounted onto skis and pushed down Main Street.

Worm Turners The inaugural World Worm-Charming Championships took place in Cheshire, England, in 1980. The winner charmed 511 worms out of his 10-ft (3-m) square plot of ground in the allotted half-hour. Worms are coaxed to the surface by vibrating garden forks and other implements in the soil. Water may also be used but competitors must first drink a sample. This rule was created following a number of incidents where water was laced with dishwashing liquid, a stimulant that irritates the worm's skin and drives it "illegally" to the surface.

Frozen Pole Daniel Baraniuk from Gdansk in Poland claimed a new pole-sitting record in November 2002 after spending 196 days and nights on his 8 ft (2.5 m) perch. Baraniuk outlasted nine rivals to win the World Pole-Sitting Championship at Soltau and the first prize of over $20,000 (£11,500). His closest rival had fallen off his pole a month earlier. Baraniuk came down only because spectators started to dwindle with the onset of winter.

In the annual Wife Carrying Competition in Helsinki, Finland, contestants have to carry their wives over a 240-yd (220-m) obstacle course.

Ironing Bored?

Fed-up with the mundane routine of ironing, Phil Shaw of Leicester, England, set about making the chore more interesting. Joined by like-minded people, he sought increasingly hazardous places to erect his board—on a mountainside, in the back of a car, in a canoe, in an underground pothole cavern, underwater, and even on top of a bronze statue!

The result was "extreme ironing," which, in the words of Shaw, "combines the thrill of an extreme sport with the satisfaction of a well-pressed shirt." The first Extreme Ironing World Championships took place in Munich, Germany, in 2002. Eighty competitors from ten countries were judged on the degree of difficulty they could create for themselves in order to iron. They were tested on their ability to cope with five arduous ironing tests on a variety of fabrics and in different environments, ranging from rocky to forest, urban to water. They were judged on their creative ironing skills as well as the creases in the clothing. One ironed while surfboarding on a river, another while hanging upside down from a tree!

• • • Ripley's • • • Believe It or Not • • •

Under trying conditions, a Russian woman tries to keep her balance in the cold waters of the Mangfall River, Bavaria, during the Extreme Ironing World Championships.

PRESSING CASES

- A South African duo won a photographic competition by ironing while suspended from a rope across a mountain gorge

- A British pair set a new altitude record by ironing at 17,800 ft (5,425 m) on Mount Everest

- Australian Robert Fry threw himself off the side of a cliff in the Blue Mountains with an iron, a board, laundry—and a parachute!

Throw-Away Phone

Ten thousand people turned up at a park in London, England, in 2003 to take part in the first Cell Phone Olympics—a three-day event covering a range of activities involving cell phones. Competitors had to prove their skill at picture and text messaging, playing a game, and throwing a cell phone as far as possible. The winner was 11-year-old Reece Price from Essex. He sent an 80-character text message in 56 seconds, a picture message in 21 seconds, scored 11,365 points on Tony Hawks Pro Skater 4, and hurled an old cell phone 114 ft (35 m)!

Kissing was included as one of the athletic events in the ancient Olympic Games.

A Touch of Class East Dublin, Georgia, is home to the annual Redneck Games, where contestants test their skills at activities such as bobbing for pig's feet, seed spitting, armpit serenading, and dumpster diving! The winner proudly gets to display a trophy made from an empty, crushed, and mounted Bud Light beer can!

The Kenley-on-Todd Regatta is held in the town of Alice Springs in Australia's Northern Territory in the dry riverbed of the Todd River.

Something to Shout About On National Hollerin' Contest day, Spivey's Corner, North Carolina, comes alive with the noise of shouting and hollering as contestants each raise their voices for four minutes to demonstrate their skills. The contest marks the town's tradition of hollering to neighbors, whereby they would yell to one another when in need of help, or to call in the livestock, and families would holler between houses to let each other know that all was well.

> **"teams race along the riverbed in bottomless canoes"**

COLES NEW WORLD

An Indonesian contestant encourages his racing hermit crab by blowing on it at festivities in Jakarta, while spectators cheer on the crustacean racing.

Sinking Feeling College students from all over the U.S.A. gather once a year in Virginia at the Concrete Canoe Competition hosted by The American Society of Civil Engineers. Students must build a canoe out of concrete that will float and be light enough to be paddled without too much effort.

Do You Come Here Often? Speed dating contests involve hundreds of eager men spending seven minutes impressing women. Women armed with score cards mark "yes" or "no" as the men move from chair to chair in a bid to impress the ladies with their conversation. At the end of the contest, score cards are analyzed and any man who achieved two yes scores gets the opportunity to impress further in a telephone conversation.

Odors Afoot! For one day in March in Vermont the air is filled with the smell of foul, rotten sneakers! Children from all over the country gather to show off their smelliest pair of sneakers in an attempt to win a $500 (£290) savings bond and a year's supply of Odor-Eater™ products if their sneakers smell the worst.

- Around 150 contestants show up in the town of Laufach, Bavaria once a year to take part in the International Alpine Countries Finger Pulling Championships. The object of the contest, which is organized into different classes in all weights, is to drag your opponent across the table.

Porridge from Heaven September in Oatmeal, Texas, features an annual festival that can draw up to 10,000 participants taking part in oatmeal sculpture contests, oatmeal cook-offs, and oatmeal eat-offs! Women over the age of 55 might impress the crowds during the Miss Bag of Oats pageant. But the highlight for the crowd is when it starts to rain oatmeal! Up to 1,000 lb (454 kg) of the cereal is dropped from an airplane!

Dig It! Angel Fire, New Mexico, is host to the annual World Snow Shovel Race. Contestants enter into one of the three categories. Those participating in the basic production category have to try to control their snow shovels as they ride them down the 1,000 ft (305 m) course at speeds of up to 60 mph (97 km/h). The modified class allows contestants to attach their shovel to all manner of items, such as a bobsleds, luges, or even fireworks. However, in the modified unique class anything goes! Past entries have included an entire living room, a doghouse, and a chicken sandwich all shooting down the slope!

TREADING WALKING
Carrying heavy stones to keep them underwater and without the aid of breathing apparatus, the hardy contestants in the underwater walking race in Polynesia must follow a 70 yd (64 m) course, which is marked out on the seabed by wooden pegs. The contestants have to walk the course and are not allowed to swim. Spectators are able to watch from boats, as the shallow waters are very clear.

Diver Goes the Distance

At the 2003 Edinburgh marathon, an athlete wearing a 130-lb (59-kg) deep-sea diving suit set a world record for the slowest marathon time ever. Lloyd Scott, a 41-year-old former firefighter from London, crossed the finish line in the Scottish capital six days, four hours, 30 minutes, and 56 seconds after setting off.

When running future marathons, Scott plans to swap his diving suit for a medieval suit of armor!

The previous year he had taken five days to complete the London and New York marathons in the diving suit, but in Edinburgh he was hampered by an attack of food poisoning. He walked for an average of nine hours a day, covering half a mile every hour, but one day he managed only one mile because of stomach cramps. Not content with his mammoth achievements, Scott then spent two weeks in Loch Ness, Scotland. Using the old-fashioned diving suit for its intended purpose, he waded through 26 mi (42 km) of murky water!

HIDDEN TALENTS

- Singer Billy Joel in his youth was a welterweight boxing champion

- Author Edgar Allan Poe was a long jumper

- Singer Johnny Mathis in 1955 was ranked 85th in the world for the high jump

- Fidel Castro was voted Cuba's best schoolboy athlete in 1944. He also had an unsuccessful trial for Washington Senators baseball team

- Sir Arthur Conan Doyle, creator of Sherlock Holmes, played soccer and cricket, and scored 100 runs in his cricket debut

The slowest ever marathon runner, Lloyd Scott crosses the finish line of the 2002 London marathon.

No Frills Flight

Released in Northern France in order to make the journey back to his loft in Liverpool, Engand, Billy, a homing pigeon, took a wrong turn on his first overseas flight and ended up in New York! What should have been a 375-mi (603-km) jaunt across the English Channel, instead became a 3,500-mi (5,632-km) transatlantic marathon. Billy's co-owner John Warren released him from Fougeres in Brittany on June 6, 2003, expecting him to arrive in Merseyside, England, within seven hours. When Billy still hadn't appeared two weeks later, Warren gave the two-year-old bird up for dead, only to receive a phone call saying that he had flown into the Staten Island coop of Joseph Ida. Puzzled by the British markings on the metal rings around the bird's legs, Ida began an exhaustive search of pigeon clubs and eventually tracked down Billy's owners. The battered bird—exhausted and covered in mud—became an overnight celebrity in New York and was rewarded with a flight home courtesy of British Airways.

The winners of the 25th Carrier Pigeon Olympics bask in the glory of winning such awards as "fastest carrier pigeon" and "nicest carrier pigeon."

Lost Balls A staggering 820,000 golf balls are sold worldwide every day.

The Other Cheek Face slapping was once a sport in the U.S.S.R.

Antler Antics Ice skates used 3,000 years ago in Scandinavia were made from reindeer bones.

Fish Wins Olympic freestyle swimmers reach speeds of 5 mph (8 km/h). However, the fastest fish, the sailfish, can swim at 68 mph (109 km/h) over short distances—13 times faster than a human.

Bowled Over A bowling pin needs to tilt only 7.5 degrees in order to topple.

Bob McCambridge of Vale, Oregon, High School knocked out both himself and his opponent with one blow! Reeling from the punch, his opponent fell into the ropes with such force that the corner post was torn from the ring— and struck McCambridge in the back of the head. Both boys were counted out and the fight was declared a draw.

Known as "soccerhead," this avid soccer fan alters his hair color according to the game he is watching. He even has the hexagons of a soccer ball tattooed onto his head.

Faster Age The average speed of Count de Dion, the winner of the first motor race—the Paris to Rouen Trial of 1894—was 11.66 mph (18.76 km/h). When Gil de Ferran won the 2003 Indianapolis 500, his average speed was 156.29 mph (251.52 km/h).

Who's Counting? A regulation golf ball has 336 dimples.

Croc Shot A golf club in Uganda allows a free drop if a ball comes to rest near a crocodile.

TWELVE-MILE KICK

When a ten-year-old boy playing soccer in the playground of Wilberlee Junior and Infants School, Huddersfield, England, aimed for the goal, he had no idea that his shot would travel an amazing 12 mi (19 km)! The wayward shot soared over the 7-ft (2-m) tall school wall and began rolling down a steep hill. A kindly motorist stopped to retrieve the ball but, attempting to return it with a drop kick, watched in horror as the ball bounced off a wall and into the back of a passing truck. The truck then disappeared into the distance, the driver unaware of his new cargo. Luckily, he discovered the ball at his next stop and, guessing the likely source, returned it to the school 30 minutes later.

Mike Horn took swimming to extremes when he swam 4,350 mi (7,000 km) down the Amazon River in 1998 using only a hydro-speed boat and flippers to aid him.

On a Losing Streak A naked streaker who jumped onto the ice in 2002 during a hockey game between the Calgary Flames and the visiting Boston Bruins was carried off by medics after falling heavily. Wearing only a pair of red socks, the man scaled the glass but slipped when his feet touched the ice and landed on his back with a resounding thud. He was carried off on a stretcher to cheers from the crowd but regained consciousness in time to punch the air in triumph.

Turf Luck Jockey Michael Morrissey once changed horses in the middle of a race! Riding in a steeplechase at Southwell, England, in 1953, he was thrown by his mount but landed in the saddle of another horse.

Crunch Win First prize at the ancient Olympics was a stalk of celery.

Use a Stick! The first ice hockey puck was a frozen cow patty.

German inline skater Juergen Koehler attempts to break his own speed record by holding onto the spoiler of a Porsche that is traveling at 180 mph (290 km/h) while skating.

American skydiver Jim Suber jumped from the 1,381-ft (421-m) high Kuala Lumpur Tower during the Extreme Skydiving Championship in 2003.

Small Target In 1951, as a publicity stunt, Bill Veeck, owner of the struggling St. Louis Browns baseball team, selected a 3ft 7in (1.09 m) dwarf named Eddie Gaedel, to bat against the Detroit Tigers.

Memory Shot Minneapolis basketball star Wilfred Hetzel once shot 92 baskets out of 100 tries using only one hand while blindfolded—and standing on one leg!

Bigfoot 7 ft 3 in (2.5 m) Californian Brad "Big Continent" Millard wears size 23 sneakers—the largest basketball shoes made by Nike®.

TV Rage U.S. motor racing fan Michael Melo of Boston was so angry that Fox Entertainment showed a Boston Red Sox baseball game instead of a NASCAR race that he bombarded the network with more than half a million e-mails.

Late Entry The U.S. Olympic team turned up very late for the 1896 Olympics at Athens. They had forgotten that the Greeks still used the Julian calendar, which is 11 days in advance of the Gregorian calendar!

Woodchopper James T. Blackstone of Seattle achieved a bowling score of 299.5 when a pin cracked down the middle and half of it remained standing!

Touchdown Stroke Oklahoma University halfback E. Cook once swam to a touchdown! When a blocked kick landed in the river behind the goal posts at Island Park, Guthrie, on November 6, 1904, Cook swam the ball back for an ingenious touchdown.

Barnyard Backers

Sporting teams have many weird and wonderful mascots. They range from simple stuffed toys, such as Millie the spiny anteater, which was the emblem for the 2002 Sydney Olympics, to real live animals, such as cockerels and goats!

The French rugby team's mascot Diomede watches a training session.

The U.S. Naval Academy's mascot wears team colors at a match against the University of Virginia in Maryland.

Wing and a Prayer Playing at the Bay of Quinte Club, Ontario, in 1934, golfer Jack Ackerman could not believe his bad luck when his tee shot came to rest on the rim of the hole. Just as he was cursing his misfortune, however, a butterfly landed on the ball, causing it to drop in for a hole in one.

In 1932 the Albee sisters, Connecticut trick-shot artists, played double-team billiards on the Vaudeville circuit in New York and New Jersey.

Half-Blind Winner Harry Greb held the title of world middleweight boxing champion for three years despite being blind in one eye.

Weighing a staggering 772 lb (350 kg), world sumo wrestling champion Emanuel Yarborough uses his weight against Czech female wrestler Klara Janu during the Open International Sumo Championships in April 2002.

Slippery Tactics Four players on the Sacramento State University football team in 2002 were accused of spraying their uniforms with non-stick cooking oil before a game against Montana University, in order to make themselves more difficult to tackle. The plan didn't work—Montana won 31–24.

Permanent Gold A U.S.A. team is the reigning Olympic rugby champions. They beat France in 1924—the last time rugby was featured in the Olympics.

Blunt Boot In a college accident Ben Agajanian lost four toes on his kicking foot but still became one of the greatest football kickers of all time! His football shoes are now in the NFL Hall of Fame.

Bloodthirsty! After winning the 1997 women's marathon at the Southeast Asia Games, Ruwiyati of Indonesia revealed that the secret of her success was her drinking blood from the finger of her coach, Alwi Mugiyanto, before her races.

Ballpark Figure American baseball fans consume about 26 million hot dogs a year—enough to circle a baseball diamond 36,000 times.

Ten Pin Oldtimer Bowling three times a week, Benjamin Gottlieb of Albuquerque, New Mexico, age 91, was able to maintain an average of between 120 and 125 in two leagues!

LOSING THE RACE

In 2002 a pair of short-sighted athletes competing in a race around Rotherham, England, got lost for 18 hours after forgetting their glasses. Barry Bedford and Les Huxley ended up making a 20-mi (32-km) detour into the next county because they couldn't read the route map or see the race signposts. With the other 140 runners long in bed asleep, the hapless duo eventually crossed the line at 1.30 a.m.—but only after phoning the race organizers to come and get them!

No Beef There! Each member of the 1980 Olympic gold medal Zimbabwe women's field hockey team was rewarded with a prize of a live ox!

Standing Tall At the St. Louis Olympics in 1904, the American gymnast George Eyser won six medals despite the fact that his left leg was made of wood.

Pull the Other One Ear-pulling, a sport in which twine is stretched between the ears of two people until one person yells "uncle," is an event at the World Indian–Eskimo Olympics.

Ripley's ®
MINIATURE POOL TABLE
EXHIBIT NO: 13152
CREATED BY MINIATURIST, HARVEY
LIBOWITZ USING JEWELER TOOLS

One Good Bite Having placed his false teeth on the shoreline, farmer Millard Carter was taking a drink from Louisiana's Tickfaw River when a huge jackfish leaped up and swallowed his teeth! Carter promptly went home for his rifle, shot the fish, and recovered his dentures.

Eight hundred thousand cubic ft (22,000 cubic m) of water was used to build this 50-ft (14-m) high ice rock in Russia on which ice-climbers exercise.

Bird Brained John Lambie, manager of the Scottish team Partick Thistle, admitted that he once slapped a player in the face with a dead pigeon! Pigeon fancier Lambie had taken a box of birds into his office after they had died of disease and then hit player Declan Roche with one after he began answering back.

SHOW OF STRENGTH
Before the introductions to a 1992 fight, American boxer Daniel Caruso psyched himself up by pounding his face with his gloves. Unfortunately he overdid it, broke his own nose, and was declared unfit to box!

Danish golfer Anniika Ostberg wraps up well when he competes in the World Ice Golf Championships, which attracts over 20 players from 10 countries.

How's Your Short Game?

Andre Tolme teed off on June 4, 2003, to start an extraordinary round of golf. The course Tolme was about to play measured 1,320 mi (2,124 km) long and would, he hoped, take him right across the barren wastes of Mongolia. The Californian engineer, with a handicap of 15, mapped out his unusual round following a visit to Mongolia in 2001, when he decided it was the world's most naturally formed golf course. It also possesses the world's largest bunker—the Gobi Desert. Armed with 500 balls and two clubs, he began his round at Choybalsan near the Chinese border from where it was 138,889 yd (127,000 m) due west to the first "hole." Andre's progress, however, was blocked by a sea of knee-high vegetation and he was forced to postpone completion of his round until the following spring.

Andre Tolme kept on track using a radio receiver and a compass. By August 10, 2003, he had completed nine "holes" in 5,854 shots, losing 352 balls in the process.

Last Try Scottish rugby player Easton Roy marked his retirement from the game in 2003 by scoring a try at the ripe old age of 80. Playing for the Golden Oldies against the Wolfhounds Select, grandfather Roy dived over for the try that earned his side a 5–5 draw.

"sold for his weight in shrimps"

DEAD JOCKEY WINS RACE!

RIPLEY'S

A dead jockey won a race at Belmont Park, New York City, in 1923. Frank Hayes died from heart failure just before his mount Sweet Kiss crossed the finish line.

Shelling Out In 2002 a Norwegian soccer team sold a player for his weight in fresh shrimps! Kenneth Kristensen was weighed before his transfer from the Vindbjart team to the Flekkerøy team, who then paid up in shellfish. A Vindbjart official said: "Kenneth was in top form when he left us in the winter but he has had a relaxed summer eating seafood with Flekkerøy. I think this will be a good deal for us."

Fish Story When Leonard A. Smith of Cucamonga, California, was fishing, he lost his watch overboard only to recover it later inside a fish he caught.

Ahdil is a 32-year-old extreme acrobat. His is able to balance precariously on narrow tightropes. He has also walked for 8 hours, 12 minutes on a tightrope suspended 2,200 ft (660 m) above the Tiankeng Canyon floor in China.

Golf Coast Bob Aube, 17, and Phil Marrone, 18, played golf for 500 mi (800 km), from San Francisco to Los Angeles. It took them 16 days and 1,000 golf balls!

Miraculous Survival

Ivory Hill survived an automobile accident in which a 27 in (70 cm) wooden post pierced through his chest, narrowly missing his heart!

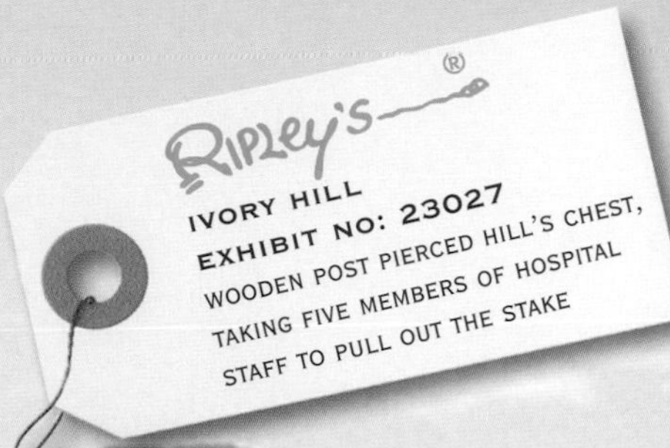

On November 17, 1941, the 28-year-old plantation worker from New Orleans lost control of his automobile while driving at night, crashing into a bridge near Thibodeux. After the accident, Hill walked for about half a mile and then traveled by car for another 15 mi (25 km) to get help—without losing consciousness or even falling down.

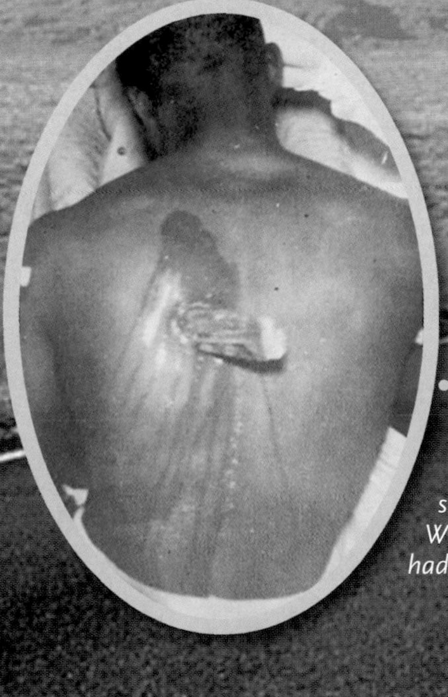

Ripley's ®

IVORY HILL
EXHIBIT NO: 23027
WOODEN POST PIERCED HILL'S CHEST,
TAKING FIVE MEMBERS OF HOSPITAL
STAFF TO PULL OUT THE STAKE

The wooden stake narrowly missed Hill's heart and smashed one lung. Within two months he had fully recovered.

TOP FIVE
CAUSES OF ACCIDENTAL DEATH IN THE U.S.A.

1 Motor vehicle crashes

2 Falls

3 Poison (excluding food poisoning)

4 Drowning

5 Fires and burns

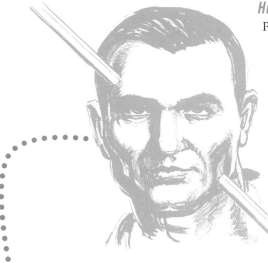

Human Missile Irving Michaels of Pennsylvania, was blown 200 ft (61 m) above his own home after crawling down a drainage pipe to ignite 5 gal (19 l) of gasoline he had poured down the pipe to smoke out a raccoon. Incredibly, he suffered only minor injuries.

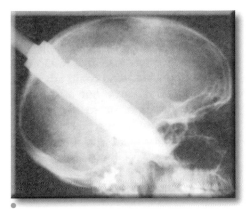

Paul Kosky survived having a 26-ft (8-m) long steel bar driven through his head, in an industrial accident. The bar entered through his left mandible in the jaw and exited through the top of his skull. He didn't lose consciousness and made a complete recovery, going back to work at the steel-plant soon after!

Inner Bomb On April 7, 1984, professional golfer Tony Cosgrave was playing a round at Baltray near Dublin when he was struck by lightning. At the hospital, surgeons discovered that his bowel had been perforated by an explosion of gases ignited by the lightning, which probably entered his abdomen through a brass belt buckle. Cosgrave recovered to resume his golf career.

In 1997, Alison Kennedy survived being stabbed in the head in a motiveless assault while traveling by train from London to Guildford, England. The 6 in (15 cm) blade missed Kennedy's brain stem and all her major blood vessels. It took surgeons 2.5 hours to remove the knife from her skull. She was left with some numbness in one arm and a level of tunnel vision, but miraculously survived the attack.

"Fall Guy" Nicholas Fagnani survived many accidents in his lifetime. He fell 55 ft (17 m) at the age of five, 60 ft (18 m) at the age of 12, fell 20 stories from the Liberty Bank building in New York, and was later hit by a fast train that threw him 300 ft (90 m) through the air.

Mass Execution On June 22, 1918, 504 sheep were killed by a single lightning strike in the Wasatch National Forest, Utah.

What'll It Be?

In 2002, a Chinese man named Li was bitten by a preserved snake when he opened a bottle of spirits. The stopper to the bottle, which was made of cork, allowed some air in, which allowed the snake to breathe during its year-long confinement.

Alcoholic drinks such as rice wine containing preserved snakes or other creatures are popular in China.

An eruption of lethal carbon dioxide gas from the bottom of Cameroon's Lake Nyos in 1986 rolled 13 mi (21 km) down a valley, killing more than 1,700 people and thousands of cattle.

Unsafe at Home Gerard Hommel was a mountaineer who survived six Everest expeditions. One day, he fell off a ladder while changing a lightbulb at home in Nantes, France. He cracked his head on the sink and died.

Safely Skewered A road construction worker in Austria was skewered on an iron rod from his groin to his armpit. He phoned his wife from the ambulance to tell her not to worry—he was going to be fine. The 7-ft (2-m) rod had missed all major blood vessels and organs. Doctors told the man he would make a full recovery.

Jack Thompson was skewered by a metal pole during a car accident—and survived.

Clean Escape Window washer Kerry Burton, 27, fell five stories in Calgary, Alberta, when his rope mechanism failed. He fell onto a bucket of water, and then bounced about 2 ft (60 cm) with the bucket wedged onto his bottom. The bucket probably saved his life.

Lucky Brake In 2002, Lisa Landau, a champion horsewoman, survived 34 hours buried in a bog after her car plunged off a road in County Wicklow, Ireland. Trapped in the upturned car, Lisa survived by breathing through an air pocket she managed to find near the brake pedal.

Staying Alive Two children survived by holding on to their dead mother's body after their plane crashed into choppy seas in the Bahamas in 2003. In the same accident, a woman held her baby above her head for an hour until the U.S. Coastguard arrived.

Doesn't Add Up Travis Bogumill was shot with an industrial nail gun that drove a 3-in (8-cm) nail all the way into his skull, but he recovered and the only difference it made is that he's not quite the math whiz he used to be.

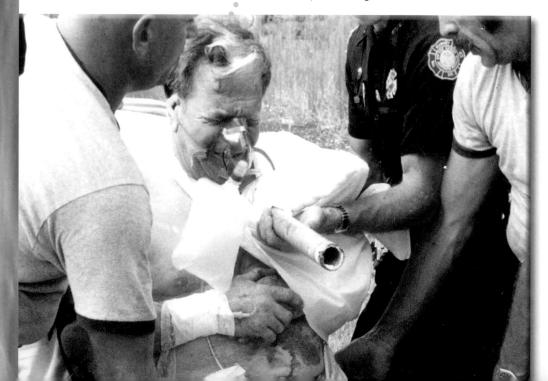

Vesna Vulovic, a stewardess on a Yugoslav DC-9 jet airliner that blew up in January 1972, survived a fall from more than 33,000 ft (10,058 m). She was paralyzed from the waist down, but later recovered and can now walk.

Shock A 25-year-old poacher in the Russian town of Tula died after putting a live electrical cable into a pond to catch fish. He forgot to disconnect the electricity before wading in to collect the fish.

Two-year-old Dwanna Lee had a miraculous escape when she was struck by a freight train and thrown 10 ft (3 m) through the air. The engine and six cars passed over her body—without injuring her.

Lover's Lock Doctors in Copenhagen spent two hours trying to pry two lovers apart after the braces on their teeth locked as they kissed passionately in a city cinema. A medic said, "It wouldn't have taken so long had they been able to stop laughing."

Stowaway Snake In 1991, a pilot lost control of his helicopter near Rock Hill, South Carolina, when he tried to step on a copperhead snake that slid out of a vent near his feet. The helicopter crashed into trees and was destroyed, and the pilot was injured.

The contents were still fresh and the ice cubes had not melted in this electric refrigerator, which was the only thing left standing after the house it was in was completely destroyed by fire.

SAFETY CUSHION

A beer belly was the hero of this man's story! Doctors who treated 264 lb (120 kg) Shaun Reaney of Birmingham, England, for serious stomach injuries inflicted by a power saw believe that his life was saved by his beer belly, which kept the blade of the saw away from his internal organs.

Death's Joy In January 2003, police in Spain chased a motorcyclist for 43 mi (69 km) at speeds of up to 112 mph (180 km/h) before he crashed. Investigators discovered that the rider had died about 30 minutes before the crash. Believe it or not, he had frozen to death.

Think Cue

Ron Fenwick was nearly snookered when he tripped onto a pile of cue sticks and was speared through the head by one of them.

When rushed to hospital, surgeons removed the cue stick by pulling it slowly out, as its shape was unlikely to cause further damage. The cue stick was not going through any organs and the only ongoing ill effects Fenwick has suffered are mild headaches and a pain in his tongue, which slightly affects his speech.

Ron Fenwick demonstrates where the cue stick entered his jaw—on the right of his head and emerged slightly behind his left ear, apparently piercing his earlobe.

TOP FIVE
SURVIVORS OF LONG FALLS

1 **Vesna Vulovic**—fell from an exploded DC-9 jetliner at 33,000 ft (10,000 m)

2 **Steve Fossett**—fell 29,000 ft (8,840 m) from his hot-air balloon

3 **Mike Hussey and Amy Adams**—descended 13,450 ft (4,100 m) with a torn parachute that had snagged on their aircraft's tail

4 **Juliane Keopcke**—fell over 10,000 ft (3,000 m) from her airplane in Peru

5 **Jill Shields**—freefell 9,515 ft (2,900 m) after her parachute failed to open

SNAKE SKIN COLLAR!

Biswajit Sawain woke up at his home in Bhubaneshwar, India, to find a cobra wrapped around his throat. Friends were too frightened to remove it, so after several hours Biswajit took a rickshaw to a nearby temple and prayed to the Hindu god Shiva, asking to be released from the reptile. Soon afterward, the snake relaxed its grip and slithered off.

Saved by Junk Food Trapped for a week in his wrecked car in December 2002, Robert Ward of West Virginia survived freezing temperatures by burning the car's manual page by page, and eating all the unopened tomato sauce, chilli and mayo packets he'd previously discarded on the car's floor.

Accident Prone American men are five times more likely to die by accident than women.

Coin-up Killers Vending machines caused 37 fatal accidents in the U.S.A. between 1978 and 1995.

ONE FOR THE RABBITS

Farmer Vincent Caroggio was hunting rabbits near Chartres, France. After killing five, he stopped for a rest, putting down the shotgun by his side. A rabbit bolted from its hole and stepped on the trigger, causing the gun to go off—killing the farmer.

Driven by Fate In 1975, Neville Ebin of Bermuda was killed when the moped he was riding was hit by a taxi. One year later, while riding the same moped, the man's brother was struck by the same taxi, driven by the same driver—who was carrying the very same passenger.

Kite Violence In 2003, the Mayor of Lahore in Pakistan banned kite-flying "dog fights" following a series of accidents that left 12 people dead and others injured. Some of the victims had had their throats cut by the glass-coated lines used by competitors to sever the strings of their rivals' kites.

Road Toll More people in the United States have died in car accidents than all the American soldiers who have died in wars since 1776 combined.

Steep Step While laying a telecommunications cable on the roof of a five-story office building in Walnut Creek, California, Ken Larsen walked backward over the edge, falling 65 ft (20 m) through tree branches. He suffered minor scratches and bruises.

Mrs. Hewlett Hodges of Sylacauga, Alabama, was actually hit by a meteorite on November 30, 1954. The 9 lb (4 kg) meteorite crashed through her roof, bounced off a radio, and struck her on the hip, causing severe bruising.

Cornish Miracle On July 6, 1979, an RAF Hawker Hunter jet fighter crashed into the English village of Tintagel, Cornwall. Although the village was crowded with tourists and parts of the plane landed within yards of a fuel tanker, no one was killed or seriously injured. Even the pilot, who had ejected into the sea, was picked up unharmed.

Nick of Time In 1988, U.S. parachutist Eddie Turner saved his unconscious colleague while they were both freefalling, by pulling the ripcord of his friend's parachute ten seconds before he hit the ground.

What Train?

A woman walking on the rail tracks at Sjömarken near Boras, Sweden, was hit by an express train moving at 60 mph (96 km/h). When the train stopped and the driver and guard went out to look for a body, they found the woman staggering about on the embankment some 650 ft (200 m) away. Two days later it was discovered that the woman was a 59-year-old patient at a local hospital. She couldn't remember the accident, and had only minor bruises on her left arm and forehead.

Hotrodder In 1991, Kelvin Page, a steelworker in Kent, England, was impaled through the head by a hot steel rod. He pulled it out with his bare hands after a workmate sawed it down to a manageable size.

Buried in Candy A 23-year-old candy factory worker in Marseilles, France, was crushed to death when a bin filled with 5,000 lb (2,270 kg) of marshmallows fell on him.

Fright Wig A 53-year-old man from Abbeville, France, stopped his car to try on an expensive new wig. He applied special glue and put on the wig, then lit a cigarette. The glue fumes ignited and the car exploded, killing him instantly.

Taking the Fall Both of Gareth Griffith's parachutes malfunctioned in a tandem jump with his instructor, Michael Costello, near Umatilla, Florida, in June 1997. Falling together from 5,500 ft (1,680 m), Costello maneuvered so that he would land first, cushioning Griffith's impact. Griffith survived, but Costello did not.

Office Pitfalls Official U.K. accident figures for 1999 reveal that calculators caused 37 office injuries, rubber bands hurt 402 people, and staplers injured 1,317 workers.

This sedan was cut in half in a collision, but its windows weren't even cracked!

Snake Charmer Turkish actor Sonmez Yikilmaz was sleeping in a tent when a black snake slipped into his open mouth. X-rays showed that the snake was still alive but Sonmez refused an operation to remove it. He opted for an ancient cure—hanging upside down from a tree while a pot of steaming milk was placed below him. The smell of the milk lured the creature back out through his mouth!

Early Morning Riser Asuncion Gutirrez, aged 100, startled her mourning family in Managua, Nicaragua, when she sat up in her coffin at her wake and asked for food. The family would have been even more shocked if it hadn't been the third time she had woken from the dead!

Flawed Diagnosis Englishman Kenneth Andrews was accidentally poisoned with the wrong medicine in 1930 following an appendix operation in Hong Kong, and was told he only had a short time to live. In World War II he was shot twice, stabbed, bitten by a rabid dog, and contracted malaria. He died in 1999 aged 106.

Won't Try That Again A man from Clermont, France, blew up his house when he added gasoline to a washing machine to try to remove a grease stain from his shirt. A spark ignited the gasoline, and blew out the first floor of his home, knocking him unconscious.

PIG IGNORANT
In Transylvania, pork rind is a traditional Christmas delicacy. Farmers inflate butchered pigs using a pump to stretch the skin, and then burn off the bristles. In 1990, a farmer from Cluj in Transylvania had the not-very-bright idea of pumping up his pig with butane gas. As soon as he applied a flame, the pig exploded, throwing him to the ground. He spent three days in the hospital recovering.

Twin Tragedy A tragic double accident killed twin brothers in Finland in 2002. The first brother died when hit by a truck as he was crossing the road on a bike. Two hours later and 1 mi (1.5 km) away, the second brother was killed by another truck as he crossed the same road.

HE'S NO PIKER
Dan Droessler of Platteville, Wisconsin, needed 60 stitches after a 36-in (14-cm) pike bit his foot as he dangled it over the side of his canoe on Twin Valley Lake. Droessler pulled his foot into the canoe with the pike still attached. He had to pay the Wisconsin Department of Natural Resources a $10.55 (£6) special permit fee in order to keep the fish and have it stuffed.

> **" Shot twice, bitten by a rabid dog, poisoned, and had malaria! "**

Braving a Brushfire

Rajendra Kumar Tiwari of India demonstrates his ability to balance more than a dozen lighted candles in his moustache.

Performance artist Rajendra Kumar Tiwari has even had two teeth extracted to make balancing the candles easier.

The Allahabad-based performer twirls his moustache to the rhythmic beat of traditional Indian music without twitching a muscle in the rest of his body. Tiwari says: "I stop eating or drinking anything at least two hours before a moustache dance because food makes it difficult to control your breathing, and that hurts in getting the right balance for the moustache."

HE'S A CORKER!

John Pollack, a speechwriter for former president Clinton, sailed a boat made from 165,000 corks 165 mi (266 km) down Portugal's River Douro in 2002. Pollack has been collecting corks for 30 years but was helped on the 17-day voyage by a donation of 150,000 corks from the Cork Supply Company of California.

Someone's Barking In 2003, Indianapolis dog lover Ilia Macdonald purchased a luxury bathroom for her french poodle, Pierre Deux. His toilet lid is wrapped in chiffon with a purple feather boa border and the room is adorned with a specially commissioned $400 (£200) painting that features a note supposedly written by Pierre to his girlfriend Gigi. Pierre relieves himself on disposable diapers arranged on the floor.

OBSESSIVE BEHAVIOR

- Rather than spotting trains, a man from Yorkshire, England, spots cement mixers

- A paranoid man from Oxnard, California, was so convinced that police were watching him that he dissected his pet guinea pig to remove what he believed was a hidden camera!

- A man from Leicestershire, England, transformed his flat into the interior of the *Starship Enterprise*

Up a Tree A couple who lived in a tree house near San Francisco for 12 years were finally evicted in 2002. Besh Serdahely, 58, and Thelma Cabellero, 50, met at a San Francisco soup kitchen and originally spent their honeymoon in the tree before making it their home.

Daredevil Dachshund Skydiver Ron Sirull performed at the Air and Space Show at Vandenberg Air Force Base, California, in 2002— accompanied by his pet dachshund. "Brutus the Skydiving Dog," as he is billed, wears goggles and rides in Sirull's jumpsuit and, according to his owner, is "totally turned on" by the experience.

Pickle Pride Residents of a village in Michigan hold an annual parade to celebrate Christmas pickles. The specialities of the festival, staged in Berrien Springs, are chocolate-covered gherkins.

Laying Down the Law Judge John Prevas of the Baltimore Circuit was so angry when vital evidence at an attempted murder trial in August 2002 wasn't handed in on time that he ordered Detective Michael Baier to do 25 push-ups in court!

In 1934, four-year-old Billy Crawford made several gigantic leaps in Cleveland, Ohio, while he was harnessed to a gigantic balloon that made him almost weightless.

Valencian priest Francisco Javier Serra (left) conducted an underwater reading of the Bible in September 2000. He and his two companions dived to a depth of 33 ft (10 m) in the Moraig creek off Alicante, Spain.

"Bible reading takes place 33 ft below water"

Some folks take car care a little too seriously! Torsten Baubach from Wales covered his mini with tiger print fur.

Don't Look Back Indian taxi driver Harpreet Devi is unique among cabbies—for he drives everywhere in reverse! He started driving backward when his car got stuck in reverse gear and he had to drive 35 mi (56 km) home. He has been driving his taxi in reverse for two years and has covered over 7,500 mi (12,070 km) at speeds of up to 25 mph (40 km/h).

Just Broken In In October 2003, 81-year-old Jusuf Sijaric from the town of Novi Pazar in southern Serbia revealed that he had been wearing the same pair of shoes for the past 60 years! He said he wanted to leave them to a museum when he dies.

Champion Liar In January 2003, Sandi Weld beat off several hundred rivals to become the winner of the 72nd World Champion Liar Contest by claiming that her sheep produced steel wool when she moved to Iron Mountain, Michigan.

Eight-year-olds Stephanie Larson (left) and Garrett Gilley won first place in the Tide Dirtiest Duo competition for children held in Santa Monica, California, in November 2000. Contestants had to tackle a stain-a-thon obstacle course ranging from chocolate pudding to peanut butter and jelly.

Dirty Diet Hao Fenglan, a 78-year-old Chinese woman has eaten dirt since the age of eight. In that time she has consumed over 10 tons of soil. She says she feels physical discomfort if she doesn't eat some dirt every day of her life.

Spirit of Give and Take North Carolina businessman Mike Jeffcoat played Santa over the Christmas holiday in 2002 by taping 300 $1 dollar bills to his office window accompanied by a note, which read: "Please take only what you need. Remember others." All the money had completely disappeared within 35 minutes.

Clowning Around In 2002, Spanish lawyer Alvaro Neil, 36, from Asturias, Spain, gave up his job and sold his car in order to cycle around South America dressed as a clown. Within 19 months he had ridden 19,200 mi (31,000 km) through ten countries.

Hidden Resident In July 2003, staff at a garbage dump in Berlin, Germany, discovered a man who had been living there undetected for ten years. His 3-ft (0.9-m) high hideaway contained a mattress, shelves, and a cupboard!

Feeling Peckish Gerben Hoeksma, 58, from the Netherlands, has a very unusual diet. For the past 11 years he has eaten three meals a day—of pigeon food. He says the meals are nutritious, healthy, appetizing, and cheap.

Lofty Intent In November 2002, pastor Steve Coad made his home on top of an advertising billboard above Highway 19 in Pinellas Park, Florida, and announced that he wouldn't be coming down until he had raised $23,000 (£12,600) for charity. He said: "I have a port-a-potty, a tent, a little TV, a mobile phone, baby wipes, toothpaste, and deodorant."

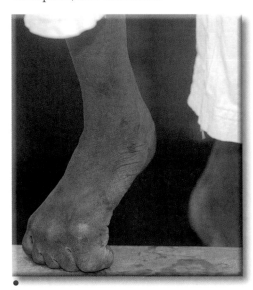

On March 27, 2003, K. Vasantha Kumar, a 25-year-old university student, walked up the 310 steps of a 16-story building in Madras, India, solely on his curled toes. The climb took him just three minutes.

DEVOTED TO DONUTS
Richard Ahern and his son Christopher spent two nights sleeping in a van in October 2002 just to make sure they would be the first people in Newington, Connecticut, to buy a new kind of donuts. The pair were first in the line when Krispy Kreme's new store opened, and were duly rewarded with a year's supply of donuts.

Singe Trim Bombay barber Aqueel Kiratpuri has abandoned using scissors to trim customers' hair in favor of burning the locks off with a candle flame. The "candle cut" revives an old Indian tradition and takes about an hour. It also reduces mess as the hair simply burns away.

Slice of Life Mike Uris from New Jersey ate a medium pizza and drank four diet cokes from the same takeout stand almost every day for over five years. He estimated that between 1997 and 2002 he ate roughly 2,000 pizzas from his local Domino's store.

Out of Time Machine A Missouri man was found guilty of stealing transformers from a power company, with which he hoped to build a time machine that would help him predict future lottery numbers.

MC MANIAC
Peter Holden, 40, from Washington, D.C., is the ultimate McDonald's fan. He eats an average of two McDonald's meals a day and by April 2002 had eaten at over 11,000 of the 13,500 McDonald's restaurants in North America. On a recent 54-day business trip, he ate at 125 new McDonald's restaurants.

Brainstorm In October 2003, San Francisco artist Jonathan Keats registered his brain as a sculpture and began selling futures contracts on its six billion neurons, offering buyers the rights to any creativity it might produce if science learns how to keep it alive after his death.

Echo Grey poses with her pet great dane, named Jagger, after the Fantasy Fest Pet Masquerade competition, which takes place annually at Key West, Florida. Grey airbrushed herself and Jagger so they looked like tigers and won a prize in the "most exotic" category.

• *Fruit takes on a new shape at a Tokyo market where cubic watermelons are sold.*

Worrying Warrior

The Confederate army general Thomas "Stonewall" Jackson, who would not eat pepper because he thought it would hurt his left leg, always sat rigidly upright because he believed that his internal organs were misaligned, and rode into battle with his right arm held above his head, because he believed that it greatly improved the flow of blood to his brain.

NEAR DEATH EXPERIENCES

• Belgian pensioner Jos Thys is the only man who can be said to have enjoyed his own funeral. For his 68th birthday in February 2003, his family invited 250 friends to his funeral party, even though he was still very much alive, because he had always wondered what his funeral would be like

• A man in Romania, who tried to take his own life by hanging from a rope was so appalled at the quality of the rope, after relatives had cut him down from the tree, that he planned to complain to a consumer rights authority

Ultimate Squash
In 2002, Jim Bristoe, a 42-year-old electrician from Elletsville, Indiana, built a cannon designed to fire a pumpkin one mile. With a 30-ft (9-m) barrel and powered by a 700-gal (2,600-l) air tank, the cannon is capable of blasting projectiles at a speed of 900 mph (1,450 km/h). During tests it fired a pumpkin through the rear of a Pontiac car!

Flying Finger
Farhat Khan from India can type 60 words per minute using just one finger! He can also type in both Hindu and English at this speed.

" Maize grew all over a man's body "

Indian police constable Shyamial Bundele decided to lie down for days waiting for maize to grow over his mud-covered body! His objective for doing this was to raise money for the construction of a temple near Bhopal.

Churchgoers from a village in the Netherlands have created a replica of their local church—made from 10,000 Edam cheeses! The cheese church stands 13 ft (4 m) high and 30 ft (9 m) long!

Cow-Eyed A Missouri family woke one morning to find 13 eyeballs in their back yard! Tests revealed that they were from cows, but no one knew how they got there!

Time Traveler? Forty-four year old Andrew Carlssin made a $350 (£200) million fortune in just two weeks on Wall Street, having started with only $800 (£400)! Not surprising, the Securities and Exchange Commission became suspicious and accused him of insider dealing. Carlssin made a four-hour long confession about how he was a time traveler from the year 2256 and so knew what the best investments were. Naturally the officials on the case weren't at all convinced of Carlssin's story, but it does seem strange that no record can be found of an Andrew Carlssin anywhere before he turned up as an adult in 2003!

Swallowing Pride For years, John "Red" Stuart of Philadelphia was the only man in the U.S. who could swallow an automobile axle. Now he has announced that because his Adam's apple has turned to bone, axles will no longer fit down his throat and he has decided it is safer to swallow samurai swords and bayonets!

Pet Pursuit To draw attention to his search for the family's missing pet dachshund, Summer Sausage, Rick Arbizzani of Florence, Illinois, took to the streets in 2003 dressed as Scooby Doo! Alas, nine months later there was still no sign of the dog.

Mayor Pays Up As the result of a lost bet in 2002, Mel Rothenburger, mayor of Kamloops in British Columbia, attended a council meeting dressed as a pink rabbit!

Ganesh Bhagat Chourasia, from Calcutta, suspends ten bricks weighing 77 lb (35 kg) from his moustache. The shopkeeper is working toward lifting more than 110 lb (50 kg)!

Raman Andiappan can husk a coconut with his teeth in 37.67 seconds. He is seen here demonstrating his skills in Madras, India!

Plane Crazy

Some couples choose to marry in the presence of Elvis, others choose to marry underwater, but these options were not exciting enough for Justin Bunn and Caroline Hackwood from Cirencester, England.

Justin Bunn and Caroline Hackwood got married while wing-walking on biplanes flying at great heights.

The bride and groom took their vows and were married by Reverend George Bingham while flying at 10,000 ft (3,050 m) over Rendcombe Airfield, England.

Something Borrowed

Japanese bride Yuko Osawa can afford to smile following her marriage to Ikuo Kine at Kakegawa City in 2000. For she was wearing the "Millennium Bra," spun in 24-carat gold thread, studded with 15 carats of diamonds and worth 200 million yen ($2 million).

This $2 million dollar bra, developed by lingerie maker Triumph® International Japan, was loaned to the Japanese couple for their wedding.

First Fight Newlyweds Marcia Alarcon and Carlos Alarcon-Schroder were jailed in Des Moines, Iowa, in 2001 after brawling over whose parents they would visit first!

Dig This Elaine Hesketh was expecting to leave the church at Manchester, England, in 2003, in a chauffeur-driven limousine—but instead traveled to the reception at 5 mph (8 km/h) while sitting in the bucket of a giant mechanical excavator. The unusual mode of transport was the idea of bridegroom Gary Hesketh, a former JCB driver (J.C. Bamford —makers of heavy-duty, drivable machinery).

Fit to be Tied Chinese bride Xu Fei is such a fitness fanatic that she wore a bikini on her wedding day in 2003 and performed an exercise workout for guests. She met her husband-to-be, Wang Xiaohu, at a gymnasium in Nanjing.

Set in Stone In 1976, Los Angeles secretary Jannene Swift officially married a 50-lb (23-kg) rock in a ceremony witnessed by over 20 people.

Bride Corinna Heimann and bridegroom Klaus Karrenberg prepare to climb down the 463-ft (141-m) high Frankfurt Office Center, Germany, during the 2001 skyscraper festival. A priest conducted their wedding ceremony at 98 ft (30 m) above the ground.

DROP-IN CEREMONY

Skydiving enthusiast Jason Stieneke found a novel way of arriving for his wedding to Peggy Sue Cordia in June 2002. He jumped from a plane and parachuted down to land on a lawn outside the church in Cape Girardeau, Missouri. Apart from a grass stain on his tuxedo, he was unhurt. The wedding photographer and best man also parachuted to the church, but the bride preferred to arrive by car.

One hundred and sixty couples from across China got married on October 12, 2002, in a mass wedding at the Juyongguan Pass on the Great Wall, north of Beijing. The event, the fourth of its kind on the Great Wall of China, was broadcast on the Internet.

Shotgun Wedding The Serbian wedding tradition of firing guns into the air in celebration brought an unexpected result in October 2003 when guests unwittingly shot down a small plane that had been flying low over the party at Ratina, near Belgrade.

Aged Divorce In 1984, 97-year-old Simon Stern from Wisconsin was divorced from his 91-year-old wife Ida.

Eli Cuellar (right) and her bridegroom Juan Videgain exchanged vows in an underwater aquarium of San Sebastian, northern Spain, on March 10, 2001.

Out of Place In 1993, a man shot a fellow guest dead at a wedding reception at Long Beach, California, because he was unhappy with the seating arrangements.

Nine-year-old Karnamoni Hasda (left) married a dog at a special ceremony at Khanyan, India, in June 2003. According to Santhal tribal custom, if a child's first tooth appears on the upper gum, he or she can only be saved from serious illness by marrying a dog.

"Underwater wedding ceremony"

In an Icy Grip

In 1914, relentless pack ice trapped the ship *Endurance* as Irish-born explorer Ernest Shackleton and his 27-man crew attempted to cross Antarctica. They spent the next four months marooned on an ice-floe.

Finally they took to lifeboats and made a perilous, nine-day voyage to Elephant Island. Shackleton then took five men in an open boat on a 17-day journey through some of the most stormy waters on Earth to South Georgia Island, where he led two of his men on a 36-hour trek over treacherous glaciers to reach a whaling station. He was able to borrow a ship in an attempt to rescue the remaining stranded crew members. He eventually reached the castaways on August 30, 1916. Amazingly, over the entire ordeal, not a single life was lost.

Shackleton borrowed a ship and spent the last four months of the ordeal trying to rescue the 22 men stranded on Elephant Island.

The Endurance was trapped in pack ice and held for ten months before it finally sank.

Meat on the Hoof During the French army's retreat from Moscow in the bitter winter of 1812, some soldiers survived by using their horses as living larders. They cut slices of flesh from their mounts to eat, but because the temperature was way below freezing, the blood froze instantly. The horses were so numb that they didn't feel pain.

Cold War Cow In November 1960, an American rocket launched from Cape Canaveral, Florida, veered off course and crashed in Cuba, killing a cow. The Cuban government gave the cow an official funeral as the victim of "imperialist aggression."

The Japanese television game show Endurance dared contestants who were brave enough to fight their fears, or carry out feats that pushed their strength and willpower to the very limits. Feats included hanging for hours on end with a cage of rats inches above, or being strapped into a box with live scorpions edging their way towards the contestants.

Baked Survivor In the summer of 1905, Mexican Pablo Valencia survived seven days in southwestern Arizona, without water, in temperatures up to 200°F (95°C). When he was found, his body was blackened and shrivelled, his eyes unblinking—but he recovered.

Tanya Streeter, seen here in a yoga pose, became the world's freediving champion in 2003. She was able to dive to depths of up to 525 ft (160 m) underwater.

Cut It Or Die

Rock climber Aran Ralston used a pen-knife to cut off part of his own arm to free himself after being trapped under a 1,000-lb (454-kg) boulder for five days in a canyon in Canyonlands National Park, Utah. Ralston was trapped on April 26, 2003, and spent three days trying to lever the boulder off himself. When his food ran out, he resorted to amputation. Carrying the severed limb, Ralston then careered 60 ft (18 m) to the bottom of the canyon and walked about 5 mi (8 km) before finding help.

Fifteen Weeks in Broken Boat

More than three months after setting out for a three-hour sail to Catalina Island in 2002, 62-year-old Richard van Pham of Long Beach, California, was rescued off the Pacific coast of Costa Rica. Van Pham had drifted more than 2,500 mi (4,000 km) south after a storm dismasted his boat, and his engine and radio failed. He survived on rainwater, fish, and turtles. When picked up by the United States patrol vessel *McClusky*, van Pham was grilling a seagull using wood from his own boat as fuel.

Van Pham (left) was rescued by the United States patrol vessel McClusky, after being adrift for three and a half months.

Richard van Pham spent his time adrift off the Pacific coast in this battered sailboat, which had been damaged by high winds.

Up and Away In 1979, Peter Strelzyk and Guenter Wetzel and their families escaped from Communist East Berlin in a hot-air balloon stitched together from curtains and bedsheets, and inflated with a home-made gas burner.

During an aborted 1975 space mission, the Russian crew of Soyuz-18A endured forces of 21 G—five times greater than the G-forces that cosmonauts must withstand during routine maneuvers.

Ski Plunge In extreme skiing, which involves hurtling down near-vertical slopes, Harry Egger of Austria set a world record, reaching speeds of 155 mph (250 km/h) in 1999.

Faithful Mailman August Sutter, aged 83, delivered mail over the same route in rural Illinois for 64 years, covering more than a million miles in this time!

Air Drop American round-the-world balloonist Steve Fossett was rescued uninjured from the Coral Sea after his hot-air balloon ruptured at an altitude of 29,000 ft (8,840 m).

Aargh A 62-year-old Korean man choked to death after swallowing a live octopus—which is a popular snack in Korea. The octopus was still alive when doctors removed it.

Hold Your Breath The Ama pearl divers of Japan make up to 100 dives each day to depths of around 66 ft (20 m) without suffering ill-effects.

Mid-Air Grab Thrown out of his exploding bomber in April 1944, Australian pilot Joe Herman struck something in mid-air. Grabbing the object he had collided with, Herman found himself hanging onto the legs of upper gunner John Vivash, whose parachute had just opened. Both men landed under the single parachute, sustaining only minor injuries.

SOFT LANDING

RAF Flight Sergeant Nicholas Alkemade was on a bombing mission over Germany in 1944 when his Lancaster bomber was hit by enemy fire. Faced with the choice of burning to death in the blazing bomber or jumping without a parachute from 18,000 ft (5,486 m), Alkemade chose to jump. He passed out during the fall and woke to find himself in a snowdrift, with only a twisted ankle, tree branches having broken his fall. The hardest part was convincing the German patrol that found him how he came to be there without a parachute.

Tragic Ascent
In 1875, French scientist Gaston Tissandier made a balloon ascent to about 35,000 ft (10,700 m). Although the balloon was equipped with primitive oxygen equipment, Tissandier and his two colleagues lost consciousness before they could use it. Tissandier survived, but both his companions perished.

Man Whips Horse
In 2002, American sprinter Tom Johnson raced a horse and rider for 50 mi (31 km) across a desert in the United Arab Emirates. Johnson came home in 5 hours 45 minutes, beating the horse by just 10 seconds. The horse had stopped for an hour during the race to eat, drink, and rest.

Jet Chokes
On June 24, 1982, a British Airways Boeing 747 cruising at an altitude of 37,000 ft (11,278 m) flew through a volcanic ash plume from Galanggung volcano on Java. Ash sucked into the engines caused all four engines to cut out. The plane went into a steep glide for 15 minutes, dropping to 13,000 ft (3,962 m), but at the last minute Captain Eric Moody and his crew were able to restart the engines and make an emergency landing at Jakarta airport.

Epic Journey Home
In February 1924, six months after Frank and Elizabeth Brazier lost their pet collie Bobbie in Wolcott, Indiana, the dog turned up back home in Silverton, Oregon, having made an incredible 3,000 mi (4,830 km) journey.

The Ultimate Leap
On August 16, 1960, Colonel Joseph W. Kittinger Jr. jumped from a balloon at 102,800 ft (31,333 m)—more than 19 mi (31 km) high—to set the high altitude parachute jump world record. It took Colonel Kittinger more than 13 minutes to finally reach the ground.

Hans Graas saved his three companions when they plunged into a crevice from a rock projection while climbing the 12,834-ft (3,912-m) Piz Palu mountain in Switzerland. Graas saved them by leaping off the other side of the rock as they fell, in order to create a balance by counter-pulling on the rope to which they were all attached, preventing them from all falling off the one side.

While journeying around the world, British yachtsman Tony Bullimore (right) survived for five days trapped under his boat after it capsized in the icy Southern Ocean in 1997.

Women Conquer Asia

It took four British women, Sophia Cunningham, Lucy Kelaart, Alexandra Tolstoy, and Victoria Westmacott, eight months to ride horses and camels across Uzbekistan, Kygyzstan, and two-thirds of China, traveling over four deserts and two mountain ranges on horse- and camel-back.

While on their 4,300-mi (6,920-km) journey, the women experienced extremes of temperature, frozen contact lenses, and Chinese shepherds eager to trade 1,000 camels for one of the girls!

The four intrepid travelers arrived in Xi'an, China, on their camels after the adventurous eight-month journey.

High-flying Hobo A 23-year-old Chinese man, on July 29, 1998, survived temperatures of about −80°F (−50°C) and a shortage of oxygen at an altitude of 32,800 ft (9,998 m) in the wheel well of a jumbo jet. The man was on a three-hour flight from Shanghai to Tokyo.

CRAWL FOR LIFE

While descending from the summit of Siula Grande, a 20,850-ft (6,355-m) peak in the Peruvian Andes, British climber Joe Simpson fell and smashed his knee. His partner, Simon Yates, lowered Simpson down the mountain on a rope, but Simpson slipped over the edge of a cliff and plunged into a deep crevasse. Yates had little choice but to cut the rope to avoid being pulled down himself. After a long, fruitless search for Simpson's body Yates returned to base camp, about 6 mi (10 km) away. Miraculously, Simpson had survived the fall, and in the next three days he pulled himself out of the crevasse and crawled back to base camp.

Thin Air Pioneers In 1862 British balloonists James Glaischer and Henry Coxwell ascended to a height of 28,770 ft (8,770 m) without oxygen— nearly the same altitude as the summit of Mount Everest.

This Mahatma Gandhi devotee painted himself silver to symbolize a statue, and walked for nearly 100 mi (160 km) in India in 1992 to commemorate Gandhi's famous Freedom March.

Ignoring the Cold

A Nepalese pilgrim who followed a 1960 American expedition in the Himalayas walked barefoot in the snow at 15,000 ft (4,570 m). He slept in the open in temperatures that fell to −20°F (−30°C), wearing only cotton pants, a shirt, and an overcoat.

Interrupted Nap

Chad Dillon from Indiana was in a dumpster, sleeping off a big night out, when he was collected by a garbage truck. He managed to escape when his screams were heard. He had head, chest, and arm injuries from being compacted three times.

Taking the Heat

In an 18th-century experiment, an English scientist named Blagden voluntarily shut himself in a room that had been heated to 221°F (105°C)! With him he had a dog, some eggs, and a piece of raw steak. Fifteen minutes later, Blagden and the dog emerged unharmed, but the eggs had been baked hard and the steak cooked.

LAST MAN STANDING

Japanese soldier Lt. Hiroo Onoda refused to surrender for 29 years after World War II was over, claiming that stories of Japan's defeat were propaganda. It wasn't until his former commanding officer flew to Lubang, the remote Philippines island where Onoda was holed up, and ordered him to lay down his arms, that he finally emerged from the jungle on March 19, 1972.

Bungee Ticket

A Canadian man was arrested after trying, without success, to bungee jump onto a cruise ship passing under a Vancouver bridge.

Thawed Out Well

Anna Bagenholm, a 29-year-old Norwegian skier, was trapped in an icy river for more than an hour. By the time she was rescued, her body temperature had fallen to 57°F (14°C)—that's 43°F (23°C) below normal. Pronounced clinically dead, she was taken to Tromso University Hospital where a resuscitation team managed to revive her. Eight months later, the only lingering effect was a tingling in Anna's fingers.

Double Miracle

Juliane Koepcke, a German teenager, had not one but two miraculous escapes after the airliner she was on broke up in a storm over Peru on Christmas Eve, 1971. First, she survived the fall of more than 10,000 ft (3,000 m). Then, despite a broken collarbone and other injuries, she walked for 11 days through the rainforest before finally finding help.

Seventy-six year old Indian, Prahlad Jani, claims to have survived 68 years without eating or drinking. A band of devotees have formed to pay homage to this man who claims his survival under such circumstances is due to divine inspiration. To prove his claim of surviving without food or drink, he agreed to go under surveillance at his local hospital, where they were unable to refute his claims.

Fire in the Hole In 1993, Stanley Williams, an American volcanologist, was taking measurements inside the Colombian volcano Galeras when it erupted, incinerating six of his colleagues and three tourists. Fiery debris fractured Williams' skull and broke his legs, but two female fellow volcanologists braved the explosion and mounted an amazing rescue effort to carry him off the mountain.

Speed Climb Most climbers take four days to reach the summit of Mt. Everest from Base Camp, but in May 2003, Sherpa Lhakpa Gelu made the ascent in just under 11 hours, beating the previous best time—also held by a Sherpa—by nearly two hours.

Indonesian magician Alford escaped from chains and shackles while immersed in a tank full of sharks at Seaworld in Jakarta in June 2003. He was underwater for a total of 1 min, 50 sec.

❝ *Walked a tightrope for 22 days* ❞

Chinese tightrope walker Adili Wushouer in 2002 stayed on a tightrope above Jinghai Lake in the suburbs of Beijing, for 22 days.

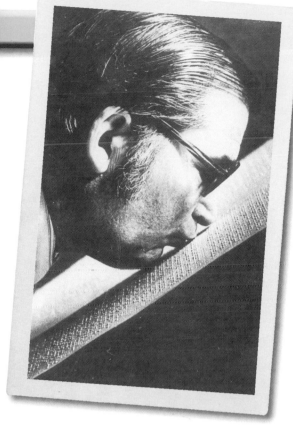

Girl Tackles Python Six-year-old Marlie Coleman of Cairns, Australia, was awarded the RSPCA's humane award for saving her kitten from a scrub python in 2003. The python had grabbed her kitten Sooty in her backyard, and when Marlie tried to make it let go, it sank its teeth into her lip, hanging on until Marlie's mother heard the screams and shook the snake off.

Julius Rosenburg, age 5, of Winnipeg, Manitoba, Canada, snatched his three-year-old sister from the jaws of a bear then growled at the animal until it fled.

Steady Climb Matthew Palframan, a dyslexic who could not speak until he was three years old and who, as an adult, only has the reading age of a child, won a place at Oxford University, England, in 2002 to study chemistry.

Genius Dreamer Albert Einstein, one of the greatest scientists of all time, was described by a teacher as "mentally slow, unsociable, and adrift forever in his foolish dreams."

Slow Start As a student John Maynard Keynes, one of the most influential economists of the 20th century, regularly got the lowest marks in his economics class.

Jim Abbott, born with only one hand, became a major league baseball player in the 1990s. Among the teams he pitched for were the California Angels, the New York Yankees, and the Chicago White Sox. During his career he pitched a no-hitter.

Diving Champ At the age of 90, Viola Krahn won the 10 ft (3-m) springboard diving competition at the United States Master's Indoor Championships in Brown Deer, Wisconsin.

Mini-Grandmaster In 2002, Sergei Karjakin, a 12-year-old Ukrainian boy, became the youngest grandmaster in chess history.

Early Starter Wolfgang Amadeus Mozart composed his first piano pieces at the age of five years!

Red Bottom Line

A Bolivian street vendor hangs out red underwear in preparation for the New Year season's increase in sales.

In some countries, such as Bolivia, many people wear red underwear on New Year's Eve, as it is believed to bring good luck in the following year.

In Poland, red underwear has also been accredited with helping to bring success to students writing exams. A study published in the Polish media in 2003 reported that students wearing red underwear were more likely to pass their exams than fellow students sticking to more conservative colors. Lingerie shops in Poland saw a huge increase of sales as students flocked to buy red underwear in a bid to guarantee exam success!

Lucky the chicken survived a truck crash in 2002 that killed 2,000 chickens on board. He fled into the undergrowth when the truck overturned on the highway on its way to the slaughterhouse.

Dave Clements was extremely lucky when he survived a fall in 2001 after his parachute failed to open. His fall was broken when he landed on an aircraft hangar, leaving him with just a fractured arm.

Lottery Lifesaver Patrick Gayle of Harrisburg, Pennsylvania, survived being shot at when a bullet lodged in 80 lottery tickets that were stuffed in his breast pocket.

Good Luck Fails An Italian man picked a four-leaf clover on a clifftop in Vibo Marina, then slipped on the wet grass and plunged 150 ft (46 m) to his death.

Price of Greed In 1977, a man was knocked down by a car in New York, but fortunately was uninjured. A bystander told him it would be a good idea to pretend he was hurt and claim the insurance money, so he lay down in front of the car again. No sooner had he done so than the car rolled forward and crushed him to death.

Safe and Warm Twenty-seven percent of past female winners of the British National Lottery keep their winning tickets in their bras.

Poor Judgment A 25-year-old motorist in New Zealand was driving to court to face a charge of driving while under suspension, when he crashed into a car driven by a man who turned out to be the judge assigned to hear his case.

Ill-Fated Revival When a New York woman was pronounced dead from heart disease, preparations for her burial began. At the funeral parlor she "came back to life," sat up in her coffin, and asked what was going on. The woman's daughter promptly dropped dead of shock.

Choice Number The number seven is the most popular number chosen by lottery players.

Bruiser the dog fell 200 ft (61 m) from a cliff in Dorset, England, but miraculously survived!

DETERMINED TO SUCCEED
World-class Canadian rower, Silken Laumann survived a near-fatal collision with a pair of rowers, while training for the 1992 Olympics. Despite a skin graft, and five operations in just ten days, Silken made an unbelievable come-back when she won the bronze medal in the single's finals the same year.

Bite Worse than Bark A beech tree near a churchyard in Suffolk, England, had a skull carved in its trunk, and many villagers thought it was cursed. A local farmer cut down the tree, sceptical of the curse. He cut his hand badly on his chainsaw, and when he stepped on a nail, his foot turned septic. He developed jaundice and was rushed to the hospital, where he died.

Shortlived Triumph In Foggia, Italy, Armando Pinelli, 70, won his argument with another man over who should sit in the only chair in the shade of a palm tree, but when he sat down, the tree toppled over and killed him.

Single Strokes of Luck

The odds of hitting a hole-in-one in golf are 1 in 15,000—but some lucky golfers manage to achieve this, including five-year-old Mason Aldrege who, in 2002, hit a 106-yd (97-m) hole-in-one at Eagle's Bluff Country Club in Bullard, Texas. However, the record for the youngest golfer to hit a hole-in-one is held by three-year-old Jake Paine of Orange County, California. A much older, 76-year-old Felicity Sieghart hit two holes-in-one in the same round at Aldeburgh Golf Club, England, in 2003.

In 2001, lucky eight-year-old Greg Law scored a hole-in-one at Oldmeldrum Club in Scotland.

Lip Reading Micaela Velasco, 101 years old, was declared dead by a doctor in Zamora, north-west Spain. A few hours later, undertakers were preparing her for burial when they saw her lips move. Three days later, she was "as fit as a lady of her age can be."

Gee, Thanks After purchasing countless losing raffle tickets, balding Chris Calver of Newcastle–upon–Tyne, England, finally struck lucky, winning some curling tongs.

Next Stop Jail A man in Rio de Janeiro who robbed bus passengers of more than $800 (£470) alighted at the next stop only to be arrested by the commanding officer of more than 400 police officers gathered for a ceremony.

Mohammad Nasib from Pakistan tells the fortune of customers who pass by in the street, using his talking fortune-telling parrots!

LIFE IMITATES ART

In Edgar Allan Poe's 1838 fictional story *The Narrative of Arthur Gordon Pym of Nantucket*, four men adrift in a boat kill and eat a cabin boy called Richard Parker. Forty-six years later, the real-life crew of the *Mignonette* were cast adrift after their ship was sunk in a storm. After 19 days without food, the captain decided to kill and eat the 17-year-old cabin boy, whose body kept the sailors alive for 35 days until they were rescued. The unfortunate boy's name was Richard Parker.

Lovelorn Leap Devastated by her husband's suspected adultery, Vera Czermak of Prague, Czech Republic, jumped from her third-story window—and accidentally landed on him as he passed below. She recovered in hospital, but he died instantly.

Body Armor Jane Selma Soares, a Brazilian woman shot in crossfire between police and drug dealers in 2002, was saved by her silicone breast implants, which slowed the bullet up enough to prevent it from causing her serious injury.

Bank-Breaking Labor In 1873, Englishman Joseph Jaggers "broke the bank" at the Beaux-Arts Casino, Monte Carlo. It wasn't just luck. Jaggers spent time figuring out that one of the six roulette wheels was unbalanced, throwing up nine numbers more often than natural probability indicated. By the time the casino figured out Jaggers' system and redesigned the wheel, he had netted the astonishing amount of $325,000 (£191,000)!

Hail Attack Almost 5,000 holes the size of baseballs were made in a biplane during a freak hailstorm. The pilot managed somehow to fly his plane 275 mi (445 km) to land safely.

Superstitious President Franklin D. Roosevelt was a sufferer of triskaidekaphobia— the fear of the number thirteen. Incidentally, eleven plus two is an anagram of twelve plus one.

Sticky Situation Bill the plumber had to be freed by firemen after he got his head stuck in a lavatory bowl at his house in Puckeridge, Hertfordshire, England. His full name was W.C. Sticks.

War Victim The first bomb dropped by the Allies on Berlin during World War II killed the only elephant in the city's Zoo.

Sight Shock Nine years after being blinded in an accident, Edwin Robinson of Falmouth, Maine, recovered his sight after being struck by lightning on June 4, 1980.

Streaks of Luck

Bill Morgan's extraordinary run of good luck began in 1998, when the Australian truck driver won a car in a scratch lottery. He was asked to re-enact his scratchcard triumph for the benefit of a local TV station, and won another AU$250,000 (US$180,000 / £106,000) on the scratch card there and then! A spokesman for the lottery said the odds of winning both prizes were more than six billion to one. Croatian Frane Selak, over the course of ten years, escaped relatively unharmed from a train accident, a bus accident, falling from a plane, three car fires, and being knocked down by a bus in Zagreb, Croatia. Selak's extraordinary run of luck reached its peak when, in 2003, he won the Croatian lottery, winning the equivalent of £600,000 ($1 million)!

> **"*Kitten survives 105°F wash cycle!*"**

RETURN OF THE RING

A gold ring lost at a swimming pool in Colchester, England, turned up 27 years later inside an apple. The ring was discovered in 2002 by 12-year-old Jamie-Louisa Arnold when she bit into the apple. Rosalind Pike saw the ring in a press photograph and immediately recognized it as the one that she had lost during a school swimming trip in 1975. A gardening expert suggested that a bird might have picked up the ring and dropped it in an orchard, and the apple formed around it.

Sugar, an extremely lucky 12-month-old kitten, survived inside a washing machine for 45 minutes at 105°F (40°C) after accidentally being shut in the machine.

Index

13 (b) ITD/REX; 14 (t) AFP/GETTYIMAGE; 15 (l) FPL; 16 (t) Emanuel Ilan/AFP/GETTYIMAGE, (b) FPL; 17 (t) Paul Villa/FPL, (b) Mary Evans Picture Library; 18 (t) FPL, (b) Sipa Press/REX; 19 (t) Ken Webster/FPL, (b) Ken Webster/FPL; 20 (t) FPL, (b) Marina Jackson/FPL; 21 (b) FPL; 22 (t) Doug Kanter/AFP/GETTYIMAGE, (b) Matt Cambell/AFP/GETTYIMAGE; 23 (c/l) Carl de Souza/AFP/GETTYIMAGE, (t) Rus/Rex, (b) Nicolas Asfouri/AFP/GETTYIMAGE; 24 (t/r) FPL, (b) FPL; 25 (t) E. Coxon/FPL; 26 (r) Hulton-Deutsch Collection/CORBIS; 27 (b) ZZ/XXH/SPL/REX; 28 (c) Dr. B. E. Schwarz/FPL; 29 (t/l) Kevin Braithwaite/FPL, (r) Ken McKay/REX, (b) Saeed Khan/APF/GETTYIMAGE; 30 (r) Larry E. Arnold/FPL; 31 (b/r) Dr. Elmar R. Gruber/FPL, (b/l) Dr. Elmar R. Gruber/FPL; 32 (t) FPL, (b) FPL; 33 (t) SWS/REX, (b) SWS/REX; 34 (t) Cliff Crook/FPL, (b) Tony Healy/FPL; 35 (c) FPL, (b) Tony Healy/FPL; 36 (c/l) Charles Sykes/REX, (b) Charles Sykes/REX; 37 (t/l) FPL; 40 (b) Ciro Fusco/AFP/GETTYIMAGE; 41 (l) NASA/AFP/GETTYIMAGE; 42 (t) William West/AFP/GETTYIMAGE, (b) William West/AFP/GETTYIMAGE; 43 (t) Lloyd Cluff/CORBIS; 44 (b) IBL/REX; 45 (t) Alex Sudea/REX; 46 (t) Sipa Press/REX, (b) Miura Dolphins/AFP/GETTYIMAGE; 47 (t) David Hill/REX; 48 (b) Davis Factor/CORBIS; 49 (b/r) DiMaggio/Kalish/CORBIS; 50 (t) Roy Garner/REX, (b/l) AFP/GETTYIMAGE; 51 (t) Tom Bean/CORBIS; 52 (t) Jens Buettner/AFP/GETTYIMAGE; 54 (l) Bettmann/CORBIS, (r) Bettmann/CORBIS; 55 (b) Sunday Time/CORBIS SYGMA; 56 (b) Dragon/REX; 57 (b) Victor Vasenin/AFP/GETTYIMAGE; 58 (t) PIERRE VERDY/AFP/GETTYIMAGE; 59 (t) JAC/REX; 60 (b) Sipa Press /REX; 61 (r) AFP/GETTYIMAGE; 62 (t) Christopher Gerigk/AFP/GETTYIMAGE, (c/r) Gred Garay/AFP/GETTYIMAGE, (b) Kevin Schafer/CORBIS; 63 (b) Philippe Hays/REX; 64 (r) Simon Walker/REX; 65 (b) Rick Doyle/CORBIS; 66 (b) Richard Sowersby/REX; 67 (t) Paul A. Souders/CORBIS, (b) Patrick Barth/REX; 70 (c) Gregory Ochocki/Seapics.com; 71 (t) Kay Nietfeld/AFP/GETTYIMAGE, (b/r) STF/AFP/GETTYIMAGE; 72 (t) Doc White/Seapics.com, (b) Matthias Schrader/AFP/GETTYIMAGE; 73 (b/r) Universal, (b) Amos Nachoum/CORBIS, 74 (r) Jeffrey L. Rotman/CORBIS, (b) Jeffrey L. Rotman/CORBIS; 75 (r) Royalty-Free/CORBIS; 76 (t) Tom Brakefield/CORBIS, (b) Galen Rowell/CORBIS; 77 (c) Jeffrey L. Rotman/CORBIS; 79 (t) Roger Garwood & Trish Ainslie/CORBIS; 79 (b) Paul A. Souders/CORBIS; 80 (b) Martin Harvey, Gallo Images/CORBIS; 81 (t) Michael and Patricia Fogden/Corbis; 82 (t/l) Robin Utrecht/AFP/GETTYIMAGE, (t/r) Michael Freeman.CORBIS, (b) Joe McDonald/CORBIS; 83 (t) Martin Harvey, Gallo Images/CORBIS; 84 Background STT/AFP/GETTYIMAGE, (b) Pornchai Kittiwongsakul/AFP/GETTYIMAGE; 85 (t) INS News Group/REX, (b) Mohammad Ibrahim/AFP/GETTYIMAGE; 86 (t) Raed Qutena/AFP/GETTYIMAGE, (b) Jim Erickson/CORBIS; 88 (t) Yoshikazu Tsuno/AFP/GETTYIMAGE, (b) Gunner Ask/AFP/GETTYIMAGE; 89 (c/l) David A. Northcott/CORBIS, (b) Paul J. Richards/AFP/GETTYIMAGE; 91 (c) Tom Kidd/Katz; 92 (b) AFP/GETTYIMAGE; 93 (b) Keren Su/CORBIS; 95 (t/l) AFP/GETTYIMAGE; 95 (b) Roger Wilmhurst,FLPA/CORBIS, (t/r) SAM YEH/AFP/GETTYIMAGE; 96 (b) Action Press/REX; 97 (t) Courtesy of NASA, (b) AFP/GETTYIMAGE; 101 (t) Gary Roberts/REX, (c/l) FPL; 102 (b) Bettmann/CORBIS; 104 (b) Michael Friedel/REX; 105 (t) AFP/GETTYIMAGE, (b/l) ,Marc Alex/AFP/GETTYIMAGE, (b/r) Marc Alex/AFP/GETTYIMAGE; 106 (t/l) Joseph Barrak/AFP/GETTYIMAGE, (t/r) AFP/GETTYIMAGE, (b/l) Biju Boro/AFP/GETTYIMAGE; 107 (t/r) Deshakalyan Chowdhury/AFP/GETTYIMAGE; 108 (t/r) Uta Rademacher/AFP/GETTYIMAGE; 109 (t) Tim Rooke/REX, (c) Ripley's Believe It or Not! Archives, Sony Pictures Television (b) Ripley's Believe It or Not! Archives, Sony Pictures Television, 110 (b) FPL, (t/l) Ripley's Believe It or Not! Archives, Sony Pictures Television; 111 (c) Ripley's Believe It or Not! Archives, Sony Pictures Television, (b) Bettmann/CORBIS; 113 (b) AFP/GETTYIMAGE; 114 (t) Pornchal Kittiwongsakul AFP/GETTIMAGE; 116 (c) Courtesy of Michael Vine Associates/Nicky Johnson; 117 (t) Brownie Harris/CORBIS, (b) John Mclellen/REX; 118 (b) Greg Williams/REX; 119 (c/r) Dave Bebber/REX, (b/l) Gary Trotter/REX; 120 (t) Sipa Press/REX, (b) Nils Jorgensen/REX; 121 (t) Mark Campbell/REX; 122 (t) AFP/GETTYIMAGE, (b) Paul Cooper/REX; 123 (b) Charles and Josette Lenars/CORBIS; 124 (t) Gamma/Katz; 126 (t/l) Issouf Sanogo/AFP/GETTYIMAGE, (t/r) Issouf Sanogo/AFP/GETTYIMAGE, (b) Issouf Sanogo/AFP/GETTYIMAGE; 127 (t) Jerry Daws /REX; 130 (t/r) David Hartley/REX, (b) REX; 131 (t) Simon Ward/REX, (b) Yoshikazu Tsuno/AFP/GETTYIMAGE; 132 (t) Sipa Press/REX; 133 (t) Sutcliffe News/REX, (b) Jimin Lai/AFP/GETTYIMAGE; 134 (b) TDY/REX; 135 (t) Anupam Nath/AFP/GETTYIMAGE; 136 (t) Henry McInnes/REX; 137 (t) Toru Yamanaka/AFP/GETTYIMAGE, (b) Ripley's Believe It or Not! Archives, Sony Pictures Television; 138 (t/l) Rabih Mograbi/AFP/GETTYIMAGE, (t/r) AFP/GETTYIMAGE, (b) Jiji Press/AFP/GETTYIMAGE; 139 (t) Nijmegen University/AFP/GETTYIMAGE, (b/l and b/r) Torsten Blackwood/AFP/GETTYIMAGE; 140 (t) Gero Breloer/AFP/GETTYIMAGE, (b) AFP/GETTYIMAGE; 141 (t) Oregon State University/AFP/GETTYIMAGE; 142 (t and c) Adrian Dennis/ AFP/GETTYIMAGE; 143 (b) Patrick Bernard/AFP/GETTYIMAGE; 144 (t) Nicholas Asfouri/AFP/GETTYIMAGE, (b) Indranil Mukherjee/AFP/GETTYIMAGE; 145 (l) Yoshikazu Tsuno/AFP/GETTYIMAGE; 146 (t) Martial Trezzini/AFP/GETTYIMAGE; 147 (t/l) Mike Nelson/AFP/GETTYIMAGE, (b/r) Yoshikazu Tsuno/AFP/GETTYIMAGE; 148 (t) AFP/GETTYIMAGE, (b/r) Nigel Snowdon/REX; 149 (t) Gero Breloer/AFP/GETTYIMAGE, (b) AFP/GETTYIMAGE; 150 (t) Hector Mata/APF/GETTYIMAGE, (b/r) Giorgio Benvenuti/AFP/GETTYIMAGE; 151 (t) Courtesy of South West News Service; 152 (t) Jean pierre Clatot/AFP/GETTYIMAGE; 153 (t) TA/REX; 154 (t) Craig Beruldsen/AFP/GETTYIMAGE, (b/l) Bettmann/Corbis (b/r) Robert Holmes/CORBIS; 155 (b) Frederic J. Brown/AFP/GETTYIMAGE; 156 (t) AFP/GETTYIMAGE, (b) Ludovic Maisant/CORBIS; 157 (t) Ciro Fusco/AFP/GETTYIMAGE, (b) Stephen Frink/CORBIS; 160 (b) Layne Kennedy/CORBIS; 161 (b) Tony Kyriacou/REX; 163 (t) Gideon Mendel/CORBIS; 165 (t/l) Ashley Gilbertson/AFP/GETTYIMAGE, (t/r) Ulrich Perrey/AFP/GETTYIMAGE, (b) Robyn Beck/AFP/GETTYIMAGE; 166 (b) Robyn Beck/AFP/GETTYIMAGE; 167 (t/r) AFP/GETTYIMAGE, (b) Joern Pollex/AFP/GETTYIMAGE; 168 (t) James Leynse/CORBIS, (b) Frederic J. Brown/AFP/GETTYIMAGE; 169 (t/r) Sourav/AFP/GETTYIMAGE; 170 (b) Courtesy of Warner; 172 (l) Idranil Mukherjee/AFP/GETTYIMAGE; 173 (t) Sipa Press /REX; 174 (b) Bill Keogh/AFP/GETTYIMAGE; 175 (t) Bill Keogh/AFP/GETTYIMAGE; 175 (b) Bill Keogh/AFP/GETTYIMAGE; 176 (t) Sven Nackstrand/AFP/GETTYIMAGE, (b) Stefan Puchner/AFP/GETTYIMAGE; 177 (b/r) Peter Parks/AFP/GETTYIMAGE; 178 (t/r) Pictorial Press Ltd; 179 (t) Nils Jorgensen/REX; 180 (t) Carsten Rehder/AFP/GETTYIMAGE, (b) Maria Laura/REX; 181 (b) Moma/AFP/GETTYIMAGE; 182 (b/l) James Fraser/REX; 183 (t/r) Courtesy of Polygram, (c/r) Courtesy of Polygram, (b) Entertainmant/New Line; 184 (t/l) Pictorial Press Ltd, (t/r) Pictorial Press Ltd, (b) Columbia/Goldcrest; 185 (c) Pictorial Press Ltd; 186 (t/r) Pictorial Press Ltd, (c) Universal/Miramax, (b/l) Entertainment/New Line; 187 (t/l) Entertainment/New Line, (b) Pictorial Press Ltd; 190 (b) Chris George/CORBIS, (c/l)Thierry Zoccolan/AFP/GETTYIMAGE; 191 (t) AFP/GETTYIMAGE, (c/r) Stephen Jaffe/AFP/GETTYIMAGE, (b) Olivier Morin/AFP/GETTYIMAGE; 192 (t) Richard T. Nowitz/CORBIS, (b) Joel Nito/AFP/GETTYIMAGE; 193 (t/r) Marcus Fuehrer/AFP/GETTYIMAGE, (b/l) Valerie Hache/AFP/GETTYIMAGE; 194 (b) AFP/GETTYIMAGE; 195 (t) Gerard Malie/AFP/GETTYIMAGE; 196 (c/t) AntonioBat/AFP/GETTYIMAGE; 197 (t) J. C. Cardenas/AFP/GETTYIMAGE; 198 (t/r) J. Fesl/AFP/ GETTYIMAGE, (b) Galen Rowell/CORBIS; 199 (t) Paolo Cocco/AFP/GETTYIMAGE, (b) Hector Mata/AFP/GETTYIMAGE; 201 (t) AFP/GETTYIMAGE, (b) Christian Thalheimer/AFP/GETTYIMAGE; 202 (t) Henny Ray/AFP/GETTYIMAGE, (c/r) Mohammed Sarji/AFP/GETTYIMAGE; 203 (t/r) PA Photos, (b) EPA European Press Agency/PA Photos; 204 (b) Raveendran/AFP/GETTYIMAGE, (t) Sipa Press /REX; 205 (b) Courtesy of Chris Pritchard, (t) Courtesy of Chris Pritchard; 206 (t/l) Kimmo M Nytl/AFP/GETTYIMAGE, (b/r) Victor Drachev/AFP/GETTYIMAGE; 207 (t) Gamma/Katz, (b) Tommi Korpihalla/AFP/GETTYIMAGE; 208 (t) Frank Maechler/AFP/GETTYIMAGE; 209 (t/l) Nokia, (b) Patrick Ward/CORBIS; 210 (t) AFP/GETTYIMAGE, (b) Wolf-Dietrich Weissbach/AFP/ GETTYIMAGE; 211 (b) Gerry Penny/AFP/GETTYIMAGE, (t) Doug Kanter/AFP/GETTYIMAGE; 212 (t) Michael Kupferschmidt/AFP/GETTYIMAGE, (b/l) Alistair Berg/Katz; 213 (t) AFP/GETTYIMAGE, (b) Herbert Spies/AFP/GETTYIMAGE; 214 (t) Jimin Lai/AFP/ GETTYIMAGE, (b/c) Damien Meyer/AFP/GETTYIMAGE, (b/r) Lowell Georgia/CORBIS; 215 (b/l) Petra Masova/AFP/GETTYIMAGE; 216 (b/l) Anatoly Maltsev/AFP/GETTYIMAGE; 217 (t/l) Courtesy of Andre Tolme, (t/c) Courtesy of Andre Tolme, (b) AFP/GETTYIMAGE; 221 (t/r) PNS/REX, (b) Roman Soumar/CORBIS; 222 (t) Peter Turnley/CORBIS; 223 (t) AFP/GETTYIMAGE; 224 (b) IPC Magazines:Whats On TV/REX; 225 (t) Bettmann/CORBIS; 227 (b) AFP/GETTYIMAGE; 228 (b) J.G. Morell/AFP/GETTYIMAGE; 229 (t) SWS/REX, (b) John T. Barr/AFP/GETTYIMAGE; 230 (l/c) Dibyangshu Sarkar/AFP/ GETTYIMAGE, (b/r) Andy Newman/AFP/GETTYIMAGE; 231 (t) Jiji Press/AFP/GETTYIMAGE, (b) AFP/GETTYIMAGE; 232 (t/l) Jeroen Oerlemans/REX; (b/l) Dibyangshu Sarkar/AFP/GETTYIMAGE; (b/r) Sourvav/AFP/GETTYIMAGE; 233 (c) Peter Macdiarmid/REX; 234 (t) Yoshikazu Tsuno/AFP/GETTYIMAGE, (b) Katja Lenz-Pool/AFP/GETTYIMAGE; 235 (t) AFP/GETTYIMAGE, (l/c) Deshakal Yan Chowdhury/AFP/GETTYIMAGE, (b) AFP/GETTYIMAGE; 236 (t/r) Pictorial Press Ltd, (b) Pictorial Press Ltd; 237 (t) Philip Dunn/REX, (b) Christophe Simon/AFP/GETTYIMAGE; 238 (t) AFP/GETTYIMAGE, (c/r) AFP/GETTYIMAGE, (b) NASA/AFP/GETTYIMAGE; 239 (r) AFP/GETTYIMAGE, (b) AFP/GETTYIMAGE; 240 (b) Lucy Kelaart/REX; 241 (t) Lindsey Hebberd/CORBIS, (b) AFP/GETTYIMAGE; 242 (t) Bay Ismoyo/AFP/GETTYIMAGE, (b) AFP/GETTYIMAGE; 243 (b) John Zich/AFP/GETTYIMAGE; 244 (t) AFP/GETTYIMAGE, (b) Paul Watts/REX; 245 (t) Jeremy Durkin/REX, (b) Matt Morton/REX; 246 (t) Helen Osler/REX, (b) Jewel Samad/AFP/GETTYIMAGE; 247 (b) Neil Hall/REX

FPL – Fortean Picture Library

All other photos are from Corel, MKP archives, PhotoDisc, and Ripley's Entertainment Inc.